Beginning iOS 3D Unreal Games Development

Robert Chin

Apress®

Beginning iOS 3D Unreal Games Development

Copyright © 2012 by Robert Chin

ISBN-13 (pbk): 978-1-4302- 4035-8

ISBN-13 (electronic): 978-1-4302- 4036-5

Printed and bound in the United States of America 9 8 7 6 5 4 3 2 1

President and Publisher: Paul Manning
Lead Editor: Michelle Lowman
Development Editor: Chris Nelson
Technical Reviewers: Thomas Havlik and David Franson
Editorial Board: Steve Anglin, Ewan Buckingham, Gary Cornell, Louise Corrigan, Morgan Ertel, Jonathan Gennick, Jonathan Hassell, Robert Hutchinson, Michelle Lowman, James Markham, Matthew Moodie, Jeff Olson, Jeffrey Pepper, Douglas Pundick, Ben Renow-Clarke, Dominic Shakeshaft, Gwenan Spearing, Matt Wade, Tom Welsh
Copy Editor: Lori Cavanaugh
Compositor: MacPS, LLC
Indexer: SPi Global
Artist: SPi Global
Cover Designer: Anna Ishchenko

Distributed to the book trade worldwide by Springer Science+Business Media, LLC., 233 Spring Street, 6th Floor, New York, NY 10013. Phone 1-800-SPRINGER, fax (201) 348-4505, e-mail orders-ny@springer-sbm.com, or visit www.springeronline.com.

For information on translations, please e-mail rights@apress.com, or visit www.apress.com.

Apress and friends of ED books may be purchased in bulk for academic, corporate, or promotional use. eBook versions and licenses are also available for most titles. For more information, reference our Special Bulk Sales–eBook Licensing web page at www.apress.com/bulk-sales.

Any source code or other supplementary materials referenced by the author in this text is available to readers at www.apress.com. For detailed information about how to locate your book's source code, go to http://www.apress.com/source-code/.

Contents at a Glance

Contents

About the Author

Robert Chin has a bachelor of science degree in computer engineering and is experienced in C/C++ and UnrealScript. He has written 3D games in C/C++ using the DirectX and OpenGL graphics APIs for the Windows platform. He has served as an Unreal UDK consultant and written UDK UnrealScript-based programs for clients, including an entire commercial game coded specifically for the iOS platform.

About the Technical Reviewers

David Franson has been involved in networking, programming, and 2D and 3D computer graphics since 1990. He is the author of *2D Artwork and 3D Game Modeling for Game Artists* (Cengage, 2002) and *The Dark Side of Game Texturing* (Course Technology, 2004). He has also produced digital artwork for 3D video games, film, and television.

Thomas Havlik is the lead developer at Action Mobile as well as the website administrator and a programmer at Raw Games.

Acknowledgments

I would like to thank Chris Nelson for providing critical suggestions as to the direction of this book and for serving as the development editor. I would also like to thank technical reviewers Thomas Havlik and David Franson. I would also like to thank Jennifer Blackwell who helped keep me on track with reminders on when material was due in her role as coordinating editor. Finally I would like to thank Michelle Lowman who helped me get this book contract in the first place by presenting my proposal to the Apress editorial board.

Introduction

The release of the Unreal Development Kit is really the first time a powerful 3D commercial game engine has been available to the masses of ordinary people for free. The underlying technology has been used for numerous high-quality commercial triple-A games that you see in the retail stores in the United States and around the world. The UDK contains the Unreal Engine 3 3D graphics engine and related tools that would normally cost hundreds of thousands of dollars. The only limitation is that the C/C++ source code used to create the UDK is only available to those who pay the full license fee. Thus, you can not modify the UDK engine itself.

This book provides an introduction to using this technology, including the UnrealScript language, for creating 3D iOS games. I have used the technology extensively and used it to create a full commercial physics puzzle type game for iOS similar to the iOS game Angry Birds. It is a powerful tool that is excellent for iOS development. My intention here is to give others a quickstart guide for creating their own iOS games and share game frameworks I've developed that readers can use as the basis for their own work.

Who This Book Is For

This book is for people that want to use the Unreal Development Kit (UDK) to create 3D games for Apple's iOS platform. This includes devices such as the iPhone, iPad, and iPod Touch. This book also is useful for people that want to develop games on the PC platform with the UDK since much of what is covered in this book would apply to creating a game for the PC as well.

This book assumes the reader has some experience with an object-oriented programming language like C++ or at least some programming experience in general. However, several basic game frameworks are presented in this book as a means to help those who are not professional programmers build their own game using the frameworks as a starting point.

It is also assumed that the reader has some basic knowledge of how to use an iOS device since the final game created using the UDK will be played on the actual iOS device.

General Layout of the Book

Before we cover the general layout of this book there are some key points that the reader should note. First, this book is not designed to cover every feature of the UDK since that would realistically involve a set of books, not just one. This book concentrates on the programming side of game development using the default set of assets that come with the UDK. Also, in terms of programming, this book is not meant to provide a full reference to the UnrealScript programming language. This book also isn't intended as a general introduction to iOS development. We have mentioned links to web sites that provide additional useful information throughout this book. Some of the more important ones are listed in the "Other Resources" section at the end of this introduction.

The general format of this book is to discuss UDK topics and then demonstrate these topics in the form of a "Hands-On Example" in which we show you how to develop an UnrealScript program along with the creation of any levels that are needed. We take you, step by step, through these examples along with showing you how to set up any configuration files that are required.

We start with overviews of the UDK and UnrealScript, including a practical coding example. Then we work through key topics with hands on examples and culminating with a complete sample game. Some of these topics rely on 3D math concepts that are reviewed and demonstrated in a separate chapter. Then, in the latter part of the book we present game frameworks which are actually small working games that you can modify and use to build your own custom games. Game frameworks include a physics game, a first-person shooter game, a third-person shooter/adventure game, and a top-down shooter/role playing game.

Other Resources

Epic Games provides a wealth of resources you can use to supplement what you learn in this book:

- Epic's UDK Mobile home page:
  `http://udn.epicgames.com/Three/MobileHome.html`

- Getting Started: Developing Mobile Projects:
  `http://udn.epicgames.com/Three/GettingStartediOSDevelopment.html`

- iOS Provisioning Overview:
  `http://udn.epicgames.com/Three/AppleiOSProvisioning.html`

- Distributing iOS Applications:
  `http://udn.epicgames.com/Three/DistributionAppleiOS.html`

- UnrealScript Language Reference:
  `http://udn.epicgames.com/Three/UnrealScriptReference.html`

Chapter 1

UDK Overview

This chapter covers the basic background information needed to get started with Unreal 3D games development for iOS and for the hands-on examples that follow in subsequent chapters. To start, we take a quick tour of the Unreal Development Kit (UDK) and familiarize those new to Unreal with the development environment. We cover the Unreal Editor, which is where levels are built and assets within the UDK are imported and managed. Some examples of UDK assets are textures, materials, static meshes, skeletal meshes, and sound cues. These are all covered in this chapter. Finally, information specific to game development on the iOS platform using the UDK is also covered. Readers who already use Unreal might want to jump ahead to this section.

Getting Started

The first thing you need to do is go to the UDK's website, located at http://udk.com, download the June 2011 Beta version of the UDK (approximately 1.5 GB) that is used in this book, and install it on your computer. The code examples in this book work correctly with the version of the UDK presented in this book at the time of the writing. The UDK is currently still in the Beta phase and new versions of the UDK are being released about every month. After downloading the executable, run the program to install the UDK. At least Microsoft Net Framework 3.1 is required and will be installed on your system if not detected. You can also download UDK Remote at http://itunes.apple.com/us/app/udk-remote, which helps with testing your iOS games.

Unreal Editor Overview

Once you have the UDK installed, go to the Start bar and navigate to where you installed the UDK and run the UDK Editor. Once the Unreal Editor is loaded, you should see something similar to Figure 1–1. The Editor is where you build your game levels, as well as manage and manipulate the game assets used in the level. You can run your game on the iOS mobile previewer from the Unreal Editor, as well as set the specific game type to be played.

Figure 1–1. *UDK Startup Screen*

Click the Close button inside the Welcome to UDK box to get started. On the right hand side there is a window with many different tabs.

The Generic Browser

I won't go over all the buttons and toolbars in the Unreal Editor UI. We'll discuss all that in context as we work through the book. It is important to take a look at the Generic Browser, however, especially the Content Browser, covered in detail later in this section, and the Actor Classes tab.

As you can see in Figure 1–1, there are six tabs:

- Content Browser. The Content Browser tab is the main interface by which users import, select, and manipulate UDK assets. This tab is discussed in greater detail later in this chapter.

- Actor Classes. The Actor Classes tab contains a list of the UnrealScript classes in the UDK and is subsequently discussed, since it has several elements that will be important early in the book.

- Levels. The Levels tab manages the levels in your world that can consist of one level or many levels that are streamed.

- Scene. The Scene tab displays objects in the current level in table form where you can click on the name of an object and bring up its properties in a side panel.

- Layers. The Layers tab allows you to organize the actors in your level so you can view certain groups of actors and hide others.

- Start Page. The Start Page tab contains internet content related to the UDK, such as documentation, news, community forums, etc.

Now let's take a look at the Actor Classes tab in a bit more detail before moving on to the Content Browser.

Actor Classes Tab

The Actor Classes tab, shown in Figure 1–2, displays the Unreal Script classes currently available. This is where new classes you create appear after you integrate them into the UDK system, as well as classes that are part of the UDK code base.

The term Actor generally refers to an object created from the Actor class or an object created from a class derived from the Actor class. The Actor class is important, because it implements many items needed for gameplay, including code needed for:

- Displaying an object

- Animating an object

- Performing physics and world interaction

- Making sounds

- Creating and destroying the Actor

- Broadcasting messages

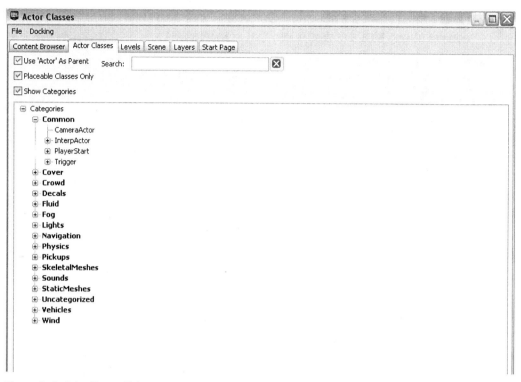

Figure 1–2. *Actor Classes Tab*

There are three checkbox options in this tab:

- Use 'Actor' as Parent. Check "Use Actor as Parent" to view only classes that use Actor as a base class. In other words, only classes built from the Actor class. If you uncheck this box, then all classes in the UDK system will be displayed. The class Object will be displayed as the root of the new tree, since Object is the base class of all other classes.

- Placeable Classes Only. If you check the "Placeable Classes Only" checkbox, then only classes that you can place in a game level using the Unreal Editor will be displayed. If you uncheck this box, then both placeable and not placeable classes will be displayed.

- Show Categories. Checking the "Show Categories" checkbox will group and display the classes in different categories like Physics and Navigation.

There is also a search function in which you can search the tree by class name. We use this tab and discuss its features in more detail later in the book.

Now let's turn to the Content Browser.

The Content Browser and UDK Assets

The Content Browser tab is the starting point for importing and manipulating game content in the UDK system. Game content can be sounds, textures, and 3d computer images used in your game. Click the Content Browser tab to change focus to the Content Browser (see Figure 1–3).

Figure 1–3. *UDK Content Browser*

Importing New Content

You can import new content into the UDK system by clicking the Import button in the lower left hand corner of the Content Browser Tab and can preview that content in the section of the browser where you see the previous images. Clicking the Import button brings up a window in which you can navigate to where your asset is, select it, and then load it into the UDK system. Examples of assets that can be imported from outside the UDK and placed into the UDK system are:

- Sound files in .wav format
- Texture files in .bmp, .pcx, .png, and .tga formats
- Static and Skeletal mesh files in .fbx format
- Movies in .bik format
- Shockwave movies in .swf and .gfx formats

Searching for UDK Assets

You can also filter the objects displayed by name, as well as type. In the upper right side of the Content Browser there is a search box in which you can type the game asset name to search for that is located next to a pair of arrows (see Figure 1–4). There is a section below that with the heading Object Type that contains two subsections named "Favorites" and "All Types." Currently, all of the assets in the game, regardless of type, are displayed, since the "All" checkbox is checked.

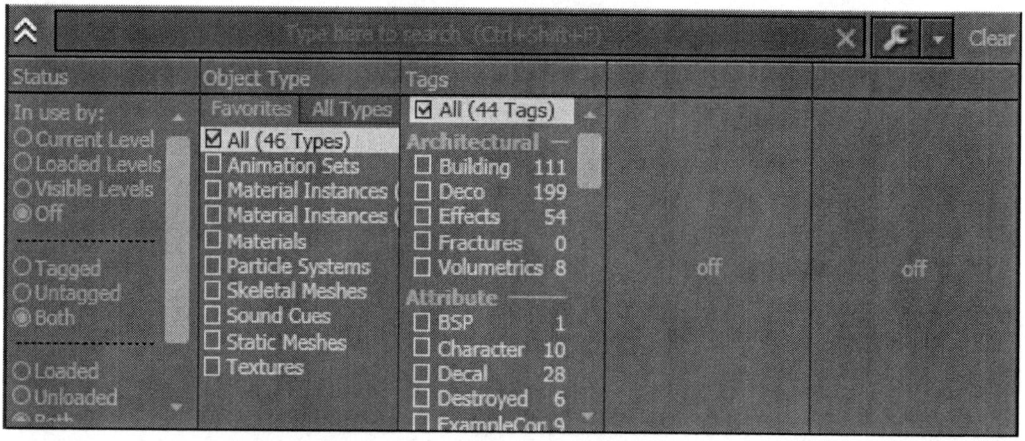

Figure 1–4. *Asset Search Filtering Section of the Content Browser*

Let's search for textures that have "blockwall" as part of their name. Click the Textures checkbox under the Favorites subsection. Next, type in the word "block" to search for textures that contain the word "block" in their name. Finally, under the Packages section of the Content Browser located in the lower left hand corner, select the UDKGame package. Your Content Browser should look something like Figure 1–5.

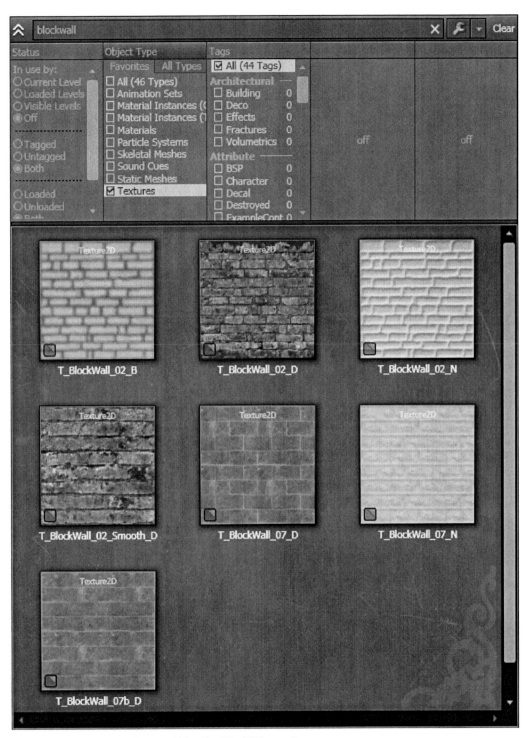

Figure 1–5. *Searching for Textures Using the "Block" Keyword*

You can double click these texture assets, and a texture's properties window will pop up, giving you more information about each texture asset. For example, click the texture called "T_BlockWall_02_D," and the Texture Properties window shown in Figure 1–6 opens.

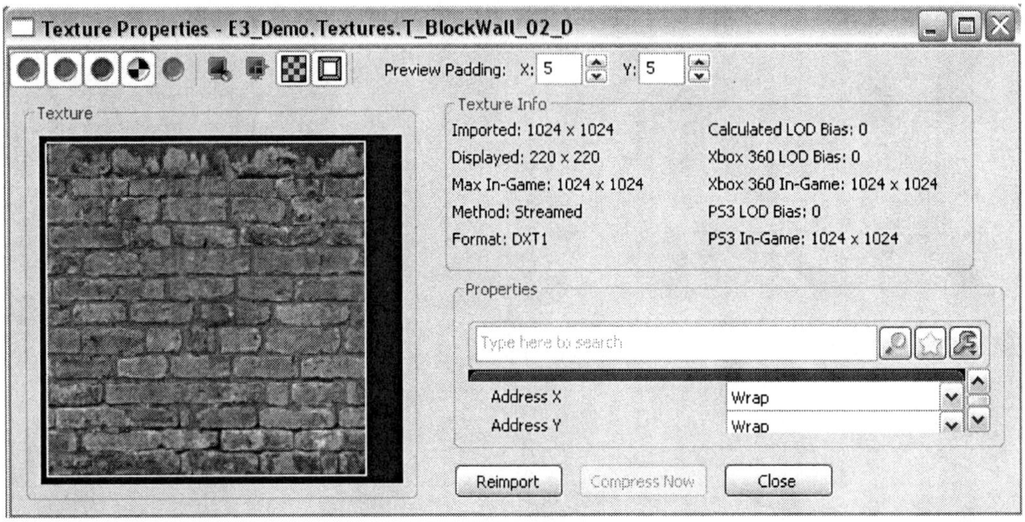

Figure 1–6. *Texture Properties*

UDK Texture Assets

Textures for iOS platforms need to be square. That is, the length in pixels must equal the width in pixels for the texture, such as 512x512 pixels. Textures are generally created outside the UDK system in a paint program like Adobe PhotoShop or PaintShop Pro and saved in a graphics file format, such as windows bitmap (.bmp), that the UDK system can understand and import in. Once inside the UDK system, textures can serve as the building blocks for UDK materials.

Uncheck the Textures checkbox and check the Materials checkbox. Find the material called "M_BlockWall_02_D" and double click it. This will bring up the Unreal Material Editor, and you should see something similar to Figure 1–7.

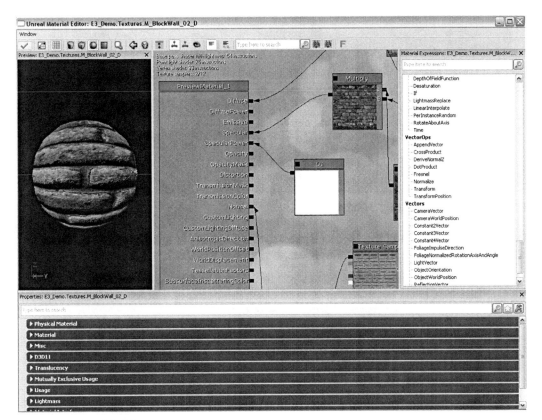

Figure 1-7. *Materials Editor*

UDK Material Assets

The Material Editor is used to create new materials using textures. In the leftmost part of the Material Editor, there is a 3d sphere with a texture applied to it. You can rotate the sphere by clicking it, pressing the left mouse button, and moving the mouse. You can move the sphere forward and backward by clicking it, pressing down the right mouse button, and moving the mouse forward and backward. The texture used for the sphere is the same texture just viewed, which is T_BlockWall_02_D. Verify this is the case by scrolling through the bottom portion of the Material Editor until you come to the Mobile property section. Click the Mobile property if the subproperties are not already displayed (see Figure 1-8).

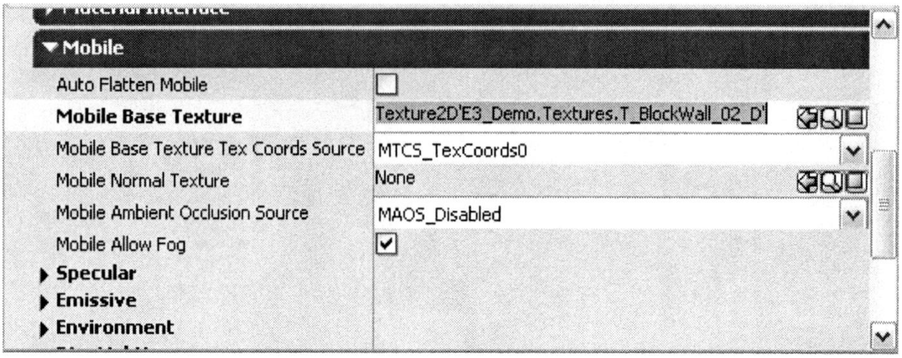

Figure 1–8. *Setting Textures in the Material Editor*

On the right hand side of the Mobile Base Texture property is a set of buttons. These buttons are also used in many other fields throughout the UDK:

- Arrow. The arrow button allows you to select a texture in the content browser, and then click this icon to place the name of that texture here so it can be used as the Mobile Base Texture.

- Magnifying Glass. The magnifying glass button allows you to find the object currently in the field by clicking the icon. When you do this, it should take you to the Content Browser and highlight the texture "T_BlockWall_02_D".

- Clear Screen. The clear screen button clears the Mobile Base Texture property field.

UDK Mesh Assets

A UDK material can be used to provide the surface covering for a mesh, either a static mesh or a skeletal mesh. A mesh is the actual 3d object consisting of a collection of vertices that can be placed in a game level. A skeletal mesh also includes moving parts, called bones, which are generally used to animate a 3d character. The material is what gives the surface of a mesh color and texture.

Now, let's look at an example.

1. Go back to the **Object Type ➤ Favorites** subsection, check Static Meshes, and make sure to uncheck all the other boxes.

2. Type "Cube" into the search box to only display static meshes that have "Cube" as part of their name.

3. Finally, go to the Packages section and click the Engine package. You should see a static mesh called "Cube" in the browser. Double click this item to bring up the Unreal Static Mesh Editor (see Figure 1–9).

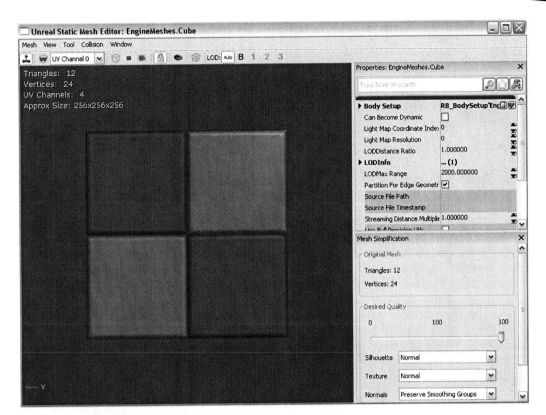

Figure 1-9. *The Static Mesh Editor*

4. You can rotate the cube by first selecting the left hand side of the Mesh Editor that contains the cube. Hold down the right mouse button and move the mouse around to rotate the cube.

5. Hold down the left mouse button and move the mouse back and forth to move the cube view back and forth. Static meshes are meshes without any moving parts.

6. You can view the material this cube is using by going to the LODInfo property section on the right hand side of the viewer, locating the material property, and then clicking the magnifying glass button (see Figure 1-10). This will take you to the Content Browser, and the material used on this mesh will be highlighted.

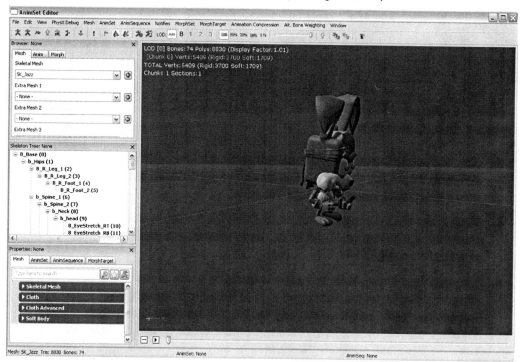

Figure 1-10. *Setting Materials in the Static Mesh Editor*

7.   As before, double click the material in the content browser to bring up this material in the Unreal Material Editor.

Now, let's search for skeletal meshes in the UDK. Check the Skeletal Meshes box under the Object Type ➤ Favorites, making sure all the other checkboxes are unchecked. Type "Jazz" in the search box and change the Package to search in to UDKGame. You should see a skeletal mesh called "SK_Jazz" in the content browser. Double click this skeletal mesh to bring it up in the Unreal AnimSet Editor (see Figure 1–11).

Figure 1-11. *The AnimSet Editor*

You can also set the material for this skeletal mesh. In the lower left hand corner of the AnimSet Editor, under the Mesh tab, you can set the Material property for this skeletal mesh under the Skeletal Mesh category (see Figure 1–12).

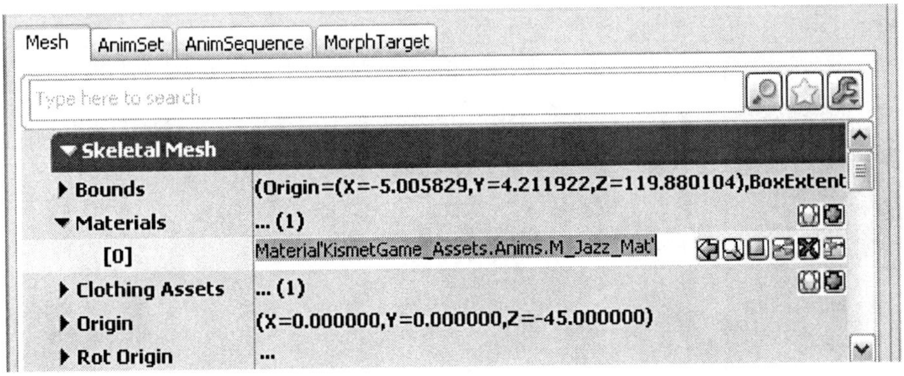

Figure 1-12. *Setting Materials in the AnimSet Editor*

You can also use the magnifying glass button to find the current material in the Content Browser, as well as set a new material from the Content Browser using the Arrow button.

In summary, textures are created in paint programs outside the UDK system and are imported into the UDK system via the Content Browser. These textures can be used to create materials inside the Unreal Material Editor. These materials can then be applied to static meshes via the Static Mesh Editor and skeletal meshes via the AnimSet Editor.

In addition to textures, materials, static meshes, and skeletal meshes, there are two other important game assets within the Content Browser, Particle Systems and Sound Cues.

UDK Particle System Assets

Particle Systems consist of an emitter and the particles that they emit. These are useful for such things as explosions and trails that projectiles leave when fired.

Let's take a look at one.

1. In the Object Type subsection, select Particle Systems as your object type, making sure all the other options are unchecked.

2. Type "fire" as the search filter term, making sure the UDKGame package is highlighted in the Packages section of the Content Browser.

3. Double click the fire particle system displayed to bring up Unreal Cascade, as shown in Figure 1-13.

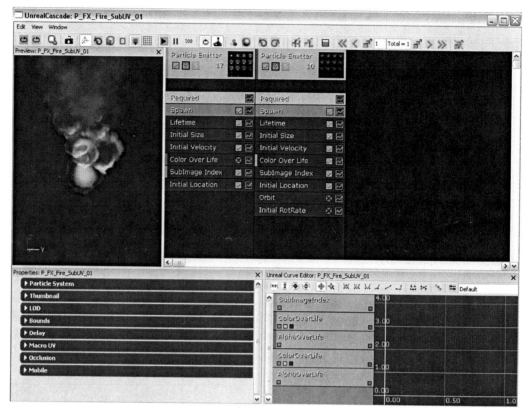

Figure 1–13. *Unreal Cascade*

Unreal Cascade has many options for creating your own custom emitters. Such things, including particle type, particle speed, and particle direction, can be customized. For now, let's not get into the details, but just know that custom emitters can be easily created from within the UDK system.

UDK Sound Cue Assets

Now, let's search for sound cues. Select Sound Cues as the Object Type you will search for by checking its box. You can double click a sound cue to hear it. You can also edit the sound cue in the Sound Cue Editor by right clicking the Sound Cue you want to edit and selecting the "Edit Using Sound Cue Editor" option (see Figure 1–14). This should bring up the Sound Cue Editor shown in Figure 1–15.

> **NOTE:** You can also access the editor for other game assets like static meshes, materials, etc. by right clicking that asset and selecting "Edit Using EditorType". The EditorType will depend on the asset, such as "Edit Using Material Editor" if the asset selected is a material.

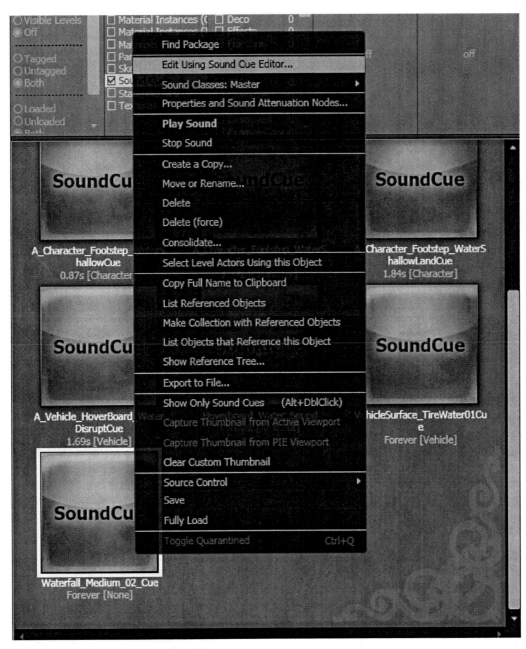

Figure 1–14. *Selecting the Sound Cue Editor*

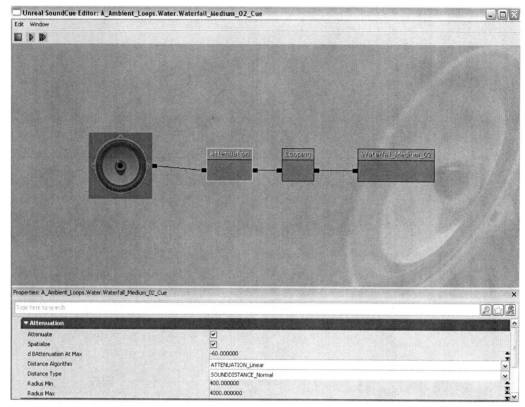

Figure 1–15. *Sound Cue Editor*

The Sound Cue Editor allows you to mix different sound samples into a single sound cue. For example, the sound editor has options for looping a sound and generating a random sound from a group of sounds.

IOS Specific UDK Information

There are certain differences to keep in mind when developing game for the iOS platform. The major differences involve saving data, preparing textures for an iOS device, and the types of player controls available to the user. We will return to the information discussed in this section later in the book and use it in the numerous hands-on examples.

Saving Data on an iOS Device

Some ways of saving data through the UDK system work on the PC-based game and even on a game on the Mobile Previewer but not on an actual iOS device. For example, using config files to save data will work on a PC-based game and even on an iOS-based game using the Mobile Previewer but will not work on the actual device. The best way to solve this problem is to use the basic save game object feature of the UDK. This method works on both the PC side and the iOS platform.

The idea of the basic save object is to put all the information you need to save into a class. Create a new object of this class and save the needed information into variables in this class object. You then save this object to a file. Once a file is created, then you can load this information back into this class variable.

Create a new class that will hold the variables you want to save to a file. For example, create a new file called PlayerInfo.uc and type the following into it.

```
class PlayerInfo extends Actor;
```

This declares a new class, called PlayerInfo, which is derived from Actor. Type in the following variables that will be the information saved to the new file.

```
var int PlayerLevel;
var float PlayerAgility;
var string PlayerName;
var bool PlayerInfected;
```

Save this file and open the class file that needs to use this information. Declare a class reference variable that uses the PlayerInfo class.

```
var    PlayerInfo    PlayerRecord;
```

Next, create a new object of this class using the Spawn command and set PlayerRecord to point to it.

```
PlayerRecord = Spawn(class'PlayerInfo');
```

In the same file that you declared the PlayerRecord variable, add the following two functions that will be used to save and load the data in PlayerRecord to a file. The filename that it is saved in is PlayerData.bin.

```
function SavePlayerRecord()
{
    class'Engine'.static.BasicSaveObject(PlayerRecord, "PlayerData.bin", true, 1);
}
function LoadPlayerRecord()
{
    class'Engine'.static.BasicLoadObject(PlayerRecord, "PlayerData.bin", true, 1);
}
```

Textures on an iOS Device

Textures on the iOS platform must be square. The length of the texture must be equal to the width of the texture in pixels. For example, texture sizes of 512x512 and 1012x1012 are both square textures.

Player Input Controls on an iOS Device

The UDK supports three types of input: built in virtual joysticks, touch input, and motion input The MobilePlayerInput class and the MobileInputZone class handle player input for the iOS device and are located in the Development\Src\GameFramework\Classes under your main UDK installation directory, which is by default UDK\UDK-2011–06. The easiest way to handle touch input is through setting and processing different input zones in your game through the MobileInputZone class. If you need a greater degree of control, then use the MobilePlayerInput class. However, for most uses, MobileInputZones will be adequate. In each of the hands-on examples in this book, we guide you on how to configure the mobile input controls for that specific example. So don't worry if you don't understand everything in this section. We guide you on exactly how to set up your mobile input controls when the time comes.

Setting Up Virtual Joysticks

To use virtual joysticks, the first thing you need to do is configure the input zones for your virtual joysticks. To do this, open the Mobile-UDKGame.ini file located in the \UDK\UDK-2011–06\UDKGame\Config directory of your UDK installation using a plain text word processor like Windows Notepad.

Type the following in the file. This defines joystick input zones for the first hands-on example we cover at the end of Chapter 2. The first line indicates that this configuration will belong to Example1Game type game located in the Example1 directory. For each new game type that uses joysticks, you must create a similar set of configurations.

```
[Example1.Example1Game]
```

The following sets up a GroupName defined as an "UberGroup" and two input zones, called "UberStickMoveZone" and "UberStickLookZone".The order in which you define the zones is important, since input captured by the first zone in the list is not passed along to subsequent zones. This might be a problem if you have overlapping zones.

```
RequiredMobileInputConfigs=(GroupName="UberGroup",RequireZoneNames=("UberStickMoveZone",
"UberStickLookZone"))
```

Next, we need to define the zones. The following line defines the block of configurations to follow as data for the UberStickMoveZone.

```
[UberStickMoveZone MobileInputZone]
```

Some of the more important configurations are subsequently discussed.

The InputKey defines the name of the inputkey to send to the input subsystem for input in the vertical direction. In this case, pushing this stick up or down will move the player forward or backward.

```
InputKey=MOBILE_Aforward
```

The HorizontalInputKey defines the name of the inputkey to send to the input subsystem for input in the horizontal direction. For this stick, this means that movements right or left will move the player right or left in a side to side manner suitable for strafing an enemy while facing it.

```
HorizontalInputKey=MOBILE_Astrafe
```

The Type indicates the kind of zone this is. This zone type is set to be a virtual joystick:

```
Type=ZoneType_Joystick
bRelativeX=true
bRelativeY=true
bRelativeSizeX=true
bRelativeSizeY=true
X=0.05
Y=-0.4
SizeX=0.1965
SizeY=1.0
bSizeYFromSizeX=true
VertMultiplier=-1.0
HorizMultiplier=1.0
bScalePawnMovement=true
RenderColor=(R=255,G=255,B=255,A=255)
InactiveAlpha=0.25
bUseGentleTransitions=true
ResetCenterAfterInactivityTime=3.0
ActivateTime=0.6
DeactivateTime=0.2
TapDistanceConstraint=5
```

Next, you need to configure the Joystick for turning the player left and right and moving the view up and down. Add the following definition for the UberStickLookZone. For vertical movements, an inputkey of value MOBILE_AlookUp is sent to the input system, indicating that the player should look up or down. For the HorizontalInputKey that tracks horizontal movements, the MOBILE_Aturn value is sent to the input system, which indicates the player should turn left or right.

```
[UberStickLookZone MobileInputZone]
InputKey=MOBILE_ALookUp
HorizontalInputKey=MOBILE_ATurn
Type=ZoneType_Joystick
bRelativeX=true
bRelativeY=true
bRelativeSizeX=true
bRelativeSizeY=true
VertMultiplier=-0.5
HorizMultiplier=0.35
X=-0.2465
Y=-0.4
SizeX=0.1965
SizeY=1.0
bSizeYFromSizeX=true
RenderColor=(R=255,G=255,B=255,A=255)
InactiveAlpha=0.25
bUseGentleTransitions=true
ResetCenterAfterInactivityTime=3.0
ActivateTime=0.6
DeactivateTime=0.2
TapDistanceConstraint=5
```

After you finish entering the previous information, make sure to save the file. Also it would be good practice to write protect it, as well to prevent the UDK system from overwriting your changes.

The virtual joysticks themselves should look like the transparent round circles shown in Figure 1–16.

Figure 1–16. *Virtual Joysticks*

Setting Up Touch Input

Now let's add in touch input for things like swipes and taps. To do this, we need to add in some more configurations to the Mobile-UDKGame.ini file that we added our joystick configuration info in earlier. First, add in "UberLookZone" to the zone names in the RequiredMobileInputConfigs section. Make sure you put the new zone at the end of the zone list. This new zone will take up the entire screen. Remember that input goes sequentially from the first listed input zone to the last. If you list the UberLookZone first, then all input will be processed by that zone and none will get to the zones that follow. This would make the virtual sticks unusable.

```
[Example1.Example1Game]
RequiredMobileInputConfigs=(GroupName="UberGroup",RequireZoneNames=("UberStickMoveZone",
"UberStickLookZone","UberLookZone"))
```

Next, add in the zone definition for the UberLookZone as follows. As with the joysticks, the InputKey refers to the up and down movements and the HorizontalInputKey refers to the left and right movements. Note that the Type is ZoneType_Trackball. Also note that the X and Y values are set to 0, which indicates the zone starts at the top left hand corner. The bRelativeSizeX and bRelativeSizeY values are set to true, and the SizeX and SizeY are set to 1, which means the size of the zone is full screen.

```
[UberLookZone MobileInputZone]
InputKey=MouseY
HorizontalInputKey=MouseX
TapInputKey=MOBILE_Fire
Type=ZoneType_Trackball
bRelativeSizeX=true
bRelativeSizeY=true
X=0
Y=0
SizeX=1.0
SizeY=1.0
VertMultiplier=-0.0007
HorizMultiplier=0.001
Acceleration=12.0
Smoothing=1.0
EscapeVelocityStrength=0.85
bIsInvisible=1
TapDistanceConstraint=32
```

Once you setup the touch input zone, you will need to set up the callback function that will process the touch input for your zone. First, you need to create a new player controller that derives from SimplePC.

```
class Example1PC extends SimplePC;
```

In this new player controller, you need to create the callback function that has the same format as the subsequent SwipeZoneCallback in terms of parameters and a Boolean return value. The EventType is ZoneEvent_Touch when the user first touches the screen. As the user moves his or her finger across the screen, the EventTypes become ZoneEvent_Update to indicate these touches are an update to a touch still in progress. Finally, the ZoneEvent_UnTouch EventType that indicates that the user has lifted his or her finger off the screen is received and the current touch is finished.

```
Function bool SwipeZoneCallback(MobileInputZone Zone,
                                float DeltaTime,
                                int Handle,
                                EZoneTouchEvent EventType,
                                Vector2D TouchLocation)
{
    local    bool    retval;

    if (EventType == ZoneEvent_Touch)
    {
    }
    else
    if(EventType == ZoneEvent_Update)
    {
    }
    else
    if (EventType == ZoneEvent_UnTouch)
    {
    }
    return retval;
}
```

Next, you need to actually set the delegate OnProcessInputDelegate that controls touch input. Create a SetupZone function like the subsequent example that sets the touch input delegate to your custom callback function.

```
function SetupZones()
{
    Super.SetupZones();
    // If we have a valid player input and game class, configure the zones
    if (MPI != None && WorldInfo.GRI.GameClass != none)
    {
        LocalPlayer(Player).ViewportClient.GetViewportSize(ViewportSize);
        if (FreeLookZone != none)
        {
            FreeLookZone.OnProcessInputDelegate = SwipeZoneCallback;
        }
    }
}
```

Motion Input

For motion input, you need to use the delegate:

```
delegate OnMobileMotion(PlayerInput PlayerInput,
                        vector CurrentAttitude,
                        vector CurrentRotationRate,
                        vector CurrentGravity,
                        vector CurrentAcceleration);
```

located in the MobilePlayerInput class. As before, you need to set up a callback function to handle the player input.

```
function MobileMotionCallback(PlayerInput PlayerInputMobile,
                        vector CurrentAttitude,
                        vector CurrentRotationRate,
                        vector CurrentGravity,
                        vector CurrentAcceleration)
{
    // Code to handle Motion Input
}
```

Next, you need to set the delegate to point to your custom callback function. Depending on your iOS device, some motion input values will be unavailable or unreliable. For example, yaw measurement, acceleration, and gravity are only valid if the iOS device has a gyroscope.

```
MPI.OnMobileMotion = MobileMotionCallback;
```

PC to iOS Setup

In this section, we will give you a quick rundown of how to set up your completed UDK game to run on an iOS device. In addition to the overview in this section, you should reference the extensive resources provided by Epic Games which are listed in the "Other Resources" section in this book's Introduction.

iOS Requirements

Games developed using the UDK can run on the following types of iOS devices:

- iPhone 4
- iPhone 4s
- iPhone 3GS
- iPad
- iPad2
- iPod touch 4th generation
- iPod touch 3rd generation (except for 8 GB 3rd generation devices.)

These devices must be running iOS 3.2 or later.

Apple Developer's License

In order to run games on an actual iOS device, you need to register as an Apple developer. Apple charges $99 per year for this. You can register at the following URL:

`http://developer.apple.com/programs/ios/`

Participating in the Apple Developer program also entitles you to a variety of resources and enables you to distribute applications via the App Store.

Provisioning

Provisioning refers to the generations of keys, certificates, and mobile profiles needed to run a UDK game on an actual iOS device. We won't go into detail about provisioning here, but Epic Games provides detailed instructions at the following site:

`http://udn.epicgames.com/Three/AppleiOSProvisioningSetup.html`

Running the UDK Game on the iOS Device

In order to play a game developed in the UDK on an actual iOS device, you need to package the game and then deploy it to the iOS device. After obtaining an Apple developer's license and doing the required provisioning, follow these steps to run your game on an iOS device.

> **NOTE:** This is the process for running default UDK game types. If you create a game with a custom type, as we'll do in this book, see the following section for some additional preparatory steps.

1. Connect your iOS device to your PC that is running the UDK.

2. Bring up the Unreal Frontend (see Figure 1–17).

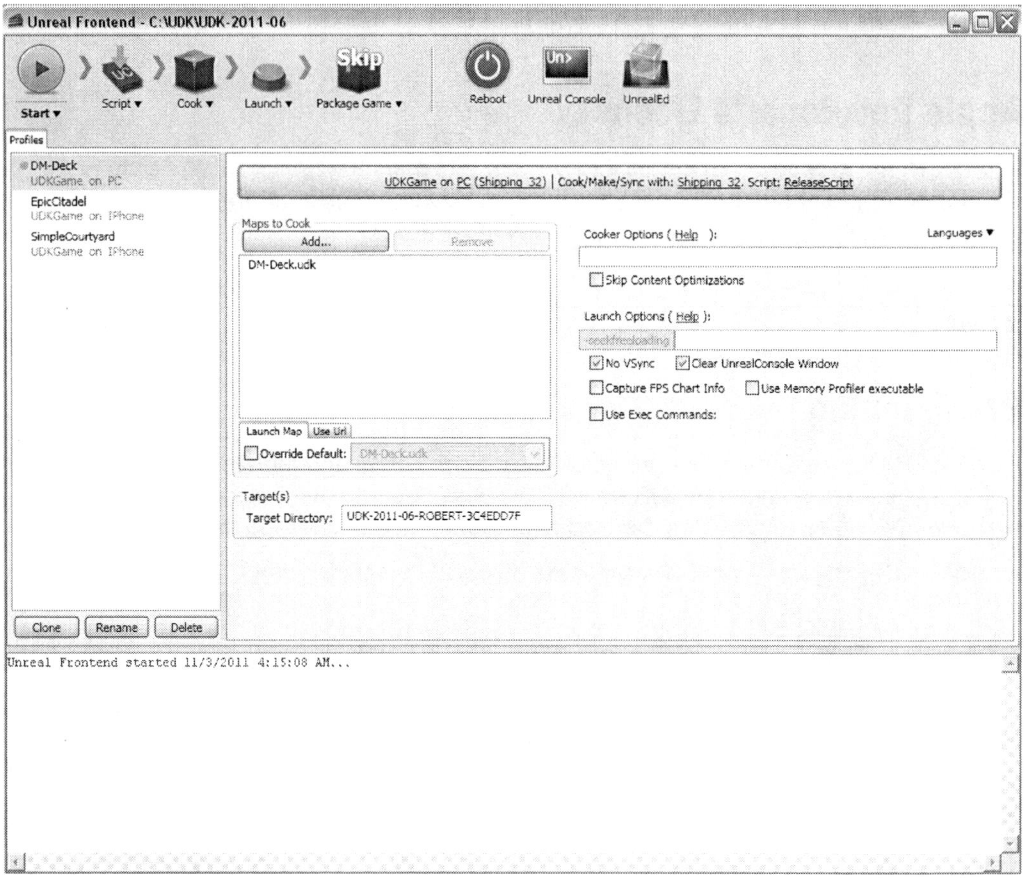

Figure 1–17. *Unreal Frontend*

3. Change the deployment platform setup from the default PC platform to the iOS platform. To do this, first press the Configuration button shown in Figure 1–18. This brings up a window shown in Figure 1–19.

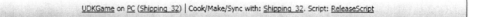

UDKGame on PC (Shipping_32) | Cook/Make/Sync with: Shipping_32. Script: ReleaseScript

Figure 1–18. *The Configuration button*

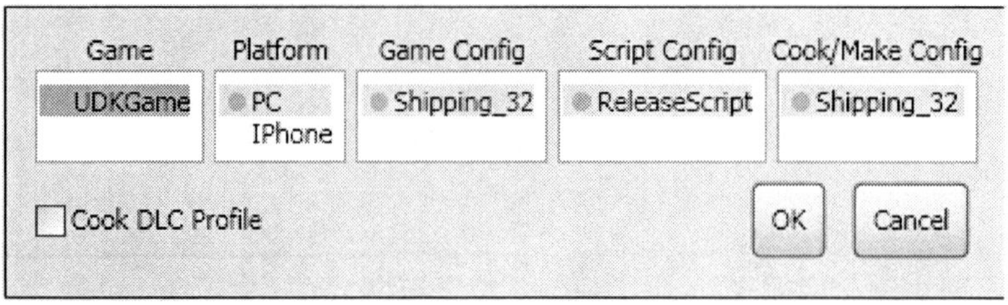

Figure 1–19. *The Default PC Deployment Setup*

4. Change the settings to those shown in Figure 1–20.

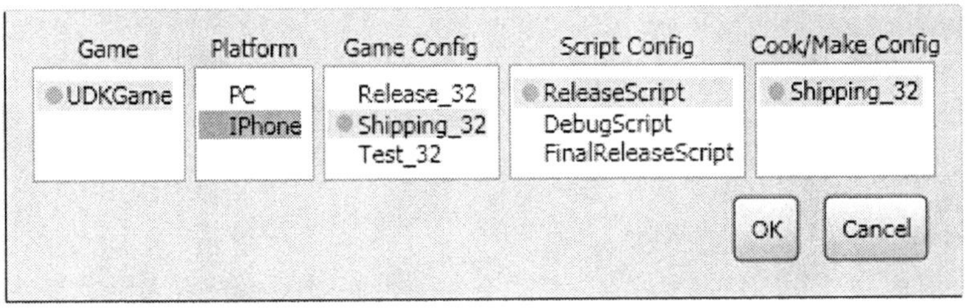

Game	Platform	Game Config	Script Config	Cook/Make Config
●UDKGame	PC **IPhone**	Release_32 ●Shipping_32 Test_32	●ReleaseScript DebugScript FinalReleaseScript	●Shipping_32

OK   Cancel

Figure 1–20. *The iOS Deployment Setup*

5. Click the OK button. The Mobile section should become visible below the Configuration button.

6. In the Mobile section, change the Packaging Mode to Default as shown in Figure 1–21.

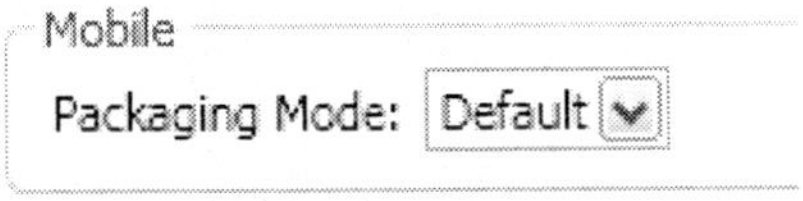

Mobile

Packaging Mode: Default ☑

Figure 1–21. *Packaging Mode*

7. Next you need to add the UDK level maps that you want to cook and place in the package that you deploy to your iOS device. Figure 1–22 shows the Maps to Cook section.

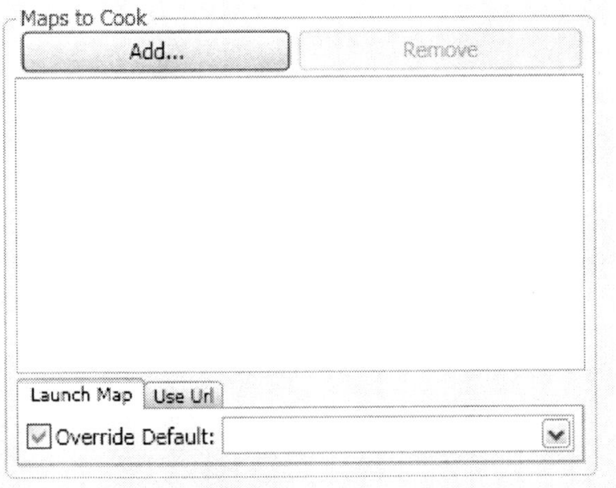

Maps to Cook

Add...   Remove

Launch Map | Use Url
☑ Override Default: ☑

Figure 1–22. *Adding Maps to Cook*

8. Click the Add button to bring up a list of the maps available on your computer (see Figure 1–23). You select the maps you want add from this list.

*

[* and ? are wildcards]

DM-Deck.udk
EnvyEntry.udk
EpicCitadel.udk
ExamplCh7Map.udk
ExamplCh7MapNavMeshMany.udk
ExamplCh7Map-PathNodes.udk
ExamplCh8MapNavMeshMany.udk
Example1Map.udk
Example2Map.udk
Example3-1Map.udk
Example3-2Map.udk
Example3-3Map.udk
Example3-4Map.udk
Example3Map.udk
Example4Map.udk
Example5Map.udk
Example6Map.udk
Example7Map.udk
Example7PathNodesMap.udk
Example8NavMeshMap.udk
Example9-HUD.udk
ExampleCh10Map.udk
ExampleCh10Map-backup.udk

Found 64 files.

[Add Selected Maps]   [Cancel]

Figure 1–23. *Selecting Maps*

9. Select the UDK level map or maps that you want to include, and then click Add
    Selected Maps to add the map(s). The added map(s) should show up as in
    Figure 1–24.

Maps to Cook

[Add...]   [Remove]

DM-Deck.udk

Launch Map | Use Url
☑ Override Default: DM-Deck.udk

Figure 1–24. *After Adding a Map*

10. Make sure that Override Default is checked. Then, from the drop-down box, select the map that you want to bring up by default when the game is first started.

11. The final thing to do is to make sure the entire build pipeline is active (which means that none of the pictures representing the Script, Cook, Package and Deploy processes have "Skip" written over them) and then click on the Start button (see Figure 1–25). If one of the processes is disabled, you can enable it by clicking on it and selecting Step Enabled from the drop-down box.

Figure 1–25. *Starting the Deployment Pipeline from Frontend*

This will compile, cook, package, and deploy your game to the iOS device where you can run it like any other iOS application. At this point the icon representing your UDK game should appear on your iOS device ready to run.

NOTE: Epic Games provides more information on cooking content at
`http://udn.epicgames.com/Three/ContentCooking.html`

Configuring Custom Game Types

In the hands-on examples in this book, we will first create, compile, and then run the UnrealScript program in the Mobile Previewer. You will also create the level in the Unreal Editor that uses this script. After making sure that the example works on the Mobile Previewer, you are ready to follow the steps in the preceding section to deploy it to an actual iOS device. Since we use custom game types in our examples, however, you will need to perform a few additional steps *before* completing the steps from the preceding section.

TIP: In terms of compiling your script, it does not matter if the Frontend is set for iOS or PC deployment. You can have your Frontend set for the PC and still compile and run your UnrealScript program in the Mobile Previewer.

First, you need to set the game type that will be played in the deployed version of the example. In order to do this, you need to change the Mobile-UDKGame.ini and the DefaultGame.ini configuration files located in

`C:\UDK\UDK-2011-06\UDKGame\Config`

and set the specific default game that is used in the hands-on example. (If you are using a different version of the UDK your default directory will be different.) For example, change the DefaultGame and DefaultServerGame configurations to the following to play the game type for the hands-on example in Chapter 2:

```
[Engine.GameInfo]
DefaultGame=ExampleCh2.ExampleCh2Game
DefaultServerGame=ExampleCh2.ExampleCh2Game
```

Next, we need to add the package that contains the code for this new game type to the list of packages that are cooked and deployed to the iOS device.

In the UDKEngine.ini configuration file add the following entries under the existing headings:

```
[Engine.PackagesToAlwaysCook]
Package=ExampleCh2

[Engine.StartupPackages]
Package=ExampleCh2
```

Next, in the DefaultEngine.ini configuration file, add the following entries under the existing headings:

```
[Engine.PackagesToAlwaysCook]
+Package=ExampleCh2

[Engine.StartupPackages]
+Package=ExampleCh2
```

Now you are ready to perform the steps from the preceding section.

> **NOTE:** Be sure to return to this chapter when you are ready to deploy any of the examples from this book to your iOS device, and complete the steps in this section and then those from the preceding section.

Summary

In summation, we took a brief look at the key features of the UDK system. We took a look at the Unreal Editor and the associated subprograms and UDK assets, such as textures, materials, static meshes, and skeletal meshes. We then discussed important UDK development aspects that differ from the iOS platform and the Windows PC platform. We discussed how saving data and using textures differ on the PC platform and the iOS platform for the UDK. We also covered the different types of player input specific to developing games on the iOS platform. Finally, we went through the basics of the PC to iOS setup for your game.

Chapter 2

UnrealScript Overview

In this chapter we will cover the UnrealScript programming language that is used to develop games for the UDK. We will cover key information concerning the UnrealScript programming language as well as Kismet which is the graphical version of that language. Such topics as data types, functions, classes, and operators are briefly discussed to give you a quick working understanding of the UnrealScript language. You will also learn how to create and compile your UnrealScript using the Unreal Frontend. There are also many hands-on examples that apply UnrealScript throughout the book and an appendix with additional UnrealScript language information. If you are already familiar with UnrealScript feel free to skip over the language review in this chapter directly to the Hands-on Example at the end of this chapter.

Finally, we'll work through a hands-on example in which you'll create your first iOS objects that you can select and receive information about using the UDK Mobile Previewer.

Kismet or UnrealScript?

Kismet is a more limited and less flexible graphical version of UnrealScript. There may also be memory and performance issues with using Kismet on older iOS devices. At least one poster on the iOS development forum on the official UDK message board complained that older iOS devices would only run his game if most of the Kismet was stripped out. The game would crash otherwise. He concluded that either it was a memory issue related to Kismet or a performance issue where a Kismet sequence was causing the game to crash. In the end he decided to only release his game for newer iOS devices and was looking for an UnrealScript programmer to convert all of his Kismet code to UnrealScript.

Kismet is more limited than UnrealScript in that it:

- Does not allow direct access to the UDK's base code with direct access to classes such as Object, Actor and so on.

- Does not allow the creation of certain variable types such as structures.

- Does not allow the creation of new classes that are derived from the UDK's base classes.

- Does not allow loading and saving Kismet sequences to separate files for merging together Kismet code from different programmers on a large project.

UnrealScript is able to do all of the above listed items.

However, for smaller games, demos, or prototypes that use little Kismet like the Jazz Jackrabbit game demo that ships with the UDK, Kismet can work well. Another area where Kismet works well is in simple level and location specific items like moving platforms, doors, gates including doors and gates that require the player to push a button to activate or unlock. Kismet will be discussed further in Chapter 6 as it relates to opening doors and locked gates.

To access the Kismet Editor first bring up the Unreal Editor. Once the editor is up and running, click the button that contains a "K" in it that is located in the Unreal Editor at the top middle portion in the first row of buttons (see Figure 2–1).

Figure 2–1. *Unreal Kismet Editor button and Matinee button*

After clicking on the "K" button, the Unreal Kismet Editor shown in Figure 2–2 should start.

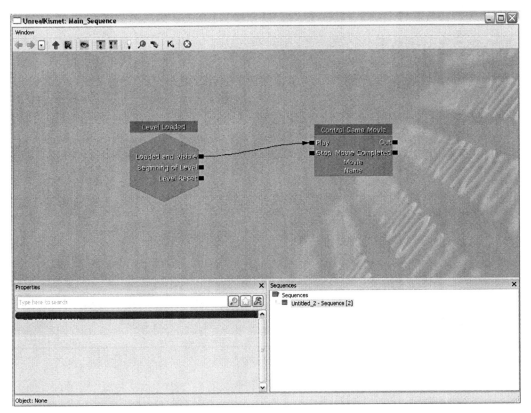

Figure 2–2. *Unreal Kismet Editor*

You may be wondering why we included the Unreal Matinee button with the Kismet button. The reason is that in order for Kismet to work in moving the doors, platforms, and gates we need to specify the specific locations where you want the object to move to. In order to do that we need to use Unreal Matinee. If you click on the Matinee button it will list all the Matinee sequences for the level. If there are Matinee sequences in the level you can click on one to bring up Matinee and load that sequence in. Another way to access Matinee is to bring up Kismet and right-click with your mouse and select "New Matinee" to create a new Matinee node. Then double-click on the Matinee graphic node to bring up the Matinee sequence associated with that node. See Figure 2–3.

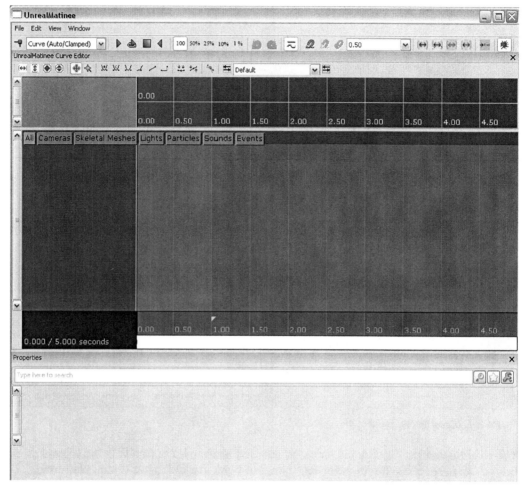

Figure 2–3. *Unreal Matinee*

Kismet is good for rapid prototyping of small games or demos, and certain things like the control of gates and doors when used with Matinee. Kismet is very limited in its access to underlying UDK base code and lacks the ability to create new classes that are derived from UDK base classes as well as being unsuited for large projects with many different programmers and large amounts of code. UnrealScript is suitable for large and small projects and gives you the flexibility and expandability you want in your UDK game.

Overview of UnrealScript

UnrealScriptUnrealScript was designed to combine features from C/C++ and Java and to add in new features such as States to create a programming language that was specifically designed for creating games.

Key features of UnrealScriptUnrealScript are:

- Single inheritance—All class objects derive directly or indirectly from a single class, which is Object. Actor is a class that derives from Object. Most important game classes like Pawn and Controller are derived from Actor. Multiple inheritance is not supported

- Support for States—An object can execute different code based on what current state it is in. UnrealScript basically implements a finite state machine as part of its built-in language features.

- No crashes when accessing "None" references - UnrealScriptUnrealScript handles accessing a None object reference (which is similar to NULL in C/C++) by logging the error should a crash occur. This alone saves much time in game development.

- Automatic garbage collection—Objects that are not used (unreferenced) are eventually deleted by UnrealScript's built-in garbage collector. This automatically regains memory that would otherwise be lost.

- Latent Functions—These are functions that require game time to execute and must finish executing before returning. Some examples are Sleep() which allows the Actor to suspend all code execution for a certain amount of game time or game ticks before continuing and MoveTo() which moves the actor to a target destination. Latent functions may only be called from within a State block and not within a function even if the function is located inside a State block.

- UnrealScript objects execute script independently—Each object in the game is updated simultaneously. For example, a game object may be executing a latent function such as a MoveTo() command but another object can access a function in this game object at the same time.

NOTE: UnrealScript is about 20 times slower than C/C++ in execution speed. So the key to creating an efficient UnrealScriptUnrealScript program is to only use UnrealScript to handle key events that you want to customize such as when two Actors collide with one another for example.

The Unreal Engine is basically a virtual machine. UnrealScript runs on this virtual machine and thus there is an extra layer of overhead required to convert UnrealScript code into code that is understood by the CPU processor running the Unreal Engine. This is one reason why UnrealScript is much slower than C/C++ which are compiled into machine language and optimized to run on a certain CPU such as Intel. The benefit of this is that UnrealScript is platform independent which means that you can take your UnrealScript code and create games on other platforms besides the PC.

UnrealScript is an object-oriented language similar to C++. This book assumes that you have a basic understanding of object-oriented programming (OOP).

> **NOTE:** If you need a refresher or introduction to OOP with C++, a good reference book is *Programming: Principles and Practice Using C++* by Bjarne Stroustrup (Addison-Wesley, 2008). Stroustrup is the original designer and implementer of the C++ programming language. Another good book on C++ is by Ray Lischner called *Exploring C++: The Programmer's Introduction to C++* (Apress, 2008). For those newer to programming, an alternative would be *Sams Teach Yourself C++ in 24 Hours* by Jesse Liberty (Sams, 2011).

The following sections give you a brief working look into the UnrealScript language itself in terms of basic variables, functions, classes, and data types. Certain aspects of UnrealScript, such as its object-oriented nature and inheritance, will not be discussed in depth because you are expected to have knowledge of this already. It is not a complete reference to the UnrealScript language. We will also be going more deeply into the language as the book progresses.

> **NOTE:** For a full official reference on UnrealScript please check out:
>
> http://udn.epicgames.com/Three/UnrealScriptReference.html

UnrealScript Comments

There are two kinds of comments styles in UnrealScript: the single line comments starting with "//" and the multi-line comments enclosed by "/* */".

- //—Single line comments begin with double slashes. The following is an example of a single line comment:

  ```
  // This is an example of a single line comment
  ```

- /* */—Multi line comments begin with a slash followed by an asterisk and end with an asterisk followed by a slash. The following is an example of this multi-line comment:

  ```
  /* This is an
  example of
  a multi line
  comment */
  ```

UnrealScript Variables

Data in a class is held in variables. In the UnrealScript language variables can be of many different types such as integer, floating point, Boolean, string, as well as references to class objects.

Scope Modifiers

All variables in UnrealScript must specify a scope which is either var or local.

- var—The specifier var indicates this variable is global to the class it is declared in.

- local—The specifier local indicates that this variable is declared within a function.

Variable Types

There are many different variable types in the UnrealScript language including types like int and float that hold numbers. Strings can hold characters. Boolean variables can hold the values true or false. An Object reference can hold a reference to a class object. Structures can comprise any of the above mentioned types.

- int—The int type holds an integer value. The following declares a local function variable of type int.

  ```
  local int dist2goal;    // Declares a local variable of type int
  ```

- float—The float type holds a floating point value. The following declares a local function variable of type float.

  ```
  Local float MinimumForce;    // Declares a local variable of type float
  ```

- bool—The bool type holds a boolean value of true or false. The following declares a global class variable of type bool.

  ```
  Var bool bdestroyed;    // Declares a global boolean variable
  ```

- string—The string type holds a group of characters. The following declares a local function variable of type string.

  ```
  Local string Player1Name;    // Declares a local variable of type string
  ```

- enum—The enum type declares an enumerated type. The following declares and enumeration called eColors that can contain the values of Purple, Violet, or Red. The variable ColorGroup1 is declared as a variable of eColors type.

  ```
  enum eColors
  {
      Purple,
      Violet,
      Red
  };
  var eColors ColorGroup1;    // Declares a global enurmerated variable
  ```

- struct—The struct type declares a structure type that can hold any combination of the other variable types. The following declares a structure of called sPlayerInfo that contains two variables, one int variable called PlayerHeartRate and one bool variable called PlayerInfected. A variable called Player1Info is declared as a global class variable of type sPlayerInfo structure.

```
Struct sPlayerInfo
{
    var int PlayerHeartRate;
    var bool PlayerInfected;
};
var sPlayerInfo Player1Info;    // Declares a global variable of type sPlayerInfo
```

- Static Arrays—Static arrays can hold collections of objects. The length of this type of array is set at compile time and cannot be changed during program execution. Static arrays in UnrealScript are restricted to one dimension. Any variable type can be put into a static array except boolean. The following declares a global variable of type static array that holds 5 elements of objects references to an Actor.

```
Var Actor SquadMembers[5];
```

- Dynamic Arrays—Dynamic arrays can hold a collection of objects. The length of the array can change during script execution. Dynamic arrays have many functions that can manipulate items in the array. The following declares a dynamic array of type reference to an Actor.

```
Var array<Actor> SquadMembers;
```

The following code adds a new member to the SquadMembers array assuming that TempBot is an object reference variable to an Actor.

```
var Actor TempBot;
SquadMembers.AddItem(TempBot);
```

The following code finds the number of members in the array or in this case the number of members in our squad.

```
numbersquadmembers = SquadMembers.length;
```

The following code loops through the members of the dynamic array SquadMembers and returns a reference to each member through the variable TempSquadMember. In the loop each squad member can be processed one at a time.

```
Local Actor TempSquadMember;
foreach SquadMembers(TempSquadMember)
{
    // Process TempSquadMember
}
```

- Object Reference – The object reference type holds a reference to an object of type Class Object. The following declares an object reference variable to an Actor called TempActor. A new object of class Actor is created by the Spawn command and assigned to the TempActor reference.

```
Var Actor TempActor;// Declares a global reference variable to an Actor
TempActor = Spawn(class'Actor');
```

You can cast an object reference variable to a specific class to test if it refers to an object of that type. If it returns a None reference then it does not refer to an object of that class or any subclass of that class. If the returned result is not None then the returned reference will be to an object of the type of the cast.

In the following code the variable TempActor is tested to see if it is of class Pawn though a cast. The result is put into the variable TempPawn. If the conversion was successful (holding a value besides None) then TempActor was indeed a Pawn or a subclass of Pawn. If the value in TempPawn is None then the object in TempActor is not a Pawn or a subclass of Pawn.

```
Var Actor TempActor;
Var Pawn TempPawn;

TempPawn = Pawn(TempActor);
If (TempPawn != None)
{
    // TempPawn contains a reference to a Pawn
}
else
{
    // TempPawn contain a None value and does not
    // contain a reference to a Pawn
}
```

> **NOTE:** For object reference variables like TempActor above you need to make sure to either assign a valid reference to TempActor before you use it or you need to create a new object using the Spawn function built into the base UDK code. Example: TempActor = Spawn(class'Actor');

- Class Reference—A class reference variable holds a reference to a class. The format is in

```
class<BaseClass> VariableName;
```

The class reference VariableName can hold a class of type BaseClass or a subclass of BaseClass. A subclass of BaseClass would be any class that is derived from BaseClass. Remember that UnrealScript only supports single inheritance from the base class called Object. Multiple inheritances from more than one class is not permitted so determining if a class is a subclass of another is very straightforward.

The following code holds a reference to the player controller class used to spawn players. The `PlayerControllerClass` variable is then set to a custom player controller class that we will create later in this chapter.

```
var class<PlayerController> PlayerControllerClass;
PlayerControllerClass=class'ExampleCh2.ExampleCh2PC'
```

Operators

In order to perform mathematical calculations UnrealScript has the standard arithmetic operators available for you to use. UnrealScript also has many different conditional operators to test expressions for such things as equality, inequality, and so on. Each of the operators takes two expressions. Expressions can consist of a single variable or many variables and operators.

Artithmetic Operators

UnrealScript provides you with add, subtract, multiply, and divide operators that allow you to make math calculations. You can use parenthesis to group these operators together if needed.

- +, -, *, /—The standard add, subtract, multiply and divide operators

Conditional Operators

Conditional operators return a value of true or false depending on what type of conditional operator is involved and the value that the expressions evaluate to. Conditional operators are mostly used in combination with flow control statements such as if, while, and for.

- (expression1) || (expression2)—Evaluates to true if expression1 or expression2 are true. False otherwise.

- (expression1) && (expression2)—Evaluated to true if expression1 and expression2 are true. False otherwise.

- (expression1) == (expression2)—Evaluates to true if expression1 is equal to expression2. False otherwise.

- (expression1) != (expression2)—Evaluates to true if expression1 is not equal to expression2. False otherwise.

- (expression1) > (expression2)—Evaluates to true if expression1 is greater than expression2. False otherwise.

- (expression1) < (expression2)—Evaluates to true if expression1 is less than expression2. False otherwise.

- (expression1) >= (expression2)—Evaluates to true if expression1 is greater than or equal to expression2. False otherwise.

- (expression1) <= (expression2)—Evaluates to true if expression1 is less than or equal to expression2. False otherwise.

Code Execution Flow Control Statements

UnrealScript code, just like C/C++ code, executes sequentially one line after another. However, UnrealScript also has statements to control the execution of code so that it does not have to always execute sequentially.

- If Statement—If expression1 evaluates to true then the code in Section 1 will execute. If expression1 evaluates to false then the expresion2 is evaluated and if it evaluates to true then Section 2 code is executed.

```
if (expression1)
{
    // Section 1 Code
}
else if (expression2)
{
    // Section 2 Code
}
```

In the following example if PlayerHealth is less than 0 then the code within the braces is executed.

```
if (PlayerHealth < 0)
{
    // Execute code for Player's Death
}
```

- While Statement—The code within the While block is executed as long as expression1 evaluates to true.

```
While (expression1)
{
}
```

In the following example the code block is executed if PlayerHealth is less than 20 and keeps executing as long as that condition evaluates to true.

```
While (PlayerHealth < 20)
{
    // While PlayerHealth is less than 20 then execute this loop
}
```

■ For Statement—The `for` statement is composed of three sections. The first section is the variable initialization section where the initial value of the counter variable is set and optionally declared. The second section contains the expression to be evaluated. This expression is evaluated at the beginning of the `for` loop and if it evaluates to true then the code block is executed. At the end of the code block the counter variable is incremented/decremented. The expression is tested again and if it evaluates to true then the code block is executed. This continues until the expression evaluates to false then the for loop is exited.

```
for (counter variable initialization;
     (expression1);
     countervariable increment/decrement)
{
}
```

In the following example, the `for` loop counter variable is initialized to 0. If i is less than 10 then the code block is executed. The counter variable is incremented by 1 at the end of the loop.

```
For (int i = 0;  i < 10; i++)
{
    // Execute this block of code while i < 10, increase i by 1 after every loop
}
```

■ Switch/Case Statement—The switch statement is a more elegant and organized alternative to the if then else statement. Instead of many else if statements with many braces you have a neat case break pair. The expression in the switch statement is evaluated. Execution will jump to the case break block that matches the value in the case statement or will jump to the default block if there are no matches.

```
Switch (expression1)
{
    case value1:
    break;

    case value2:
    break;

    default:
    break;
}
```

In the following example, the value of ColorGroup1 is determined then that value is matched with the values Purple, Violet, or Red to determine which case break block to jump to.

```
Switch (ColorGroup1)
{
    case Purple:
        // Insert Code Here
    break;
    case Violet:
```

```
                // Insert Code Here
            break;
            case Red:
                // Insert Code Here
            break;
    }
```

Class Declarations

UnrealScript supports object oriented classes and class inheritance. In order to have one class derive from a parent class use the extends keyword. A class consists of the class heading which declares the classname followed by "the" extends keyword and the class it derives from. This is followed by the global class variables if any. Then the class functions are declared. UnrealScript classes can have many different options associated with them and these are discussed in a subsequent chapter later in this book.

The following code declares a new class of type Soldier that derives from the Actor class. Two global class variables are also declared. Each class must be put in a separate plain text file created with a program like Notepad and named after the class. This class's filename would be Soldier.uc.

```
class Soldier extends Actor;
var bool bIsSick;
var bool bHasOpenSores;
```

Functions

Functions in UnrealScript help you divide a big task into smaller more manageable pieces much like other programming languages like C and C++. UnrealScript functions have many different options and function specifiers. These will be discussed in detail in a subsequent chapter.

The following declares a basic function called TestSoldierInfected(). It takes an input parameter of type Soldier and returns a boolean value depending on weather this soldier is infected or not.

```
function bool TestSoldierInfected(Soldier TestActor )
{
    local bool bInfected;
    if (TestActor.bIsSick && TestActor.bHasOpenSores)
    {
        bInfected = true;
    }
    else
    {
        bInfected = false;
    }
    return bInfected;
}
```

States

UnrealScript has built-in support for a finite state machine. A finite state machine (or FSM) used in this book refers to a computer model that describes the behavior of computer controlled bots. An FSM can only be in one state at a time and can move to other states depending on a trigger such as a change of conditions in the game.

For example, a bot using an FSM can initially be put into an idle state then when an enemy is within a certain distance change to an attacking state and move toward the enemy and fire its weapon at it.

The following is the general format for a state. The items in brackets are optional.

```
[Auto] State[()] StateName
{
[ignores FunctionName1, FunctionName2, …]
    event BeginState( Name PreviousStateName )
    {
        // Code for BeginState Goes Here
    }
    event EndState( Name NextStateName )
    {
        // Code for EndState Goes Here
    }
    function StateSpecificFunction()
    {
        // Code StateSpecificFunction Goes Here
    }
    Begin:
    // Begin State Code
    // Put calls to Latent Functions here.
}
```

The Auto specifier for the state indicates that this state is the initial state that the actor is placed in when it is created.

The ignores keyword is optional and causes the functions specified after ignores to not be executed while the object is in this state.

The parenthesis () after the State keyword means that this state can be edited in the Unreal Editor.

The BeginState and EndState functions are part of the built in UnrealScript State system and are optional. The BeginState function is executed once when the state is first entered. The input parameter PreviousStateName holds the Name of the previous state the object was in before transitioning to the current state. The EndState function is executed once when leaving the state but before entering the new state. The input parameter NextStateName is the name of the state that is to be transitioned to after the EndState function is executed. A state does not need to declare a BeginState, or EndState but it is good to have the framework in place just in case you need to add code that has to be executed every time when a state is entered or exited.

Within a state you can define functions that only will be executed when the object is in that specific state.

The beginning of the actual state code starts at the Begin: label.

Debug Messages

One helpful way to debug your program is to have messages displayed on your screen via the Broadcast() function. UnrealScript is very flexible and will automatically convert boolean, int, float, and even class objects into a displayable format using the code below.

```
WorldInfo.Game.Broadcast(self, "Soldier Object = " @ TestActor @
                         "Soldier's Sick Status = " @ TestActor.bIsSick @
                         ", Soldiers's Open Sore Status = " @
                         TestActor.bHasOpenSores);
```

Creating and Compiling UnrealScript

UnrealScript can be created by any plain text word processing program such as Notepad. Notepad comes with the Windows operating system at no additional cost. In order to compile UnrealScript you need to start up the Unreal Frontend program. The Frontend is located in the Tool directory of your UDK installation and is labeled "Unreal Frontend". Select this program from the Start Menu bar and click on it. The Frontend window shown in Figure 2–4 opens.

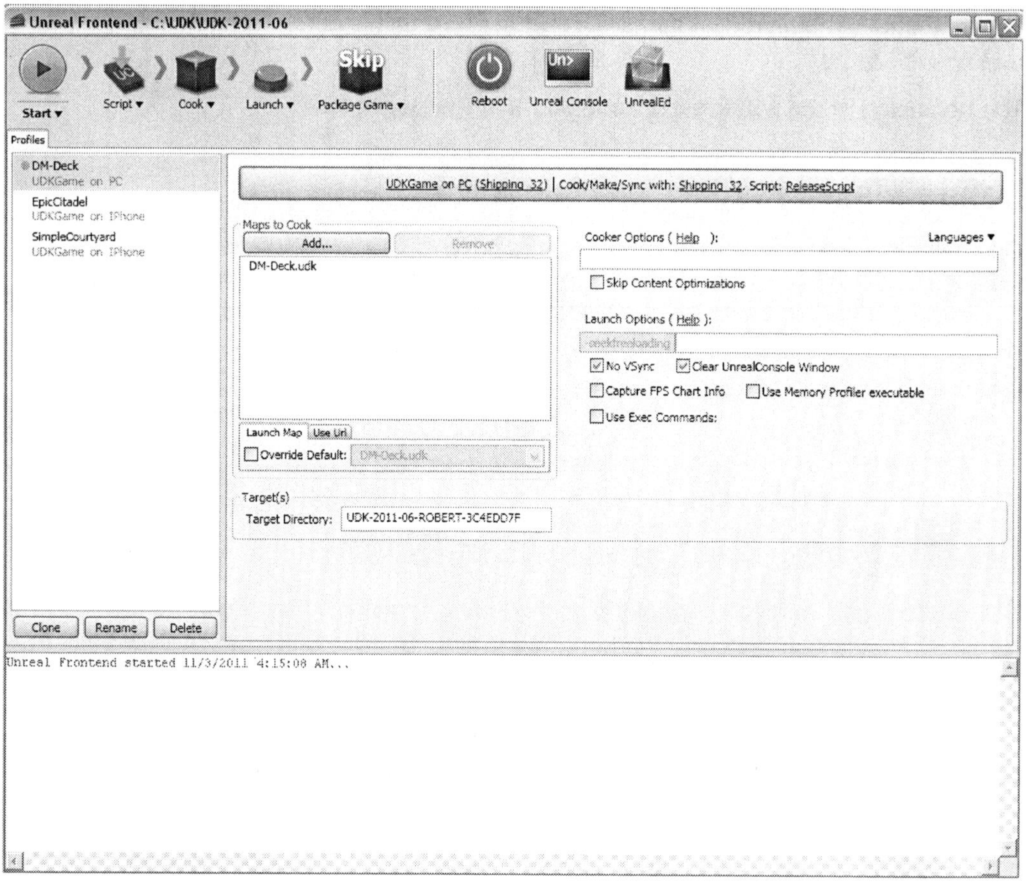

Figure 2–4. *Unreal Frontend*

In order to start the actual compiling click the Script button on the top left-hand side of the toolbar, which will highlight options for compilation (see Figure 2–5).

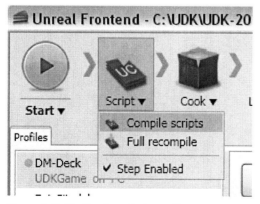

Figure 2–5. *Starting the actual compile*

The "Compile scripts" option only compiles scripts that have been changed since the last compile. The "Full recompile" option compiles all the scripts in the UDK system regardless if they have changed since the last compile or not. Once the scripts have been successfully compiled then any new classes are automatically added to the Actor Classes tab in the Unreal Editor where they can be used in building game levels.

Hands-On Example: Selecting an Object with Touch

In this tutorial you will learn how to use the iOS touch input system to pick out an actor. The first thing we need to do is create a new level for this example and put some objects in it.

1. Start up the Unreal Editor.

2. Change the object type filter in the Content Browser to search for static meshes.

3. Put static meshes of your choice into the blank level that is the default level that is loaded when the Unreal Editor comes up. One way you can do this is you can click on the static mesh you want to put into the level then drag it to where you want to place it into the level. Another way is to click on the static mesh then go to the place in the level where want to place it then right-click and select the add StaticMesh option (see Figure 2–6).

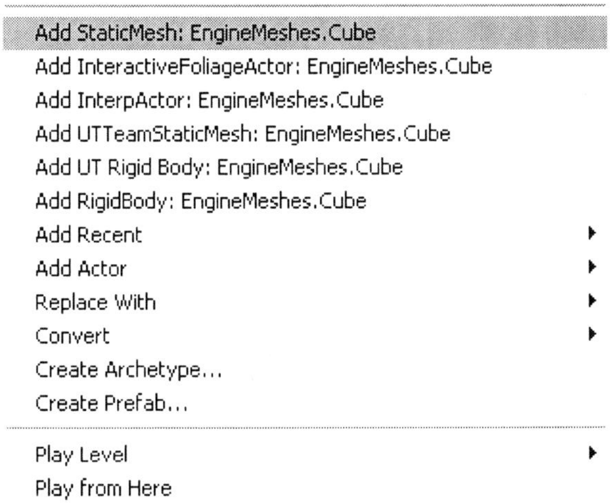

Figure 2–6. *Adding a Static Mesh to a level*

4. Make sure your static mesh also has a collision model associated with it or else it will not be detected by the user's touch.

> **NOTE:** We will discuss collision models in Chapter 4 on UDK collisions. Some examples of static meshes with collision models are SM_GEN_Foliage01_LargeTree01_Opt, SM_GEN_Ruins_512Block01, and SM_VendorCrate_01_E. The collision models are already incorporated within each of the static meshes so you don't need to set any specific collision model for the meshes since they are already part of the static mesh. You can search for these models using the search function of the Content Browser and place them in the level.

5. The next thing to do is to save the level. To do this, click "File" menu item and choose the "Save As" option which brings up the Save As file dialog box. Enter the filename as "ExampleCh2Map" and click the Save button.

Creating the Game Type

Now that we have created our map for this example we need to create the code to handle touches and code to pick an actor.

1. Create a new directory called ExampleCh2 under the Development\Src directory of the UDK installation which by default is \UDK\UDK-2011-06 on the drive you installed the UDK on.

2. Under that directory create another directory called Classes. This is where the source code from this example will be placed in.

3. Create a new file called ExampleCh2Game.uc in the Classes directory. This new class will hold information for the type of game to be played and is a subclass of the GameInfo class.

4. Add the following line to the file, which declares the new ExampleCh2Game class as deriving from FrameworkGame.

```
class ExampleCh2Game extends FrameworkGame;
```

5. Add the OnEngineHasLoaded() function to the file. This function is called when the Unreal engine has finished loading and prints out a message that our custom game type is now active.

```
event OnEngineHasLoaded()
{
    WorldInfo.Game.Broadcast(self,"ExampleCh2Game Type Active - Engine Has Loaded
!!!!");}
```

6. Add the PreventDeath() function to the file. The PreventDeath function returns true to stop our player from dying in the game.

```
function bool PreventDeath(Pawn KilledPawn,
                Controller Killer,
                class<DamageType> DamageType,
```

```
                              vector HitLocation)
{
    return true;
}
```

7. Add the SetGameType() function to the file. The SetGameType function can be used to allow only certain mapnames to be used with our gametype. For now just let all maps use our gametype.

```
static event class<GameInfo> SetGameType(string MapName, string Options, string Portal)
{
    return super.SetGameType(MapName, Options, Portal);
}
```

8. Add the defaultproperties block to the file. The important thing to take note of is that custom player controllers, custom pawns and custom HUD classes can be specified here. The PlayerControllerClass variable is set to our custom player controller that we will create next which is ExampleCh2PC.

```
defaultproperties
{
        PlayerControllerClass=class'ExampleCh2.ExampleCh2PC'

        DefaultPawnClass=class'UDKBase.SimplePawn'
        HUDType=class'UDKBase.UDKHUD'
        bRestartLevel=false
        bWaitingToStartMatch=true
        bDelayedStart=false
}
```

9. Save the ExampleCh2Game.uc file that you just added the above lines into.

Creating the Player Controller

Now let's create the player controller.

1. Create a new file called ExampleCh2PC.uc and save it in the same directory as the other file. Add in the following line to declare this new player controller class as a subclass of SimplePC.

```
class ExampleCh2PC extends SimplePC;
```

2. Add the following line to the file. PickDistance is the maximum distance that the picked item can be from the player.

```
var float PickDistance;
```

3. Add the PickActor() function to the file. The PickActor function actually does the work of finding the actor based on an input 2d touch location and maps this into the 3d world and then returns the actor touched by the player if there is one.

```
function Actor PickActor(Vector2D PickLocation, out Vector HitLocation, out TraceHitInfo
HitInfo)
{
    local Vector TouchOrigin, TouchDir;
    local Vector HitNormal;
    local Actor  PickedActor;
    local vector Extent;

    //Transform absolute screen coordinates to relative coordinates
    PickLocation.X = PickLocation.X / ViewportSize.X;
    PickLocation.Y = PickLocation.Y / ViewportSize.Y;

    //Transform to world coordinates to get pick ray
    LocalPlayer(Player).Deproject(PickLocation, TouchOrigin, TouchDir);

    //Perform trace to find touched actor
    Extent = vect(0,0,0);
    PickedActor = Trace(HitLocation,
                    HitNormal,
                    TouchOrigin + (TouchDir * PickDistance),
                    TouchOrigin,
                    True,
                    Extent,
                    HitInfo);
    //Return the touched actor for good measure
    return PickedActor;
}
```

4. Add the SwipeZoneCallback() function to the file. The following is the
    touch input callback function that calls the PickActor function and
    displays the result. If the user picks an actor then that actor's name is
    printed out, followed by the hit location where the user touches the
    object in the 3d world, and the zone that the touch occurred in.

```
function bool SwipeZoneCallback(MobileInputZone Zone,
                                float DeltaTime,
                                int Handle,
                                EZoneTouchEvent EventType,
                                Vector2D TouchLocation)
{
    local bool retval;
    local Actor PickedActor;
    local Vector HitLocation;
    local TraceHitInfo HitInfo;

    retval = true;
    if (EventType == ZoneEvent_Touch)
    {
        // If screen touched then pick actor
        PickedActor = PickActor(TouchLocation,HitLocation,HitInfo);
        WorldInfo.Game.Broadcast(self,"PICKED ACTOR   ="
                                    @ PickedActor @ ", HitLocation = "
                                    @ HitLocation @ ", Zone Touched = "
                                    @ Zone);
    }
    else
```

```
    if(EventType == ZoneEvent_Update)
    {
    }
    else
    if (EventType == ZoneEvent_UnTouch)
    {
    }
    return retval;
}
```

5. Add the `SetupZones()` function to the file. The `SetupZones` function sets the `SwipeZoneCallback` as the function that handles touch input processing.

```
function SetupZones()
{
    Super.SetupZones();
    // If we have a game class, configure the zones
    if (MPI != None && WorldInfo.GRI.GameClass != none)
    {
        LocalPlayer(Player).ViewportClient.GetViewportSize(ViewportSize);
        if (FreeLookZone != none)
        {
            FreeLookZone.OnProcessInputDelegate = SwipeZoneCallback;
        }
    }
}
```

6. Add the `defaultproperties` block to the file. Here the `PickDistance` variable is set by default to 10000.

```
defaultproperties
{
    PickDistance = 10000;
}
```

7. Save this file.

Settting up the Game Type Configuration

Now we need to set up the configuration to compile and run our game. First you need to modify the UDKEngine.ini file located in the UDKGame\Config under your UDK installation.

1. Under the `UnrealEd.EditorEngine` section add in the following line to allow our new code to be added to the compile list

```
UDKEngine.ini
[UnrealEd.EditorEngine]
ModEditPackages=ExampleCh2
```

2. Next we need to set up the mobile virtual joystick controls and touch screen input. In the same configuration directory add the following line to your Mobile-UDKGame.ini file.

```
Mobile-UDKGame.ini
[ExampleCh2.ExampleCh2Game]
```

```
RequiredMobileInputConfigs=(GroupName="UberGroup",RequireZoneNames=("UberStickMoveZone",
"UberStickLookZone","UberLookZone"));
```

> **NOTE:** You can set up a general set of configurations here for the rest of the chapters by making new
> entries for other chapters if you wish. However, some chapters will contain multiple examples and will
> require a configuration entry for each example. We will show you the details on how to set up these
> configurations in the hands-on examples in the rest of the book.

Next, we need to compile our script. Bring up the Unreal Frontend and select Compile scripts to compile our code. After the code successfully compiles then we are ready to start up the Unreal Editor.

Running the Game Type

Starting in the June version of the UDK you can select and save the game type you want associated with a level and play this level in the Mobile Previewer from the Editor.

1. Start up the Unreal Editor.

2. Select the World Properties menu item under the View Menu. This should bring up the WorldInfo Properties window shown in Figure 2–7.

Figure 2–7. *Setting the Game Type in the Unreal Editor*

3. Under the Game Type property set the Default Game Type to ExampleCh2Game from the drop-down list box.

4. Close the WorldInfo Properties window.

5. Under the Play menu select On Mobile Previewer. This should start up the Mobile Previewer with your level using the new game type ExampleCh2Game (see Figure 2–8).

Figure 2–8. *ExampleCh2Game for our first hands-on example*

Both the joysticks should be working. The right stick should turn the player left and right and move the view up and down. The left stick should move the player forward and back and side to side. You should be able to use your mouse to click on various static meshes and the Actor name, hitlocation, and zone should be printed out on the screen. An Actor name of None means that no Actor was selected. For now, ignore the message about the lighting needing to be rebuilt since this does not affect the gameplay.

Summary

In this chapter we took a brief tour of the UnrealScript language giving readers a basic working knowledge of it and saving the details for later chapters. We also took a look at Kismet and Matinee again saving the details for later chapters. Finally, a detailed hands-on tutorial was provided that pulled all this information and concepts together in an applied manner in the form of a working UDK Mobile based application where the user can pick actors by clicking on them through the Mobile Previewer.

Chapter 3

Player Controllers, Pawns, and Weapons

This chapter will cover player controllers, the player's pawn, and weapons. A pawn in the UDK represents the physical presence of a player or a computer controlled game character. Think of this as the player's body in the game. The player controller controls the pawn and translates player input into pawn movement and other actions. Information regarding these topics is presented followed by tutorials. You will find out how to:

- Use the PlayerController and Pawn classes
- Make a pawn visible using a skeletal mesh
- Use camera views
- Set and change your pawns' views
- Use the Weapon and related classes
- Add weapons to pawns from different views

Player Controller and Pawn Overview

The player input system within the UDK is divided between the player controller and the pawn. The pawn represents the player's physical presence in the game. When you need to find the player's location, or rotation you will need to find the location or rotation of the player's pawn. The player controller takes input from the player, processes this input and translates them into movement for the pawn it controls.

All player controllers must derive from the PlayerController class and all pawns must derive from the Pawn class. For programming on the iOS platform the SimplePC class can be used for the base for custom player controllers and SimplePawn can be used as the base for custom pawns. The advantage of using the SimplePC class as the base of your custom player controller is that this class already has set up joystick and touch input zones as well as some other features like footstep sounds and simulated player breathing through camera motion. The advantage of using the SimplePawn is that it features "head bobbing" which makes the camera move up and down as the player walks around. This makes the player's view more realistic. Head bobbing is done by setting the bScriptTickSpecial=true which is the default value in SimplePawn. The actual head bobbing is done in the TickSpecial() function in the SimplePawn class. To turn head bobbing off, set bScriptTickSpecial=false in a derived pawn class. The main update function for the PlayerController class is PlayerTick(), which is called at regular intervals, or "ticked" once per frame update of the game.

Here you can add in custom code to handle items unique to your particular game. For example, if a goal in your game is to retrieve a certain item then you can check for the player's possessions for this item in PlayerTick(). The way you would do this is override the PlayerTick() function in your custom player controller, execute the normal PlayerTick() function through the Super prefix and then execute your custom code afterwards. See Listing 3–1.

Listing 3–1. *Customizing the PlayerTick() function*

```
function PlayerTick(float DeltaTime)
{
    Super.PlayerTick(DeltaTime);
    // Add in additional code here for your custom player controller
    If (Jazz3Pawn(Pawn).Lives <= 0)
    {
        Gameover = true;
    }
}
```

The modified PlayerTick() function checks if the player's has more lives and if not then sets the Gameover variable to true.

The PlayerMove() function is called every time PlayerTick() is called and calculates new acceleration and rotation values for the player. This function then calls ProcessMove() which then executes the actual move. It is in the ProcessMove() function that we can change how the player's pawn responds to the player's movement input. For example, in your custom controller class if you declared a function ProcessMove() that is defined in the PlayerWalking state then this new function will override the default ProcessMove() function.

```
state PlayerWalking
{
    ignores SeePlayer, HearNoise, Bump;
    function ProcessMove(float DeltaTime,
                        vector NewAccel,
                        eDoubleClickDir DoubleClickMove,
                        rotator DeltaRot)
    {
        // Place custom code for player movement here to override the default
    }
}
```

The UpdateRotation() function is responsible for updating the controller's rotation and the pawn's rotation.

Hands-on Example: Making your pawn visible with a 3D skeletal mesh character

This tutorial will show you how to add in a skeletal mesh to your pawn to make it visible. We start off by creating a new game type and a new custom player controller. This game type will use the first-person viewpoint. Next, we configure the new custom game to run on the UDK mobile previewer and show you how to run it. Finally, we add a skeletal mesh to the player's pawn to make the pawn visible.

Creating the Default First-Person View

In this section you will create a new game type that uses the default first-person viewpoint. This section introduces the basic framework from which we will build on for future examples.

1. The first thing you need to do is create a directory for our next example. In your UDK installation directory create the following folder, `\Development\Src\ExampleCh31\Classes`. As before you will put your code into this new Classes directory. (Note that the general numbering scheme for these examples is "ExampleCh" followed by the chapter number and then an example number if there is more than one.)

2. The first class you need to create is the `ExampleCh31Game` class that defines the type of game to be played. See Listing 3–2.

Listing 3–2. *Defining the Game Type*

```
class ExampleCh31Game extends FrameworkGame;

event OnEngineHasLoaded()
{
    WorldInfo.Game.Broadcast(self,"ExampleCh31Game Type Active - Engine Has Loaded
!!!!");
}
function bool PreventDeath(Pawn KilledPawn, Controller Killer, class<DamageType>
DamageType, vector HitLocation)
{
    return true;
}
static event class<GameInfo> SetGameType(string MapName, string Options, string Portal)
{
    return super.SetGameType(MapName, Options, Portal);
}
defaultproperties
{
    PlayerControllerClass=class'ExampleCh31.ExampleCh31PC'
    DefaultPawnClass=class'SimplePawn'
    HUDType=class'UDKBase.UDKHUD'

    bRestartLevel=false
```

```
        bWaitingToStartMatch=true
        bDelayedStart=false
}
```

3. The next class is the custom player controller class ExampleCh31PC. This player controller is stripped to the bare essentials. See Listing 3–3.

Listing 3–3. *Creating a basic player controller*

```
class ExampleCh31PC extends SimplePC;

function bool SwipeZoneCallback(MobileInputZone Zone,
                                float DeltaTime,
                                int Handle,
                                EZoneTouchEvent EventType,
                                Vector2D TouchLocation)
{
    local bool retval = true;


    if (EventType == ZoneEvent_Touch)
    {
        WorldInfo.Game.Broadcast(self,"You touched the screen at = "
                                 @ TouchLocation.x @ " , "
                                 @ TouchLocation.y @ ", Zone Touched = "
                                 @ Zone);
    }


    else if(EventType == ZoneEvent_Update)
    {
    }


    else if (EventType == ZoneEvent_UnTouch)
    {
    }
    return retval;
}

function SetupZones()
{
    Super.SetupZones();

    // If we have a game class, configure the zones
    if (MPI != None && WorldInfo.GRI.GameClass != none)
    {
        LocalPlayer(Player).ViewportClient.GetViewportSize(ViewportSize);
        if (FreeLookZone != none)
        {
            FreeLookZone.OnProcessInputDelegate = SwipeZoneCallback;
        }
    }
}
defaultproperties
{
```

```
}
```

4. Next you need to set up the game and compiler for our new example. Edit the Mobile-UDKGame.ini and UDKEngine.ini files in your UDKGame\Config directory.

```
Mobile-UDKGame.ini
[ExampleCh31.ExampleCh31Game]
RequiredMobileInputConfigs=(GroupName="UberGroup",RequireZoneNames=("UberStickMoveZone",
"UberStickLookZone","UberLookZone"))
UDKEngine.ini
[UnrealEd.EditorEngine]
ModEditPackages=ExampleCh31
```

5. Now compile the code using the Unreal Frontend.
6. Start up the Unreal Editor and change the Default Game Type to ExampleCh31Game. Do this by selecting **View ➤ World Properties** to bring up the World Properties window and setting the Default Game Type property under the Game Type category.
7. Run the game on the Mobile Previewer by selecting **Play ➤ On Mobile Previewer** from the main menu and you should see something like the following in Figure 3–1.

Figure 3–1. *Default First-Person View*

You should note that by default the player's pawn is invisible. The reason for this is that there is no mesh associated with the pawn. You will add that next.

Adding a Skeletal Mesh to represent your pawn

In order to make the player's pawn visible we can add in a skeletal mesh that would move around with the player's pawn and be animated to represent the player's walking. You need to create a new class called Jazz1Pawn and the associated file Jazz1Pawn.uc. See Listing 3–4.

Listing 3–4. *Creating a visible pawn*

```
class Jazz1Pawn extends SimplePawn;

defaultproperties
{
    Begin Object Class=SkeletalMeshComponent Name=JazzMesh
        SkeletalMesh=SkeletalMesh'KismetGame_Assets.Anims.SK_Jazz'
        AnimSets(0)=AnimSet'KismetGame_Assets.Anims.SK_Jazz_Anims'
        AnimTreeTemplate=AnimTree'KismetGame_Assets.Anims.Jazz_AnimTree'
        BlockRigidBody=true
        CollideActors=true
    End Object
    Mesh = JazzMesh; // Set The mesh for this object
    Components.Add(JazzMesh); // Attach this mesh to this Actor
}
```

In the default properties a new SkeletalMeshComponent is defined and named JazzMesh. This is added to the object's Components array which attaches this mesh to the object's position and rotation. The pawn's Mesh variable is also set to the new SkeletalMeshComponent.

JazzMesh is defined by setting the key variables of SkeletalMesh, AnimSets, and AnimTreeTemplate to point to assets in the UDK system. These assets are visible from within the Content Browser.

> **NOTE:** To find the skeletal mesh used here search for a Skeletal Mesh called "sk_jazz" in the Content Browser under the UDKGame package. You should see a skeletal mesh character called "SK_JAZZ". You can double-click on this asset to bring it up in the AnimSet Editor if you desire. You can also right-click on this asset and select Copy Full Name to ClipBoard to copy this asset's name for use in your script code. Do this now and bring up a plain text editor like NotePad and paste the text. You should see the following text:
>
> SkeletalMesh'KismetGame_Assets.Anims.SK_Jazz

In the defaultproperties block of the ExampleCh31Game class change the DefaultPawnClass to point to our new pawn class Jazz1Pawn as shown below.

```
//DefaultPawnClass=class'SimplePawn'
DefaultPawnClass=class'Jazz1Pawn'
```

Recompile the code and run the game using the ExampleCh31Game game type. You should see a skeletal mesh however at the same time it blocks your view like in Figure 3–2.

Figure 3–2. *Player's default view with a skeletal mesh attached to the player's pawn*

Obviously, this is not acceptable. By default the position of the camera that represents the player's view is set directly at the pawn's location. The skeletal mesh is also set at the pawn location. This overlapping explains this blocked view.

The solution is to move the player's view backward so that the full skeletal mesh can be viewed and so that the player's view of the game is not obstructed. In order to do this we must move the camera further away from the pawn.

UDK Camera Overview

The camera system in the UDK involves the camera, the player controller, and the pawn that is controlled by the player controller. These three elements interact to move and rotate the player's pawn and the player's view of the world. The way this works is that there are functions in these classes that can be overridden by the programmer to change things like the camera position, camera rotation, or the way the player moves. Changing the camera view from a first-person view to a third-person view where your pawn is visible is easily done. You just need to override a function in the Pawn class.

The player controller takes in user input and then translates this into movement and rotation for its pawn. As discussed in the section on player controllers the functions ProcessMove() and UpdateRotation() can be overridden in a custom player controller class derived from PlayerController to provide custom movements and rotations needed for a specific camera view. Most importantly, the pawn has a function to set the camera's location and rotation called CalcCamera(). In the following tutorials we will use this function to change the camera views of our pawn.

In our player's pawn class we would override the CalcCamera() function with our own custom function where we can set the camera location and rotation based on our pawn's location, rotation, and the kind of camera view we desire. You can set the actual camera location through the out_CamLoc variable and the camera rotation through the out_CamRot variable. Both parameters are declared with the specifier out, which means that setting the value of the variable in the function sets the value of the variable in the caller function.

```
simulated function bool CalcCamera( float fDeltaTime,
                                    out vector out_CamLoc,
                                    out rotator out_CamRot,
                                    out float out_FOV )
{
    // Put in custom code here to control the camera.
}
```

Hands-on Example: Changing the view of your pawn.

In this tutorial we will show how you can change the view of your pawn so you are able to see it. What we are going to do is override the CalcCamera() function in your custom pawn class to position and rotate the camera to get our desired view.

What you need to do is add some code to your Jazz1Pawn class from ExampleCh31. See Listing 3–5.

> **NOTE:** The Jazz1Pawn class is located in the file Jazz1Pawn.uc. Remember that all UnrealScript classes must have filenames that match the class and have a .uc extension.

Listing 3–5. *Modifying the Jazz1Pawn for a third-person view*

```
class Jazz1Pawn extends SimplePawn;

var float CamOffsetDistance;
var  int CamAngle;

// Third Person
simulated function bool CalcCamera( float fDeltaTime, out vector out_CamLoc, out rotator
out_CamRot, out float out_FOV )
{
    local vector BackVector;
    local vector UpVector;

    local float  CamDistanceHorizontal;
    local float  CamDistanceVertical;

    // Set Camera Location
    CamDistanceHorizontal = CamOffsetDistance * cos(CamAngle * UnrRotToRad);
    CamDistanceVertical   = CamOffsetDistance * sin(CamAngle * UnrRotToRad);

    BackVector = -Normal(Vector(Rotation)) * CamDistanceHorizontal;
    UpVector   = vect(0,0,1) * CamDistanceVertical;
```

```
        out_CamLoc = Location + BackVector + UpVector;

        // Set Camera Rotation
        out_CamRot.pitch = -CamAngle;
        out_CamRot.yaw   = Rotation.yaw;
        out_CamRot.roll  = Rotation.roll;

        return true;
}

defaultproperties
{
    Begin Object Class=SkeletalMeshComponent Name=JazzMesh
        SkeletalMesh=SkeletalMesh'KismetGame_Assets.Anims.SK_Jazz'
        AnimSets(0)=AnimSet'KismetGame_Assets.Anims.SK_Jazz_Anims'
        AnimTreeTemplate=AnimTree'KismetGame_Assets.Anims.Jazz_AnimTree'
        BlockRigidBody=true
        CollideActors=true
    End Object
    Mesh = JazzMesh; // Set The mesh for this object
    Components.Add(JazzMesh); // Attach this mesh to this Actor

    CamAngle=3000;
    CamOffsetDistance= 484.0
}
```

The main addition is the function CalcCamera() which actually sets the camera location and rotation. The function does this through the function parameters out_CamLoc, and out_CamRot. These parameters are declared as **out** which means that when you set the values of out_CamLoc or out_CamRot these values are set in the variables that are used to call this function. By doing this a function can return many values at once to the caller.

The variable CamOffsetDistance holds the distance from the pawn to the camera. The variable CamAngle holds the angle the camera will make with the pawn. The angle is measured in Unreal Rotation units. In Unreal Rotation units PI which is 180 degrees or half a circle is approximately 32000. See Chapter 8 on 3D Math for more information.

The variable CamDistanceHorizontal determines the horizontal distance to the camera from the pawn. The variable CamDistanceVertical determines the vertical distance to the camera from the pawn.

The variable BackVector calculates the vector behind the pawn that is horizontally CamDistanceHorizontal distance away. The variable UpVector calculates the vector that is vertically CamDistanceVertical distance upward. Vectors are discussed in more detail later in this book in Chapter 8.

The variable out_CamRot.pitch controls the up and down tilt of the camera which is set to the CamAngle.

Recompile the code and run the program using the ExampleCh31Game game type and you should see something like Figure 3–3.

Figure 3–3. *Third-Person View Behind Pawn*

By playing around with the camera settings in the CalcCamera() function you can easily create other custom camera views such as a top down camera view. For a top down camera view just fix the camera location to a point above the pawn and fix the camera rotation to point downward toward the pawn.

For example, the code in Listing 3–6 sets the camera to a top-down view of the pawn.

Listing 3–6. *CalcCamera function for a top-down view*

```
simulated function bool CalcCamera( float fDeltaTime,
                                    out vector out_CamLoc,
                                    out rotator out_CamRot,
                                    out float out_FOV )
{
    out_CamLoc = Location;
    out_CamLoc.Z += CamOffsetDistance;

    if(!bFollowPlayerRotation)
    {
        out_CamRot.Pitch = -16384;
        out_CamRot.Yaw = 0;
        out_CamRot.Roll = 0;
    }
    else
    {
        out_CamRot.Pitch = -16384;
        out_CamRot.Yaw = Rotation.Yaw;
        out_CamRot.Roll = 0;
    }
```

```
    return true;
}
```

The out_CamLoc.Z value sets the height of the camera. The out_CamRot.Yaw value sets the rotation of the camera to follow or not follow the rotation of the camera depending on the value of bFollowPlayerRotation.

UDK Weapons Overview

Using weapons in the UDK system involves the InventoryManager class, Inventory class, and the Weapon class. Weapons are actually inventory items derived from the Inventory class and held as inventory items within a player's pawn.

Inventory Manager

Each pawn has its own inventory manager that contains links to that pawn's particular inventory. In the pawn class you have the InvManager variable that holds the inventory manager.

```
var class<InventoryManager> InventoryManagerClass;
var repnotify InventoryManager InvManager;
```

The InventoryManagerClass holds the exact class to be used for the InvManager and is set in the defaultproperties block. Thus, you can create your own custom inventory manager classes and set them in your custom pawn in the pawn's defaultproperties block.

```
InventoryManagerClass=class'InventoryManager'
```

Weapon Types

In terms of weapon types the Weapon class supports three different types of weapons defined by the enumeration EweaponFireType. The three different types are:

- EWFT_InstantHit: This weapon type causes immediate damage to the object that is in the weapon's gun sights.
- EWFT_Projectile: The weapon type spawns a projectile and launches it.
- EWFT_Custom: This weapon type requires custom code to handle the firing sequence.

```
enum EWeaponFireType
{
    EWFT_InstantHit,
    EWFT_Projectile,
    EWFT_Custom,
    EWFT_None
};
```

In terms of actually firing weapons, the FireAmmunition() function in the Weapon class can be called on the weapon in order to get it to fire. This function can be used for all types of weapons including instant hit, projectile, and custom weapons. This function also processes ammo consumption. See Listing 3–7.

Listing 3–7. *Firing your weapon's ammunition*

```
simulated function FireAmmunition()
{
    // Use ammunition to fire
    ConsumeAmmo( CurrentFireMode );

    // Handle the different fire types
    switch( WeaponFireTypes[CurrentFireMode] )
    {
        case EWFT_InstantHit:
            InstantFire();
        break;

        case EWFT_Projectile:
            ProjectileFire();
        break;

        case EWFT_Custom:
            CustomFire();
        break;
    }
    NotifyWeaponFired( CurrentFireMode );
}
```

For weapons that fire projectiles you are able to fully customize the actual projectile. The class Projectile is used to define the basic projectile. You can create custom projectiles by subclassing this and creating your own class that derives from Projectile.

Weapon States

The Weapon class defines several different states. UnrealScript has built in support for the concept of states. A state is defined by the state keyword and its basic structure is similar to the following. An example of a state is the Active state in the Weapon class. See Listing 3–8.

Listing 3–8. *The Weapon class's Active state*

```
simulated state Active
{
    /** Initialize the weapon as being active and ready to go. */
    simulated event BeginState(Name PreviousStateName)
    {
        local int i;

        // Cache a reference to the AI controller
        if (Role == ROLE_Authority)
        {
            CacheAIController();
```

```
        }

        // Check to see if we need to go down
        if( bWeaponPutDown )
        {
            `LogInv("Weapon put down requested during transition, put it down now");
            PutDownWeapon();
        }
        else if ( !HasAnyAmmo() )
        {
            WeaponEmpty();
        }
        else
        {
            // if either of the fire modes are pending, perform them
            for( i=0; i<GetPendingFireLength(); i++ )
            {
                if( PendingFire(i) )
                {
                    BeginFire(i);
                    break;
                }
            }
        }
    }

    /** Override BeginFire so that it will enter the firing state right away. */
    simulated function BeginFire(byte FireModeNum)
    {
        if( !bDeleteMe && Instigator != None )
        {
            Global.BeginFire(FireModeNum);

            // in the active state, fire right away if we have the ammunition
            if( PendingFire(FireModeNum) && HasAmmo(FireModeNum) )
            {
                SendToFiringState(FireModeNum);
            }
        }
    }

    /**
ReadyToFire() called by NPC firing weapon. bFinished should only be true if called from
the Finished() function
    */

    simulated function bool ReadyToFire(bool bFinished)
    {
        return true;
    }

    /** Activate() ignored since already active
    */
    simulated function Activate()
    {
    }
```

```
/**
 * Put the weapon down
 */
simulated function bool TryPutDown()
{
    PutDownWeapon();
    return TRUE;
}
}
```

For example, when the weapon is in the `Active` state it has access to a certain set of functions unique to the `Active` state such as a custom `BeginFire()` function. The `Weapon` class can switch from one state to another through the `GotoState('StateName')` command. It also has built in functions `BeginState()` that is executed when the state is first entered and `EndState()` that is executed just before leaving the state. States are covered more in depth later in this book. Specifically, more coverage and examples of how to use states are given in Chapters 5, 7, 8, 10, 11, and 12.

Some important states in the `Weapon` class are as follows:

- `Inactive`: Weapon can not be fired and is not in use.

- `Active`: Weapon is being held by the pawn and is in use and can be fired.

- `WeaponFiring`: Weapon is being held by the pawn and is being fired.

- `WeaponEquipping`: Weapon is in this state when moving from the `Inactive` state to the `Active` state. Weapon selection animations should be done in this state. Weapon can not be fired when in this state.

- `WeaponPuttingDown`: Weapon is in the state where it is being put down and is moving to the `Inactive` state. Any weapon deactivation animations should be played in this state.

Weapon Selection

To activate a weapon from your inventory call the `SetCurrentWeapon(Weapon DesiredWeapon)` function on your inventory manger with the desired weapon. If you have a weapon active and it is different from the new weapon then the pawn will try to put the current weapon down by calling the weapon's `TryPutdown()` function. The weapon is then put into the `WeaponPuttingDown` state and then moved into the `Inactive` state. Then from there the inventory manager's `ChangedWeapon()` function is called.

If the pawn has no weapon currently active then the pawn will switch to the target weapon and activate it for use by calling `ChangedWeapon()`. This function will then call the weapon's `Activate()` function. The `Activate()` function puts the weapon into the `WeaponEquipping` state which leads to the `Active` state where the weapon is fully operational and ready to fire.

For example, to set `MainGun` as the current weapon you would use the following line of code in your pawn class.

```
InvManager.SetCurrentWeapon(Weapon(MainGun));
```

Weapon Firing

The weapon firing sequence for a player starts in the `PlayerController` class's `StartFire()` function. The `StartFire()` function associated with the controller's pawn is then called. In the `Pawn` class the `StartFire()` function associated with the pawn's current weapon is called. The weapon's `StartFire()` function calls the `BeginFire()` function which calls the `SetPendingFire()` function which sets the `PendingFire` variable array in the `InventoryManager` class to indicate that the weapon needs to fire. If the weapon is in the `Active` state then the `SendToFiringState()` function is also called. If the `FiringStatesArray` contains a valid weapon state for the requested `FireMode` then this state will be transitioned to using the command:

```
GotoState ( FiringStatesArray[FireModeNum] )
```

The default state for handling the actual firing of the weapon is the `WeaponFiring` state.

The `WeaponFiring` state then calls the `FireAmmunition()` function where the weapon is actually fired based on the type of weapon such instant hit, projectile or custom. To stop the weapon from firing you must call the StopFire() function.

On the iOS platform you can put the weapon firing code in the SwipezoneCallback() function in the player controller as shown in Listing 3–9.

Listing 3–9. *Firing a Weapon from the player controller on iOS*

```
function bool SwipeZoneCallback(MobileInputZone Zone,
                                float DeltaTime,
                                int Handle,
                                EZoneTouchEvent EventType,
                                Vector2D TouchLocation)
{
    local bool retval;

    retval = true;
    if (EventType == ZoneEvent_Touch)
    {
        // Start Firing pawn's weapon
        StartFire(0);
    }
    else
    if(EventType == ZoneEvent_Update)
    {
    }
    else
    if (EventType == ZoneEvent_UnTouch)
    {
        // Stop Firing Pawn's weapon
        StopFire(0);
    }
```

```
        return retval;
}
```

In the above example the player's pawn starts firing when the user touches the screen and stops firing when the user lifts his finger.

Hands-on Example: Adding a weapon to your pawn

In this tutorial we will be adding a weapon to the pawn from the last tutorial. The weapon will be a custom class derived from the Weapon class and fire a custom projectile that is derived from the Projectile class. We will also be creating a new InventoryManager class to manage this new weapon. Finally, in order to use this weapon we will need to modify the player controller and add code that will actually fire the weapon.

Creating the Weapon

Create a new file called "JazzWeapon1.uc" with the following code. The new class JazzWeapon1 is our custom weapon.

We are going to add to the code from the previous example so all code for this example will go to the Classes directory at:

C:\UDK\UDK-2011-06\Development\Src\ExampleCh31

See Listing 3–10 for the JazzWeapon1 code.

Listing 3–10. *Creating a Weapon*

```
class JazzWeapon1 extends Weapon;

defaultproperties
{
    Begin Object Class=SkeletalMeshComponent Name=FirstPersonMesh
        SkeletalMesh=SkeletalMesh'KismetGame_Assets.Anims.SK_JazzGun'
    End Object
    Mesh=FirstPersonMesh
    Components.Add(FirstPersonMesh);

    Begin Object Class=SkeletalMeshComponent Name=PickupMesh
        SkeletalMesh=SkeletalMesh'KismetGame_Assets.Anims.SK_JazzGun'
    End Object
    DroppedPickupMesh=PickupMesh
    PickupFactoryMesh=PickupMesh

    WeaponFireTypes(0)=EWFT_Projectile
    WeaponFireTypes(1)=EWFT_NONE

    WeaponProjectiles(0)=class'JazzBullet1'
    WeaponProjectiles(1)=class'JazzBullet1'

    FiringStatesArray(0)=WeaponFiring
    FireInterval(0)=0.25
    Spread(0)=0
}
```

The actual gun mesh is created as a SkeletalMeshComponent and assigned to the Weapon's Mesh variable and added to this object's location and rotation through the Components array.

Next a pickup mesh is defined which is the mesh that is placed into the world when the weapon is dropped by the holder.

Weapon fire types are defined by the WeaponFireTypes array in the Weapon class. For fire mode 0 we define the type of weapon that is to be fired as a projectile weapon.

```
WeaponFireTypes(0)=EWFT_Projectile
```

If the type of weapon to be used is a Projectile weapon then we need to specify the specific sub class of Projectile to use. For firemode 0 we choose the JazzBullet1 class.

```
WeaponProjectiles(0)=class'JazzBullet1'
```

The FiringStatesArray holds the state the weapon transitions to when actually firing. The weapon that uses firing mode 0 is set to the default firing state of WeaponFiring.

```
FiringStatesArray(0)=WeaponFiring
```

The FireInterval array holds the how long a shot takes for a specific fire mode. The length that a shot takes for firemode 0 is 0.25 seconds.

```
FireInterval(0)=0.25
```

The Spread refers to how much of a distance there is between shots.

```
Spread(0)=0
```

The following Figure 3–4 is a preview of our final working weapon JazzWeapon1.

Figure 3–4. *Preview of your pawn holding our custom weapon*

Creating the Bullets for the Weapon

Next we need to create a new file "JazzBullet1.uc" for our custom projectile (shown in Listing 3–11). Create this file and enter the following code into it and save it like you did before with our custom weapon class. The directory to save this new source file under would be:

`C:\UDK\UDK-2011-06\Development\Src\ExampleCh31\Classes`

Listing 3–11. *JazzBullet1 weapon projectile*

```
class JazzBullet1 extends Projectile;

simulated function Explode(vector HitLocation, vector HitNormal)
{
}

function Init( Vector Direction )
{
    local       vector  NewDir;

    NewDir = Normal(Vector(InstigatorController.Pawn.Rotation));
    Velocity = Speed * NewDir;
}

defaultproperties
{
    Begin Object Class=StaticMeshComponent Name=Bullet
```

```
      StaticMesh=StaticMesh'EngineMeshes.Sphere'
      Scale3D=(X=0.050000,Y=0.050000,Z=0.05000)
   End Object
   Components.Add(Bullet)

   Begin Object Class=ParticleSystemComponent  Name=BulletTrail
      Template=ParticleSystem'Castle_Assets.FX.P_FX_Fire_SubUV_01'
   End Object
   Components.Add(BulletTrail)

   MaxSpeed=+05000.000000
   Speed=+05000.000000
}
```

The `Explode()` function is overridden because we want the projectile to stay around for awhile and demonstrate how we can attach a particle emitter to a projectile for special effects.

The `Init()` function is called after the projectile is created and sets its starting direction and speed. Here we need to override it to set the direction it is firing to point in the direction the pawn is facing.

The actual mesh for the bullet is a `StaticMeshComponent` named `Bullet`. Here we set the `Scale3D` variable to shrink the mesh in size before it is placed into the world.

We also attach a particle emitter which is a `ParticleSystemComponent` named `BulletTrail` to this projectile. The actual name of the particle emitter is assigned to the `Template` variable. Particle emitters can be viewed in the Content Browser and viewed in Unreal Cascade.

The `MaxSpeed` variable is set to a new maximum speed from the default value. The `Speed` variable is also set to a new value from the default.

Creating the Custom Inventory Manager

Next we need to create a custom inventory manager. See Listing 3–12.

Listing 3–12. *WeaponsIM1 class*

```
class WeaponsIM1 extends InventoryManager;

defaultproperties
{
    PendingFire(0)=0
    PendingFire(1)=0
}
```

The reason we need to do this is because we need to create entries for the `PendingFire` array that holds the fire status of your weapon. By default this array is empty. You need to create these entries so that they can be set when the weapon is ready to fire.

Modifying the Player's PawnNow you need to make some changes to your custom Pawn from the last example `Jazz1Pawn`. See Listing 3–13.

Listing 3–13. *Jazz1Pawn class*

```
class Jazz1Pawn extends SimplePawn;

var float CamOffsetDistance;
var int CamAngle;
var Inventory MainGun;

simulated singular event Rotator GetBaseAimRotation()
{
    local rotator TempRot;

    TempRot = Rotation;
    TempRot.Pitch = 0;
    SetRotation(TempRot);

    return TempRot;
}

function AddGunToSocket(Name SocketName)
{
    local Vector SocketLocation;
    local Rotator SocketRotation;

    if (Mesh != None)
    {
        if (Mesh.GetSocketByName(SocketName) != None)
        {
            Mesh.GetSocketWorldLocationAndRotation(SocketName, SocketLocation,
SocketRotation);
            MainGun.SetRotation(SocketRotation);
            MainGun.SetBase(Self,, Mesh, SocketName);
        }
        else
        {
            WorldInfo.Game.Broadcast(self,"!!!!!!SOCKET NAME NOT FOUND!!!!!");
         }
    }
    else
    {
        WorldInfo.Game.Broadcast(self,"!!!!!!MESH NOT FOUND!!!!!");
    }
}

function AddDefaultInventory()
{
    MainGun = InvManager.CreateInventory(class'JazzWeapon1');
    MainGun.SetHidden(false);
    AddGunToSocket('Weapon_R');
    Weapon(MainGun).FireOffset = vect(0,0,-70);
}

///////////////////////////// Third Person View //////////////////////////////
simulated function bool CalcCamera( float fDeltaTime, out vector out_CamLoc, out rotator
out_CamRot, out float out_FOV )
```

```
{
    local vector BackVector;
    local vector UpVector;

    local float  CamDistanceHorizontal;
    local float  CamDistanceVertical;

    // Set Camera Location
    CamDistanceHorizontal = CamOffsetDistance * cos(CamAngle * UnrRotToRad);
    CamDistanceVertical   = CamOffsetDistance * sin(CamAngle * UnrRotToRad);

    BackVector = -Normal(Vector(Rotation)) * CamDistanceHorizontal;
    UpVector = vect(0,0,1) * CamDistanceVertical;

    out_CamLoc = Location + BackVector + UpVector;

    // Set Camera Rotation
    out_CamRot.pitch = -CamAngle;
    out_CamRot.yaw   = Rotation.yaw;
    out_CamRot.roll  = Rotation.roll;

    return true;
}

defaultproperties
{
    Begin Object Class=SkeletalMeshComponent Name=JazzMesh
        SkeletalMesh=SkeletalMesh'KismetGame_Assets.Anims.SK_Jazz'
        AnimSets(0)=AnimSet'KismetGame_Assets.Anims.SK_Jazz_Anims'
        AnimTreeTemplate=AnimTree'KismetGame_Assets.Anims.Jazz_AnimTree'
        BlockRigidBody=true
        CollideActors=true
    End Object

    Mesh = JazzMesh; // Set The mesh for this object
    Components.Add(JazzMesh); // Attach this mesh to this Actor

    CamAngle=3000;
    CamOffsetDistance= 484.0

    InventoryManagerClass=class'WeaponsIM1'
}
```

First we added in an Inventory item called MainGun which holds a reference to the custom weapon.

The function GetBaseAimRotation() will change the pawn's aiming to reflect our third-person viewpoint where the player's viewpoint does not move up and down.

The AddGunToSocket() function adds the custom weapon to a socket which is a dummy attachment point on the character mesh which when used with a weapon makes it appear that the character is holding the weapon. Sockets are created within the AnimSet Editor.

The AddDefaultInventory() function is automatically called when the game begins and adds in our custom weapon to the pawn's inventory.

The InventoryManagerClass variable is set to the custom InventoryManager class.

Adding to the Player Controller

In our player controller class ExampleCh31PC in the SwipeZoneCallback() function we need to add in the commands StartFire(0) for a touch event to begin firing the player's weapon and StopFire(0) for an untouch event to stop firing the player's weapon. See Listing 3–14.

Listing 3–14. *Adding to the Player Controller*

```
function bool SwipeZoneCallback(MobileInputZone Zone,
                                float DeltaTime,
                                int Handle,
                                EZoneTouchEvent EventType,
                                Vector2D TouchLocation)
{
    local bool retval = true;

    if (EventType == ZoneEvent_Touch)
    {
        WorldInfo.Game.Broadcast(self,"You touched the screen at = "
                                    @ TouchLocation.x @ " , "
                                    @ TouchLocation.y @ ", Zone Touched = "
                                    @ Zone);
        // Start Firing pawn's weapon
        StartFire(0);
    }

    else if(EventType == ZoneEvent_Update)
    {
    }

    else if (EventType == ZoneEvent_UnTouch)
    {
        // Stop Firing Pawn's weapon
        StopFire(0);
    }
    return retval;
}
```

Recompile and run the game on the Unreal Editor using our custom game type. You should now be able to touch anywhere on the screen except for the joysticks and fire your weapon. See Figure 3–5.

Figure 3–5. *Demonstration of your new weapon*

Also note how your bullets emit a fire from the particle emitter (see Figure 3–6).

Figure 3–6. *Flames come from your bullets via the fire particle emitter*

Hands-On Example: Adding a weapon to your first-person view.

In this tutorial we will be creating another custom weapon and putting it into a first-person view. First, create a new directory called ExampleCh32 under our source directory which by default is:

```
C:\UDK\UDK-2011-06\Development\Src
```

This is for the June 2011 UDK. If you are using a different version of the UDK then your directory may be different. Under this new directory create another directory called Classes. As in the previous examples you will put all the source code for this example in this Classes directory.

Creating the Weapon

Our custom weapon class is JazzWeapon2. The only difference is that this weapon will be firing a different kind of bullet as defined in the JazzBullet2 class. See Listing 3–15.

Listing 3–15. *JazzWeapon2 class*

```
class JazzWeapon2 extends Weapon;

defaultproperties
{
    Begin Object Class=SkeletalMeshComponent Name=FirstPersonMesh
        SkeletalMesh=SkeletalMesh'KismetGame_Assets.Anims.SK_JazzGun'
    End Object
    Mesh=FirstPersonMesh
    Components.Add(FirstPersonMesh);

    Begin Object Class=SkeletalMeshComponent Name=PickupMesh
        SkeletalMesh=SkeletalMesh'KismetGame_Assets.Anims.SK_JazzGun'
    End Object
    DroppedPickupMesh=PickupMesh
    PickupFactoryMesh=PickupMesh

    WeaponFireTypes(0)=EWFT_Projectile
    WeaponFireTypes(1)=EWFT_NONE

    WeaponProjectiles(0)=class'JazzBullet2'
    WeaponProjectiles(1)=class'JazzBullet2'

    FiringStatesArray(0)=WeaponFiring
    FireInterval(0)=0.25
    Spread(0)=0
}
```

Creating the Projectile for the Weapon

The code for the JazzBullet2 class is as follows. See Listing 3–16.

Listing 3–16. *JazzBullet2 class*

```
class JazzBullet2 extends Projectile;

simulated function Explode(vector HitLocation, vector HitNormal)
{
    SetPhysics(Phys_Falling);
}

function Init( Vector Direction )
{
    super.Init(Direction);
    RandSpin(90000);
}

defaultproperties
{
    Begin Object Class=StaticMeshComponent Name=Bullet
        StaticMesh=StaticMesh'Castle_Assets.Meshes.SM_RiverRock_01'
        Scale3D=(X=0.300000,Y=0.30000,Z=0.3000)
    End Object
    Components.Add(Bullet)

    Begin Object Class=ParticleSystemComponent  Name=BulletTrail
        Template=ParticleSystem'Castle_Assets.FX.P_FX_Fire_SubUV_01'
    End Object
    Components.Add(BulletTrail)

    MaxSpeed=+05000.000000
    Speed=+05000.000000
}
```

The Explode() will now change the physics model for the projectile so that when it hits another object it will fall to the ground. The Init() will now set a random spin to the object being thrown which is now a rock.

Creating the Pawn

The new pawn class is Jazz2Pawn. This pawn uses a different weapon JazzWeapon2 in the AddDefaultInventory() function. However, we don't need to change the InventoryManager class. See Listing 3–17.

Listing 3–17. *Jazz2Pawn class*

```
class Jazz2Pawn extends SimplePawn;

var Inventory MainGun;

function AddDefaultInventory()
{
```

```
    MainGun = InvManager.CreateInventory(class'JazzWeapon2');
    MainGun.SetHidden(false);

    Weapon(MainGun).FireOffset = vect(0,0,-70);
}

defaultproperties
{
    InventoryManagerClass=class'WeaponsIM1'
}
```

Creating the Player Controller

We need a new player controller class which is called ExampleCh32PC. See Listing 3–18. A lot of the code is the same as ExampleCh31PC except for the PlaceWeapon() function and the PlayerTick() function.

- The PlaceWeapon() function actually does the work of putting the weapon mesh into the first-person view. Depending on exactly how your weapon mesh is oriented your weapon rotation offsets may be different than this example.

- The PlayerTick() function is overridden and the PlaceWeapon() function is called from here to constantly update the position and rotation of our first-person weapon.

Listing 3–18. *Player Controller class*

```
class ExampleCh32PC  extends SimplePC;

function bool SwipeZoneCallback(MobileInputZone Zone,
                                float DeltaTime,
                                int Handle,
                                EZoneTouchEvent EventType,
                                Vector2D TouchLocation)
{
    local bool retval = true;

    if (EventType == ZoneEvent_Touch)
    {
        // Start Firing pawn's weapon
        StartFire(0);
    }
    else if(EventType == ZoneEvent_Update)
    {
    }
        else if (EventType == ZoneEvent_UnTouch)
    {
        // Stop Firing Pawn's weapon
        StopFire(0);
    }
    return retval;
}

function SetupZones()
```

```
{
    Super.SetupZones();

    // If we have a game class, configure the zones
    if (MPI != None && WorldInfo.GRI.GameClass != none)
    {
        LocalPlayer(Player).ViewportClient.GetViewportSize(ViewportSize);

        if (FreeLookZone != none)
        {
            FreeLookZone.OnProcessInputDelegate = SwipeZoneCallback;
        }
    }
}

function PlaceWeapon()
{
    // First Person
    local vector WeaponLocation;
    local Rotator WeaponRotation,TempRot;
    local Weapon TestW;
    local vector WeaponAimVect;

    WeaponRotation.yaw = -16000; // 90 Degrees turn = OFFSET

    TempRot = Pawn.GetBaseAimRotation();
    WeaponRotation.pitch = TempRot.roll;
    WeaponRotation.yaw   += TempRot.yaw;
    WeaponRotation.roll -= TempRot.pitch; // Swith due to weapon local axes orientation

    WeaponAimVect = Normal(Vector(TempRot));
    WeaponLocation = Pawn.Location + (40 * WeaponAimVect) + vect(0,0,30);

    TestW = Pawn.Weapon;

    if (TestW != None)
    {
        TestW.SetLocation(WeaponLocation);
        TestW.SetRotation(WeaponRotation);
    }
    else
    {
        WorldInfo.Game.Broadcast(self,"Player has no weapon!!!!!");
    }
}

function PlayerTick(float DeltaTime)
{
    Super.PlayerTick(DeltaTime);
    PlaceWeapon();
}
defaultproperties
{
}
```

Creating a New Game Type

Finally, create a new class for our new game type. See Listing 3–19.

Here, the key changes are that we set the `PlayerControllerClass` to point to the new `ExampleCh32PC` player controller class and set the `DefaultPawnClass` to `Jazz2Pawn` which will be the player's pawn.

Listing 3–19. *Game Type class*

```
class ExampleCh32Game  extends FrameworkGame;

event OnEngineHasLoaded()
{
    WorldInfo.Game.Broadcast(self," ExampleCh32Game  Type Active - Engine Has Loaded
!!!!");
}

function bool PreventDeath(Pawn KilledPawn, Controller Killer, class<DamageType>
DamageType, vector HitLocation)
{
    return true;
}

static event class<GameInfo> SetGameType(string MapName, string Options, string Portal)
{
    return super.SetGameType(MapName, Options, Portal);
}

defaultproperties
{
    PlayerControllerClass=class' ExampleCh32.ExampleCh32PC'
    DefaultPawnClass=class'Jazz2Pawn'
    HUDType=class'UDKBase.UDKHUD'
    bRestartLevel=false
    bWaitingToStartMatch=true
    bDelayedStart=false
}
```

Setting up your new Game Type

Next you need to set up the game and compiler for our new example. Edit the Mobile-UDKGame.ini and UDKEngine.ini files in your UDKGame\Config directory.

```
Mobile-UDKGame.ini
[ExampleCh32.ExampleCh32Game]
RequiredMobileInputConfigs=(GroupName="UberGroup",RequireZoneNames=("UberStickMoveZone",
"UberStickLookZone","UberLookZone"))
UDKEngine.ini
[UnrealEd.EditorEngine]
ModEditPackages=ExampleCh32
```

Running the new Game Type

Compile and run our new game using the Unreal Editor. Make sure to set your game type to ExampleCh32Game under the Default Game Type property. You should be able to move your view up and down and left and right. The weapon should be visible and you should be able to fire flaming rocks into the air (see Figure 3–7).

Figure 3–7. *Shooting flaming rocks into the air with your new weapon in a first-person view.*

Also, you should see your new projectiles bounce off of an object when it is hit. For example try to hit a static mesh object to see the rocks bounce off it and hit the ground, as shown in Figure 3–8.

Figure 3–8. *Weapon's projectiles bouncing off a sphere I*

Summary

In this chapter we have shown you how to make the player's pawn visible by adding a skeletal mesh. Then we demonstrated how to change the camera angle so you can view your pawn from the third-person perspective. Next, we added a weapon to our pawn and showed you how to set it up and fire it. Finally, we changed the view to a first-person view and demonstrated how we could place a weapon within this view and have it rotate up/down and left/right and move correctly with the player's view. In the following chapters we will build on the knowledge gained here to eventually build entire games using the UDK.

Specifically, in the next chapter which covers UDK collisions we take a look at how to create realistic complex collisions using the UDK physics engine. We also examine such topics as physics constraints that the UDK uses to bind objects together and have them behave realistically when interacting with each other and the environment.

Chapter 4

UDK Collisions

In this chapter we will cover UDK physics. The Unreal Engine features a physics engine based on the Novodex PhysX system that calculates collisions for rigid bodies based on the shape of a collision mesh. Contact points with other objects using these collision meshes are generated by the physics engine in order to produce an accurate physics simulation.

We will be learning the Unreal Physics system through a series of fun hands-on tutorials where you will learn such things as:

- How to create a KActor from a static mesh asset and making it move by applying a force to it

- How to create a KAsset from a skeletal mesh asset and making it move by applying a force to it

- How to create physics constraint that will bind different objects together using the Unreal Editor

- How to create a placeable rigid body that can be placed in a level using the Unreal Editor

- How to make an exploding wall of blocks

Collision Meshes

Collision models or collision meshes are what the physics engine uses in rigid body physics collisions. Collision meshes are critical to the behavior of an object when it collides with another object or the ground. For example, you will notice in the following tutorials that a sphere rolls across the floor of the arena while the cube does not. The difference in the behavior is caused by the structure of the collision meshes. Let's compare a collision mesh for a Cube and the collision mesh for a Sphere. The collision mesh for a Cube is also a cube in structure as indicated in Figure 4–1 of a Cube mesh in the Static Mesh Editor.

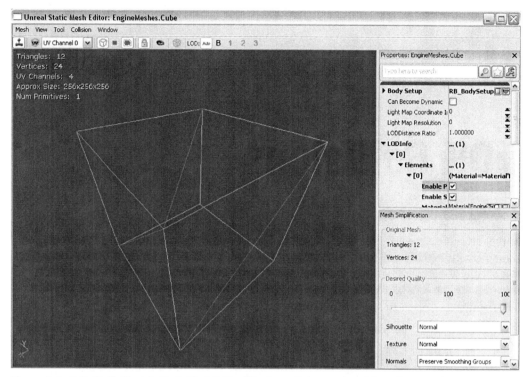

Figure 4–1. *Cube Static Mesh in Static Mesh Editor (Viewing collision mesh and the cube as a wireframe)*

For a Sphere (see Figure 4–2), the collision mesh is, of course, spherical and differs from a Cube in the same way a physical ball differs from a block. As in the real world, the different shapes behave differently when colliding with other objects.

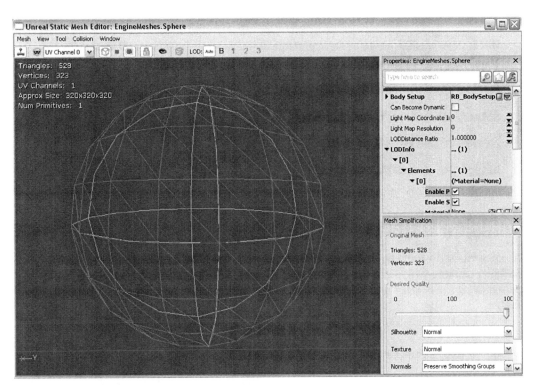

Figure 4–2. *Sphere Collision Mesh in Static Mesh Editor (Viewing collision mesh and sphere as a wireframe)*

The collision mesh generally follows the shape of the static mesh and must be convex not concave. In convex meshes all parts of the mesh are outward bending and there are no holes in the mesh. Concave meshes may have holes in them and have parts that are inward bending. You are not limited to a specific set of collision meshes. You can create your own collision meshes through a separate, free 3D modeling program like Blender available at http://www.blender.org. These meshes must be prefixed with "UCX_" which is called a "Convex Mesh Primitive" and match a corresponding regular mesh. For example, in Blender the mesh "UCX_Cube" would be the collision mesh for the mesh named "Cube". These two meshes would be placed one on top of the other so that they line up perfectly. They then would be exported in a format such as .fbx that can be imported into the Unreal UDK. The collision mesh can then be viewed in the Unreal Static Mesh Editor after selecting **View ➤ Collision** from the menu.

You can also use the feature in the Unreal Static Mesh Editor called K-DOP to generate simple collision meshes for your static mesh. However, this method is only good for a very rough collision mesh and may not be suitable for your needs. This may be especially true if you are building a physics-type game like Angry Birds that may require more precise collision detection.

> **NOTE:** Other graphics programs that can create UDK-compatible content are 3D Studio Max and Maya. Trial versions are available that last 30 days and are fully compatible.
>
> For more information on 3d Studio Max go to:
>
> http://usa.autodesk.com/3ds-max/
>
> For more information on Maya go to:
>
> http://usa.autodesk.com/maya/

Collision Objects

When simulating realistic collisions are concerned, the UDK has two main types of collision objects which are the KActor and KAsset. This section will give you a basic overview of the KActor and KAsset. Also, in the hands-on examples in this section, you will:

- Create a new KActor and apply a force to it
- Create a new KAsset and apply a force to it

KActor and KAsset Overview

In terms of meshes in the UDK system there are static meshes and skeletal meshes. Static meshes are meshes that have no bones or any flexible skeletal structure such as doors, gates, blocks, rocks, and chairs. Skeletal meshes are meshes that have bones and a skeletal structure such as characters, ropes, wires, and chains.

In terms of rigid body collisions there are two types of objects KActors and KAssets. KActors contain static meshes and can be used by the physics engine for realistic rigid body collisions using the KActor's collision mesh. KAssets contain skeletal meshes that can be used by the physics engine for realistic rigid body collisions using the mesh's collision areas that are set up in Unreal Phat. KActors and KAssets are placeable which mean that objects of these classes can be placed into a level using the Unreal Editor. You can also dynamically create new KActors and KAssets during a game but you must use the KActorspawnable class for KActors and the KAssetspawnable class for KAssets.

Creating Custom KActors and KAssets

You can create custom KActors and KAssets by creating a new class that derives from a KActor or KAsset. For example, the following class RigidBodyCube derives from the Kactor class (see Listing 4–1). In the defaultproperties a new StaticMeshComponent is created and named RigidBodyCubeMesh. The actual mesh is defined by the variable StaticMesh. The RigidBodyCubeMesh is then set as the StaticMeshComponent for this

KActor and added to the Actor's Components array which ties this mesh to the KActor's location and rotation.

Listing 4–1. *Deriving a class from the KActor class*

```
class RigidBodyCube extends Kactor
defaultproperties
{
    Begin Object Class=StaticMeshComponent Name=RigidBodyCubeMesh
        StaticMesh=StaticMesh'EngineMeshes.Cube'
    End Object
    StaticMeshComponent=RigidBodyCubeMesh
    Components.Add(RigidBodyCubeMesh)
}
```

An example of a class deriving from a Kasset is the class RopeSection that derives from a dynamic Kasset class KAssetspawnable (see Listing 4–2).A new SkeletalMeshComponent called RopeSection is created in the defaultproperties block. Here we define the SkeletalMesh and the PhysicsAsset that are used for this skeletal mesh component. RopeSection is then set as the SkeletalMeshComponent for this object and added to the Components array.

Listing 4–2. *Deriving a class from KAssetspawnable*

```
class RopeSection extends KAssetspawnable;
defaultproperties
{
    Begin Object Class=SkeletalMeshComponent Name=RopeSection
        SkeletalMesh=SkeletalMesh'physics_assets.SKM_Wire'
        PhysicsAsset=PhysicsAsset'physics_assets.SKM_Wire_Physics_02'
    End Object
    SkeletalMeshComponent=RopeSection
    Components.Add(RopeSection)
}
```

However, before we can get these KActors and KAssets to collide we need to set the collision parameters. Collision parameters are discussed later in this chapter. For now, we just wanted to introduce how you would create the general framework for a new physics object.

Applying a Force to a KActor and KAsset

In terms of applying a force to a KActor you can use the ApplyImpulse() function located in the KActor class. The ApplyImpulse() function declaration is as follows and takes in an impulse direction, impulse magnitude, and the location where to apply this force as required parameters.

```
ApplyImpulse(Vector ImpulseDir,
             float ImpulseMag,
             Vector HitLocation,
             optional TraceHitInfo HitInfo,
             optional class<DamageType> DamageType );
```

For a KAsset you must apply a force to the KAsset's SkeletalMeshComponent by using the AddImpulse() function. The actual function is located in the PrimitiveComponent class and has a declaration as follows. The `Impulse` parameter contains both the magnitude and direction of the force. The `Position` is the location where to apply the force in world space. The `BoneName` is the bone to apply the force to if this is a skeletal mesh. If bVelChange is True, then the `Impulse` will be interpreted as the change in velocity instead of a force and the mass of this object will have no effect.

```
AddImpulse(vector Impulse,
          optional vector Position,
          optional name BoneName,
          optional bool bVelChange);
```

The following examples illustrate how to apply a force to a `Kactor` and a `Kasset`.

Hands-on Example: Creating a KActor and applying a force to it

In this tutorial you will be creating a KActor from a static mesh asset using the Unreal Editor and placing this Kactor in a new level. You will then be able to apply a force to this actor by clicking on it with your mouse from within the Mobile Previewer.

Creating a new Level with KActors

The first thing you need to do is create a new level in the editor and add some KActors to the level. Follow these steps to add a sphere:

1. Bring up the Unreal Editor and the default level should pop up.

2. Create a new level by clicking on the **File ➤ Save As** menu item to save the current map as a different file. When the file Save As dialog box opens, type in **Example41Map** for the filename and click Save. This should save your map into the \UDK\UDK-2011-06\UDKGame\Content\Maps directory by default.

3. Next you need to create a KActor from a static mesh. Set your Packages section located in the lower-left-hand corner of the Content Browser to Engine.

4. Check the Static Meshes checkbox under the **Object Types ➤ Favorites** section and type **Sphere** in the search bar above that.

5. Click on the static mesh called Sphere.

6.   Right-click on an empty space in the level where you want to place this mesh and select Add Rigid Body:EngineMeshes.Sphere from the context menu (see Figure 4–3). This will place your new rigid body into the level.

Surface Properties...	F5
Find in Content Browser...	Ctrl+B
Select	▶
Cut	Ctrl+X
Copy	Ctrl+C
Paste	Ctrl+V
Paste Here	
Select Surfaces	▶
Apply Material	
Reset	
Alignment	▶
Visibility	▶
Add StaticMesh: EngineMeshes.Sphere	
Add InteractiveFoliageActor: EngineMeshes.Sphere	
Add InterpActor: EngineMeshes.Sphere	
Add RigidBody: EngineMeshes.Sphere	
Add Recent	▶
Add Actor	▶
Play Level	▶
Play from Here	

Figure 4–3. *Converting a static mesh to a rigid body*

7. The first thing you may notice is that the sphere is way too big. In order
    to make this sphere smaller as well as do some initial setup double-click
    on the sphere to bring up its properties (see Figure 4–4).

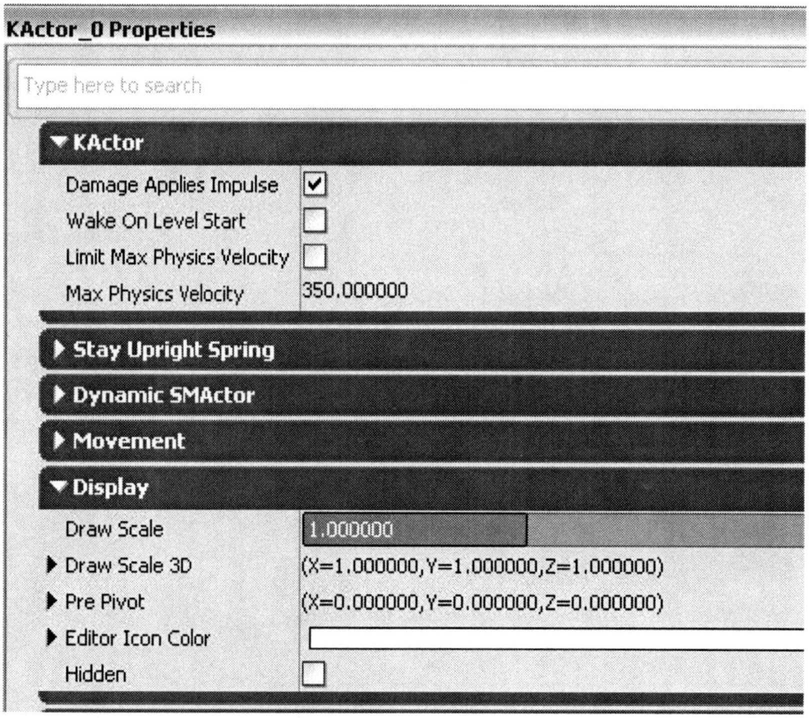

Figure 4–4. *Properties of new KActor formed from static mesh*

8. Under the KActor category click on "Wake On Level Start" checkbox to begin the physics simulation for this object when the level starts.

9. Under the Display Category change the "Draw Scale" by clicking on its input field and changing the number 1 to .10. This shrinks the size of the sphere to one tenth of its original size. You may also have to reposition the sphere so that is above ground by clicking on the up (Z Axis) of the sphere transformation widget (see Figure 4–5) and dragging the sphere upward so that it does not penetrate the ground.

Figure 4–5. *Sphere transformation widget*

Next, let's add a cube to the level using the same process we used for the sphere.

1. Change the asset search term to cube. You should see a static mesh called TexPropCube.

2. Select this asset by clicking on it with the left mouse button.

3. Place this mesh into your game level using the same procedure you used with the sphere: Right-click on the level where you want to place the cube and select Add Rigid Body: EditorMeshes.TexPropCube (see Figure 4–6).

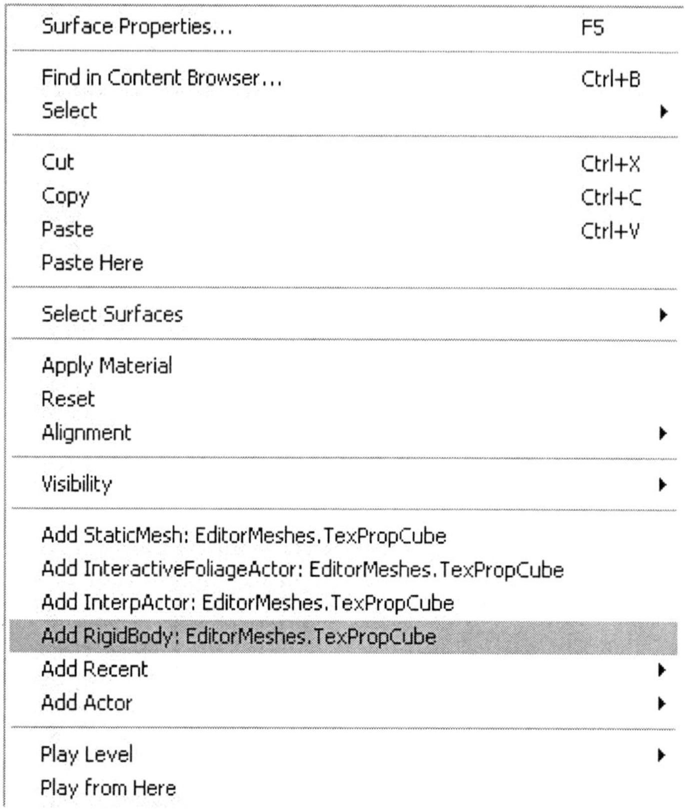

Surface Properties...	F5
Find in Content Browser...	Ctrl+B
Select	▶
Cut	Ctrl+X
Copy	Ctrl+C
Paste	Ctrl+V
Paste Here	
Select Surfaces	▶
Apply Material	
Reset	
Alignment	▶
Visibility	▶
Add StaticMesh: EditorMeshes.TexPropCube	
Add InteractiveFoliageActor: EditorMeshes.TexPropCube	
Add InterpActor: EditorMeshes.TexPropCube	
Add RigidBody: EditorMeshes.TexPropCube	
Add Recent	▶
Add Actor	▶
Play Level	▶
Play from Here	

Figure 4–6. *Converting a static mesh cube to a rigid body*

4. Again, the cube will be very big so double-click on the cube to bring up the KActor's properties.

5. Just as with the sphere check the Wake on Level Start checkbox under the KActor properties and change the Draw Scale property under the Display category to .10.

6. Move the cube using the object's transformation widget so that it is completely above ground and positioned where you want it. The transformation widget is the set of axes located at the object's center. Click and drag the X, or Y transformation axis to move the object around the arena and the Z axis to move the object up and down.

7. Now, save the level by selecting the File ➤ Save All option. Figure 4–7 shows the level with the two objects added.

Figure 4–7. *Final level with resized sphere and cube rigid bodies*

Creating the Unreal Script Code

The next thing we need to do is create a new folder for this example called
ExampleCh41 and another folder under that called Classes at C:\UDK\UDK-2011-
06\Development\Src under your UDK installation directory. This is where your source
code files will be placed. Create a new file called ExampleCh41Game .uc and save it to
your newly created folder.Save the file under the ExampleCh41Game \Classes directory
you just created.

Custom Game Type

To define the game type for this example, enter the code that follows into the file. Note
that instead of providing a large block of code at once, I'm going to walk through it a
piece at a time. Just add each new piece as we discuss it, or you can find the full code
in the book's source code.

The following declares a class ExampleCh41Game that derives from FrameworkGame.
This class defines what kind of game we will be playing:

```
class ExampleCh41Game  extends FrameworkGame;
```

The function OnEngineHasLoaded() is called once the Unreal Engine has started and outputs a message stating that this new game type is now active.

```
event OnEngineHasLoaded()
{
    WorldInfo.Game.Broadcast(self," ExampleCh41Game  Type Active - Engine Has Loaded
!!!!");
}
```

The PreventDeath function returns True indicating that the player can not die in this game type.

```
function bool PreventDeath(Pawn KilledPawn, Controller Killer, class<DamageType>
DamageType, vector HitLocation)
{
    return true;
}
```

The SetGameType function returns the current game type.

```
static event class<GameInfo> SetGameType(string MapName, string Options, string Portal)
{
    return super.SetGameType(MapName, Options, Portal);
}
```

In the defaultproperties section take special note that the PlayerControllerClass points to our custom player controller class ExampleCh41PC located in the ExampleCh41 directory. We will create the ExampleCh41PC class later.

```
defaultproperties
{
    PlayerControllerClass=class'ExampleCh41.ExampleCh41PC'

    DefaultPawnClass=class'UDKBase.SimplePawn'
    HUDType=class'UDKBase.UDKHUD'

    bRestartLevel=false
    bWaitingToStartMatch=true
    bDelayedStart=false
}
```

We have just finished creating a class that defines our custom game. The HUDType variable is set to the default class needed to display the mobile input controls. We will learn how to customize the HUD or Heads Up Display in Chapter 6.

In the next section we specify a custom Player Controller which determines exactly how the player interacts with the game.

Custom Player Controller

The next class we need to create is our custom player controller class. It is in this class we create code where the player can touch a KActor and apply a force to that KActor.

You will need to create a new plain text file called **ExampleCh41PC** in the same directory as the previous UnrealScript file. Enter the following code into this new file and save it. Again, we'll go through the code a piece at a time.

The ExampleCh41PC class is derived from SimplePC and is the class that is responsible for processing the input from the player. PC is short for "Player Controller".

```
class ExampleCh41PC extends SimplePC;
```

PickDistance holds the maximum distance that the picked object can be from the player.

```
var float PickDistance;
```

The ApplyForceRigidBody() function is where the force is actually applied to the rigid body object. See Listing 4–3.

Listing 4–3. *Applying a Force to a Rigid Body*

```
function ApplyForceRigidBody(Actor SelectedActor,
                            Vector ImpulseDir,
                            float ImpulseMag,
                            Vector HitLocation)
{
    if (SelectedActor.IsA('KActor'))
    {
        WorldInfo.Game.Broadcast(self,"*** Thrown object " @ SelectedActor @
                                        ", ImpulseDir = " @ ImpulseDir @
                                        ", ImpulseMag = " @ ImpulseMag @
                                        ", HitLocation = " @ HitLocation);
        KActor(SelectedActor).ApplyImpulse(ImpulseDir,ImpulseMag, HitLocation);
    }
    else
    {
        WorldInfo.Game.Broadcast(self,"!!!ERROR Selected Actor " @ SelectedActor @
                                        " is not a KActor, you can not apply an
impulse to this object!!!");
    }
}
```

The function takes a reference to an Actor and first tests the Actor to see if it is a KActor class object. This is done through the IsA() function which is defined in the Object class. The IsA() function returns True if the reference refers to an object of the KActor class.

If the Actor is a KActor then the KActor's class function ApplyImpulse() is called to apply an impulse to the KActor object. In this case we are applying an impulse to the SelectedActor object. In order to do this we must first convert the SelectedActor object (which is defined as a reference to an Actor) to a KActor by casting it. This is possible because KActor is a subclass of Actor. The ApplyImpulse function takes as input the force direction, the amount of the force, and the location on the object where the force is applied.

The PickActor() function does the actual work of selecting an actor in the 3d game world based on a screen input from the iOS device. See Listing 4–4.

Listing 4–4. *Picking an Actor*

```
function Actor PickActor(Vector2D PickLocation, out Vector HitLocation, out TraceHitInfo
HitInfo)
{
    local Vector TouchOrigin, TouchDir;
    local Vector HitNormal;
    local Actor  PickedActor;
    local vector Extent;

    //Transform absolute screen coordinates to relative coordinates
    PickLocation.X = PickLocation.X / ViewportSize.X;
    PickLocation.Y = PickLocation.Y / ViewportSize.Y;

    //Transform to world coordinates to get pick ray
    LocalPlayer(Player).Deproject(PickLocation, TouchOrigin, TouchDir);

    //Perform trace to find touched actor
    Extent = vect(0,0,0);
    PickedActor = Trace(HitLocation,
                        HitNormal,
                        TouchOrigin + (TouchDir * PickDistance),
                        TouchOrigin,
                        True,
                        Extent,
                        HitInfo);
    //Return the touched actor for good measure
    return PickedActor;
}
```

A 2d screen coordinate is converted to a ray that is projected into the 3d game world and if an actor is hit then that actor is returned else a None is returned. This is the exact same function as in the example in Chapter 2. The SwipeZone() callback function handles the player's input. See Listing 4–5.

Listing 4–5. *Managing input*

```
function bool SwipeZoneCallback(MobileInputZone Zone,
                                float DeltaTime,
                                int Handle,
                                EZoneTouchEvent EventType,
                                Vector2D TouchLocation)
{
    local bool retval;

    local Actor PickedActor;
    local Vector HitLocation;
    local TraceHitInfo HitInfo;

    // Variables for physics
    local Vector ImpulseDir;
    local float ImpulseMag;

    retval = true;

    if (EventType == ZoneEvent_Touch)
    {
        // If screen touched then pick actor
```

```
        PickedActor = PickActor(TouchLocation,HitLocation,HitInfo);

        WorldInfo.Game.Broadcast(self,"PICKED ACTOR = "
                                    @ PickedActor @ ", HitLocation = "
                                    @ HitLocation @ ", Zone Touched = "
                                    @ Zone);

        // Set to roughly a 45 degree angle
        ImpulseDir = Normal(Vector(Pawn.Rotation)) + vect(0,0,1);
        ImpulseMag = 100;
        ApplyForceRigidBody(PickedActor,ImpulseDir,ImpulseMag,HitLocation);
    }
    else
    if(EventType == ZoneEvent_Update)
    {
    }
    else
    if (EventType == ZoneEvent_UnTouch)
    {
    }
    return retval;
}
```

The difference between this function and the previous SwipeZone() function in Chapter 2 is that code has been added that defines the force that is to be applied to the picked object. The ApplyForceRigidBody() function is then called on this object. The force is defined so that it appears from the player's standpoint that he is kicking the object forward and upward: the *impulse direction*.

The impulse direction is defined as the sum of two vectors (see Figure 4–8). The first vector points in the direction the player is facing through the conversion of the Player's rotation to a vector through the Vector() cast:

```
Normal(Vector(Pawn.Rotation))
```

That vector is then normalized which means that the vector's magnitude is set to 1. The second vector is a vector pointing straight up with a length of 1:

```
vect(0,0,1)
```

When you add the two vectors together you get a force vector that points up and forward from the viewpoint of the player:

```
ImpulseDir = Normal(Vector(Pawn.Rotation)) + vect(0,0,1)
```

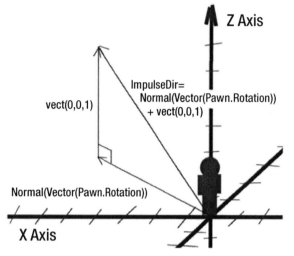

Figure 4–8. *Calculating the Impulse Direction vector*

> **NOTE:** A vector is a quantity that has a magnitude and a direction and is used to represent such things as velocities, accelerations, and forces. Vectors can be added together to produce a resultant vector that is the net result of all the vectors combined. To get a more in depth discussion of vectors, please see Chapter 8 on 3D math.

The SetupZones() function sets up the SwipeZoneCallback() function to process player input. See Listing 4–6.

Listing 4–6. *Settting up the Input Zones*

```
function SetupZones()
{
    Super.SetupZones();

    // If we have a game class, configure the zones
    if (MPI != None && WorldInfo.GRI.GameClass != none)
    {
        LocalPlayer(Player).ViewportClient.GetViewportSize(ViewportSize);
        if (FreeLookZone != none)
        {
            FreeLookZone.OnProcessInputDelegate = SwipeZoneCallback;
        }
    }
}
```

PickDistance is set to a default value of 10000.

```
defaultproperties
{
    PickDistance = 10000;
}
```

The `PickDistance` is the maximum distance that an object can be from the player in order to be "picked" by the player.

We have now finished all the coding for this tutorial. The new ExampleCh41Game class we created specified that this game will use a custom player controller called ExampleCh41PC. It is this new player controller class that allows the user to select KActor objects and apply a force to them.

Next we need to configure the mobile game setup for the UDK for compiling our new code and for playing the actual game on the mobile previewer.

Configuring the New Game Type

You need to add in the mobile control zone definitions for our game type in the file Mobile-UDKGame.ini located by default at C:\UDK\UDK-2011-06\UDKGame\Config. The following line defining the RequiredMobileInputConfigs for our game type ExampleCh41.ExampleCh41Game does that:

```
[ExampleCh41.ExampleCh41Game]
RequiredMobileInputConfigs=(GroupName="UberGroup",RequireZoneNames=("UberStickMoveZone",
"UberStickLookZone","UberLookZone"))
```

Now, open the UDKEngine.ini file located in the same directory. Under the UnrealEd.EditorEngine section heading, add in the line as below so that our new example will be added to the compilation list:

```
[UnrealEd.EditorEngine]
ModEditPackages= ExampleCh41
```

When you have finished editing the .ini files, bring up the Unreal Frontend and compile your new code.

Running the New Game Type

Start up the Unreal Editor and load in the level associated with this tutorial that you just created. Set your game type by selecting **View ➤ World Properties** from the main menu which brings up the world properties window. Under the Game Type category set the Default Game Type property to ExampleCh41Game.

Then start up the mobile game previewer by selecting the **Play ➤ On Mobile Previewer** from the main menu. (See Figure 4–9.)

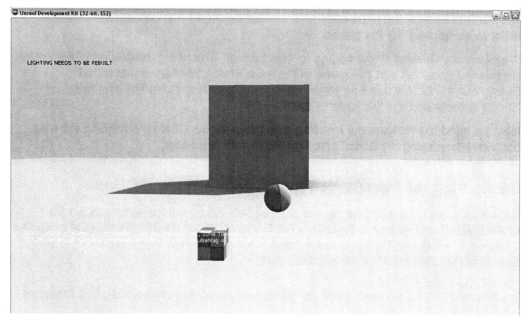

Figure 4–9. *Two KActors*

You can click on the sphere and cube to apply a force that will kick the object forward and upward. You may also need to use your mobile virtual joysticks to move the player so he can see the objects. Try moving around the arena and kicking the objects from various directions.

Hands-On Example: Creating a KAsset and applying a force to it

In this tutorial we will be creating a KAsset from a skeletal mesh asset and applying a force to this mesh. A skeletal mesh is different from a static mesh in that it is a mesh that contains moveable parts called *bones*.

Creating a KAsset

A good example of this is called SKM_Wire that is in the physics_assets.upk package that is downloadable from the official UDK website located at http://download.udk.com/tutorials/using-udk/3dbuzz_assets.zip

Unzip the file after you download it to a temporary directory.

1. Create a new directory called "3dbuzz" under the C:\UDK\UDK-2011-06\UDKGame\Content directory.

2. Copy the physics_assets.upk to this directory. This should put this new package into the Unreal Editor's content manager. Start up the Editor and check to make sure the new assets appear under **UDKGame ➤ Content ➤ 3dbuzz** directory under Packages. You may have to right-click on the 3dbuzz directory and select "Fully Load" to refresh the Content Browser's view.

3. Next, right-click the SKM_Wire in the Content Browser. Select Create New Physics Asset from the context menu shown in Figure 4–10.

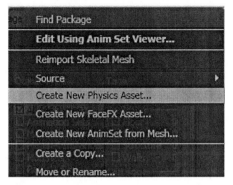

Figure 4–10. *Creating a new Physics Asset*

4. A dialog box should show up asking you to enter the package and group where to place the new asset and the name of the new physics asset itself. Enter the information requested as shown in the Figure 4–11.

Enter Package, Group and Object Name

Info

Package: 3dBuzzphysics_assets

Group: PhysicsAssets

Name: SKM_Wire_Physics_Example3

OK

Cancel

Figure 4–11. *Naming a new Physics Asset*

5. Click the OK button. Next, another dialog box shows up requesting some setup information. Accept the default options, except change the Use Verts With entry to Any Weight as in Figure 4–12.

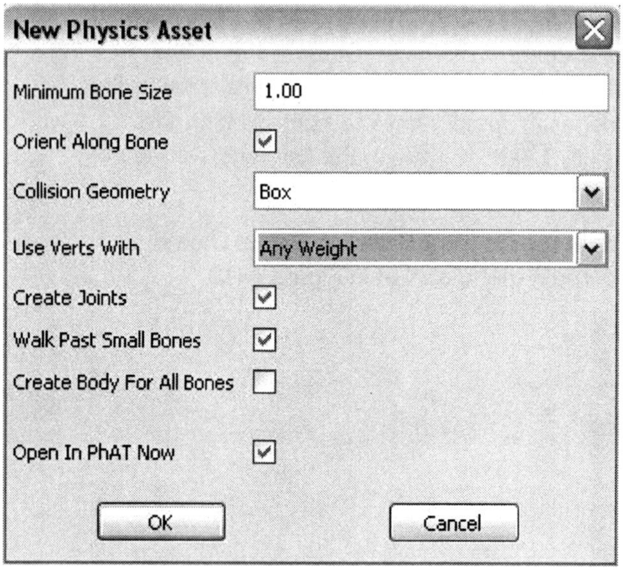

New Physics Asset   ⊠

Minimum Bone Size	1.00
Orient Along Bone	☑
Collision Geometry	Box ▼
Use Verts With	Any Weight ▼
Create Joints	☑
Walk Past Small Bones	☑
Create Body For All Bones	☐
Open In PhAT Now	☑

OK   Cancel

Figure 4–12. *New Physics Asset Setup*

6. Click the OK button and this new asset should be opened in Unreal Phat (Phat is short for Physics Assets). See Figure 4–13.

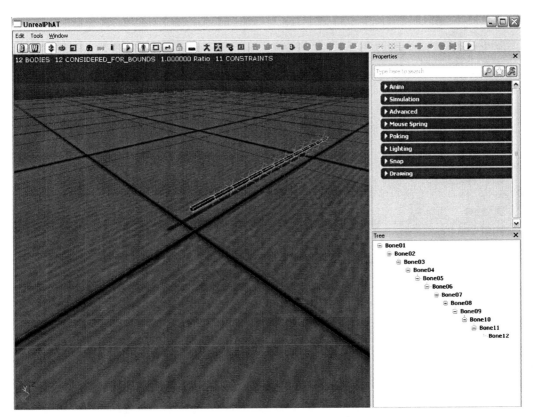

Figure 4–13. *Unreal Physics Asset with our new Asset*

Unreal Phat is used to set collision volumes and physics constraints for skeletal meshes. You should see a wire mesh that is divided by bounding boxes which enclose the separate bones that make up this wire. A bounding box is an invisible mesh that is used by the UDK Physics Engine to calculate physics collisions. Once you make sure that your wire looks similar to the above figure then close Unreal Phat window. Right-click on the new physics asset you created and select "Save" from the menu that pops up to save this asset and associated package.

Adding a KAsset to a Level

Our next step is to add a KAsset to the level. This KAsset will be the wire that we just created a physics asset for. We will also show you how exactly to put this in your level and how to set it up.

1. Load in our level map from the previous tutorial.

2. Find and then select the new physics asset you have created. Right-click on the level where you want to put this new wire and select the Add Physics Asset option. See Figure 4–14.

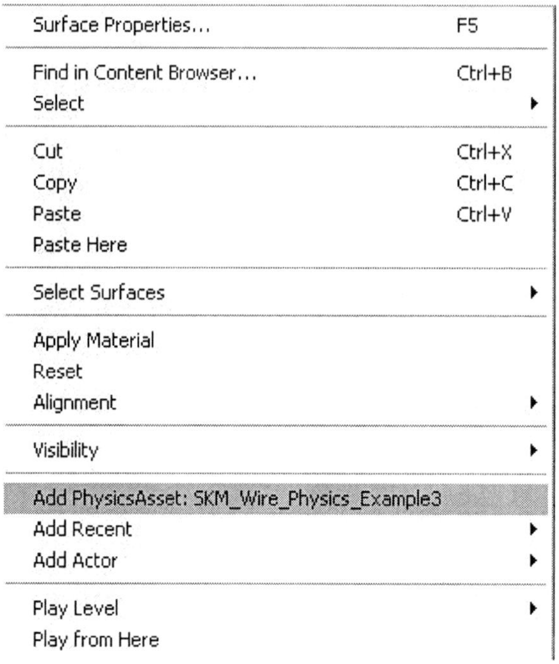

Surface Properties...	F5
Find in Content Browser...	Ctrl+B
Select	▶
Cut	Ctrl+X
Copy	Ctrl+C
Paste	Ctrl+V
Paste Here	
Select Surfaces	▶
Apply Material	
Reset	
Alignment	▶
Visibility	▶
Add PhysicsAsset: SKM_Wire_Physics_Example3	
Add Recent	▶
Add Actor	▶
Play Level	▶
Play from Here	

Figure 4–14. *Adding a Physics Asset to your level*

3. A wire mesh should be created in the level. Bring the wire up some so that you can get a better look at it using the transformation widget. See Figure 4–15.

Figure 4–15. *Level with KActors and a KAsset*

4. Next, double-click on the wire to bring up its Properties window. See Figure 4–16.

KAsset_0 Properties

Type here to search

▼ **KAsset**

▶ **Skeletal Mesh Compor** Example3Map.TheWorld:PersistentLevel.KAsset_0.SkeletalMeshComponent_11

Damage Applies Impulse   ☑

Wake On Level Start   ☐

Block Pawns   ☐

Figure 4–16. *The KAsset Properties window*

5. Click on the Wake on Level Start checkbox to begin the physics simulation for this object when the level starts and then close the window.

6. Now click on File ➤ Save As and save the level, for example, as
   Example4–2Map when the dialog box comes up.

Now that we have added the KAsset to our level, let's turn to the code.

Creating the Unreal Script Code

It's time now for you to create the code for this example. Create a new directory for this
example as you did for the previous example at
Development\Src\ExampleCh42\Classes where you will place the code for this tutorial.
Next you will define the game type and then the player controller.

Custom Game Type

The code for the new game type is almost the same as ExampleCh41. Although take
note of the new class definition ExampleCh42Game as well as the new player controller
that is derived from the PlayerController class. See Listing 4–7.

Listing 4–7. *Game Type*

```
class ExampleCh42Game  extends FrameworkGame;
event OnEngineHasLoaded()
{

    WorldInfo.Game.Broadcast(self," ExampleCh42Game  Type Active - Engine Has Loaded
!!!!");

}
function bool PreventDeath(Pawn KilledPawn, Controller Killer, class<DamageType>
DamageType, vector HitLocation)
{
    return true;
}
static event class<GameInfo> SetGameType(string MapName, string Options, string Portal)
{
    return super.SetGameType(MapName, Options, Portal);
}

defaultproperties
{


    PlayerControllerClass=class'ExampleCh42.ExampleCh42PC'

    DefaultPawnClass=class'UDKBase.SimplePawn'
    HUDType=class'UDKBase.UDKHUD'

    bRestartLevel=false
    bWaitingToStartMatch=true
    bDelayedStart=false
}
```

Custom Player Controller

Applying a force to a KAsset is a little different than for a KActor. For a KAsset you need to apply the force to the SkeletalMeshComponent of the KAsset object. Here we have specified the bone to apply the impulse to which is 'Bone06'. This would be roughly the center of the wire since the wire is divided into 12 bones. You can verify this by bringing the wire up in UnrealPhat. Please refer back to Figure 4–12 where you can clearly see the 12 bones indicated by rectangular boxes.

For the player controller for this class the only things that have changed from the last tutorial are the class definition and the ApplyForceRigidBody function. See Listing 4–8.

Listing 4–8. *Player controller class*

```
class ExampleCh42PC  extends SimplePC;
var float PickDistance;
function ApplyForceRigidBody(Actor SelectedActor,
                             Vector ImpulseDir,
                             float ImpulseMag,
                             Vector HitLocation)
{
    if (SelectedActor.IsA('KActor'))
    {
        WorldInfo.Game.Broadcast(self,"*** Thrown object " @ SelectedActor @
                                 ", ImpulseDir = " @ ImpulseDir @
                                 ", ImpulseMag = " @ ImpulseMag @
                                 ", HitLocation = " @ HitLocation);
        KActor(SelectedActor).ApplyImpulse(ImpulseDir,ImpulseMag, HitLocation);
    }
    else

    if (SelectedActor.IsA('KAsset'))
    {
        WorldInfo.Game.Broadcast(self,"*** Thrown object " @ SelectedActor @
                                        ", ImpulseDir = " @ ImpulseDir @
                                        ", ImpulseMag = " @ ImpulseMag @
                                        ", HitLocation = " @ HitLocation);
        KAsset(SelectedActor).SkeletalMeshComponent.AddImpulse(ImpulseDir* ImpulseMag,
,'Bone06');    }
    else
    {
        WorldInfo.Game.Broadcast(self,"!!!ERROR Selected Actor " @ SelectedActor @
                                       " is not a KActor or KAsset, you can not
apply an impulse to this object!!!");
    }
}
function Actor PickActor(Vector2D PickLocation, out Vector HitLocation, out TraceHitInfo
HitInfo)
{
    local Vector TouchOrigin, TouchDir;
    local Vector HitNormal;
    local Actor  PickedActor;
```

```
        local vector Extent;

        //Transform absolute screen coordinates to relative coordinates
        PickLocation.X = PickLocation.X / ViewportSize.X;
        PickLocation.Y = PickLocation.Y / ViewportSize.Y;

        //Transform to world coordinates to get pick ray
        LocalPlayer(Player).Deproject(PickLocation, TouchOrigin, TouchDir);

        //Perform trace to find touched actor
        Extent = vect(0,0,0);
        PickedActor = Trace(HitLocation,
                            HitNormal,
                            TouchOrigin + (TouchDir * PickDistance),
                            TouchOrigin,
                            True,
                            Extent,
                            HitInfo);

        //Return the touched actor for good measure
        return PickedActor;
}
function bool SwipeZoneCallback(MobileInputZone Zone,
                               float DeltaTime,
                               int Handle,
                               EZoneTouchEvent EventType,
                               Vector2D TouchLocation)
{
        local bool retval;

        local Actor PickedActor;
        local Vector HitLocation;
        local TraceHitInfo HitInfo;

        // Variables for physics
        local Vector ImpulseDir;
        local float ImpulseMag;

        retval = true;

        if (EventType == ZoneEvent_Touch)
        {
            // If screen touched then pick actor
            PickedActor = PickActor(TouchLocation,HitLocation,HitInfo);

            WorldInfo.Game.Broadcast(self,"PICKED ACTOR = "
                                    @ PickedActor @ ", HitLocation = "
                                    @ HitLocation @ ", Zone Touched = "
                                    @ Zone);

            // Set to roughly 45 degree angle
            ImpulseDir = Normal(Vector(Pawn.Rotation)) + vect(0,0,1);
            ImpulseMag = 500;

            ApplyForceRigidBody(PickedActor,ImpulseDir,ImpulseMag,HitLocation);

        }
```

```
    else
    if(EventType == ZoneEvent_Update)
    {
    }
    else
    if (EventType == ZoneEvent_UnTouch)
    {
    }
    return retval;
}
function SetupZones()
{
    Super.SetupZones();

    // If we have a game class, configure the zones
    if (MPI != None && WorldInfo.GRI.GameClass != none)
    {
        LocalPlayer(Player).ViewportClient.GetViewportSize(ViewportSize);
        if (FreeLookZone != none)
        {
            FreeLookZone.OnProcessInputDelegate = SwipeZoneCallback;
        }
    }
}
defaultproperties
{
    PickDistance = 10000;
}
```

Configuring the New Game Type

Now we need to set up the new code for compilation and setup the new game and map to run in the Mobile Previewer. Under your UDKGame\Config directory add or change entries in your Mobile-UDKGame.ini and UDKEngine.ini files to the following.

In your Mobile-UDKGame.ini file add mobile input controls for your new game.

```
[ExampleCh42.ExampleCh42Game]
RequiredMobileInputConfigs=(GroupName="UberGroup",RequireZoneNames=("UberStickMoveZone",
"UberStickLookZone","UberLookZone"))
```

In your UDKEngine.ini file, add in ExampleCh42 to the compilation list

```
[UnrealEd.EditorEngine]
ModEditPackages=ExampleCh42
```

Running the New Game Type

Bring up the Unreal Editor and load in the level with the wire. Select the View ➤ World Properties to bring up the world Properties window. Under the Game Type category set the Default Game Type to ExampleCh42Game.

Run your Mobile Game on the previewer by selecting Play ➤ On Mobile Previewer from the Editor's menu and click on the wire to apply a force. See Figure 4–17.

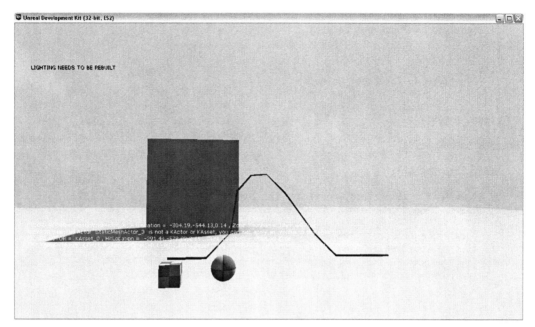

Figure 4–17. *KActors and a KAsset*

You should be able to kick around both the cube and sphere which are KActors and the wire which is a KAsset.

In conclusion, KActors and KAssets form the basis for objects providing realistic collisions. KActors are objects that are composed of static meshes and KAssets are objects that are composed of skeletal meshes. You can easily apply forces to both kinds of objects through Unreal Script and have the Unreal Physics Engine process them.

Physics Constraints

This section will discuss physics constraints. First an overview is given followed by a hands-on example where you tie several objects together and apply a force to see how those tied objects react.

Physics Constraints Overview

Physics constraints are objects that can be used to bind together different objects. Physics constraints are very flexible and have many options that can specify exactly how objects are to be tied together. With a physics constraint you can bind one actor to another or to the world itself by specifying None for that actor. If constraining a skeletal mesh you can specify which bone name to bind to.

For example, an arrow attached to a string that when fired from a bow will allow the user to retract the arrow and retrieve whatever the arrow has penetrated. The arrow would be a static mesh KActor and the string would be a skeletal mesh KAsset that are tied together via a physics constraint. The arrow would be tied to one end of the string which would be the bone at the end of the string mesh. When the arrow hits the target a dynamic constraint is generated to tie the arrow to the target which is then pulled back to the user of the bow.

Linear Constraints

Linear constraints can be hard. That is, when the two objects reach their linear limits, they stop suddenly. Linear constraints can also be soft in that instead of stopping suddenly they behave as if they are attached by a spring. Finally, linear constraints can also be set to break if enough force is applied to the constraint.

The following list provides some additional information for each type of linear constraint:

- Hard Linear Constraints—You can limit linear movement of constrained objects by setting bLimited to 1 for that axis and setting LimitSize to the limits for that axis

- Soft Linear Constraints— If bLinearLimitSoft is set to true then the linear limits make the constraint behave like a spring using the LinearLimitStiffness value to determine the extent of this behavior rather than hard limits where the object suddenly stops when it reaches this limit. The LinearLimitDamping value would then control the damping.

- Breakable Linear Constraints—You can also set if this constraint is breakable or not. If bLinearBreakable is true then this constraint can break if the force exerted on it is greater than or equal to the LinearBreakThreshold value.

Angular Constraints

Angular Constraints can be hard, soft, and breakable similar to the linear constraints except these constraints refer to angles rather than linear distance. The following list describes the several types of angular constraints:

- Hard Angular Constraints— In terms of angular movement if you set bSwingLimited to true you can limit the constrained object's angle to a cone. The values of Swing1LimitAngle and Swing2LimitAngle define the swing limited movements.

  If bTwistLimited is set to true then the twist between the two constrained bodies is limited. The value of TwistLimitAngle will then determine the limits of the twist angle.

- Soft Angular Constraints— If bSwingLimitSoft is set to true then the constraint will act like a spring instead of being a hard limit and the value of SwingLimitStiffness will determine the behavior of this spring with SwingLimitDamping controlling the damping.

If bTwistLimitSoft is set to true then the constraint acts as a spring instead of a hard limit and TwistLimitStiffness controls the spring stiffness with TwistLimitDamping controlling the damping.

- Breakable Angular Constraints—If bAngularBreakable is set to true then this constraint can be broken by twisting it apart when the force applied is greater than or equal to AngularBreakThreshold.

You can create physics constraints using the Unreal Editor and place them into the level or you can create them dynamically while the player is playing the game.

Predefined Constraints

There are already some pre-defined constraint types that set up the above values to make the constraint behave in a certain manner such as:

- Ball and Socket Constraint (RB_BSJointActor) which has its linear movement locked and its angular movements completely free.

- Hinge Constraint (RBHingeActor) which has its linear movement locked and can swing around like a door hinge.

- Prismatic Constraint (RBPrismaticActor) which has 2 out of 3 linear axes of movement locked and all of the angular movements locked. This allows it to behave similar to a sliding gate or door.

- Pulley Constraint (RB_PulleyJoinActor) which simulates a pulley where pulling down one object constrained by the pulley pulls up on the other object.

Dynamically Created Physics Constraints

You can also dynamically create physics constraints. The following is an example of creating a physics constraint using Unreal Script using the RB_ConstraintActorSpawnable class.

```
Var RB_ConstraintActorSpawnable  Constraint1;
Var Actor RopeStart,RopeSection2;

Pos = RopeSection2.Location;
Constraint = Spawn(class'RB_ConstraintActorSpawnable',,,Pos);
Constraint.InitConstraint(RopeStart, RopeSection2 , 'Bone12', 'Bone01');
```

Now that you have an idea of how constraints work, let's put them to work in a practical example.

Hands-On Example: Creating physics constraints with the Unreal Editor

In this example we will show you how to create physics constraints in the Unreal Editor. Physics constraints are what you use to tie objects together in various ways. Examples that use physics constraints include doors, sliding gates, punching bags and of course the wire we used in our previous tutorial. The wire was composed of smaller segments that were constrained together. In this example you will tie together a cube and a sphere to the ends of the wire you created in the previous example. You will then apply a force to parts of this combination and observe the reaction.

Adding New Objects to a Level

First we need to add in some new elements to our level from the KAsset example. We need to make copies of the cube, sphere, and the wire and put them together using physics constraints.

1. Start the Unreal Editor and load in the level from the previous example that contains the sphere, cube, and wire.

2. Right-click the sphere and select Copy from the context menu.

3. Right-click on the place in the level where you want to place the sphere and select Paste.

You may have to move the new object so that it does not penetrate the ground using the transformation widget. Use the same procedure to copy and paste copies of the cube and the wire in the same general area.

Constraining Objects

Once you get all the objects copied and pasted you will need to constraint these together. To do this we will use a physics constraint called a ball and socket joint. The ball and socket joint constrains the objects linearly so that the constrained objects do not move in the X, Y, and Z directions. However, the ball and socket joint is not constrained in terms of its angular movement so it is free to rotate around the X, Y, and Z axes. You can also modify these properties if you want to after you create the new constraint. To create a new ball and socket constraint change the tab in the Unreal Editor from "Content Browser" to "Actor Classes".

1. Select RB_BSJointActor under the Physics category. See Figure 4–18.

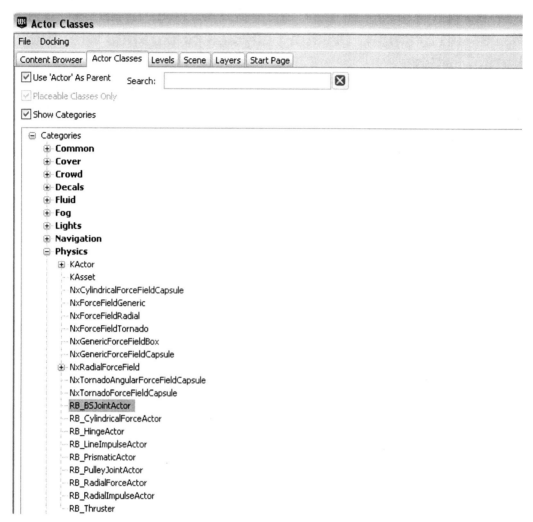

Figure 4–18. *Selecting a Ball and Socket Constraint*

   2.   Then right-click on an empty area in your level and select Add RB_BSJoint Actor Here to add it to your level. See Figure 4–19.

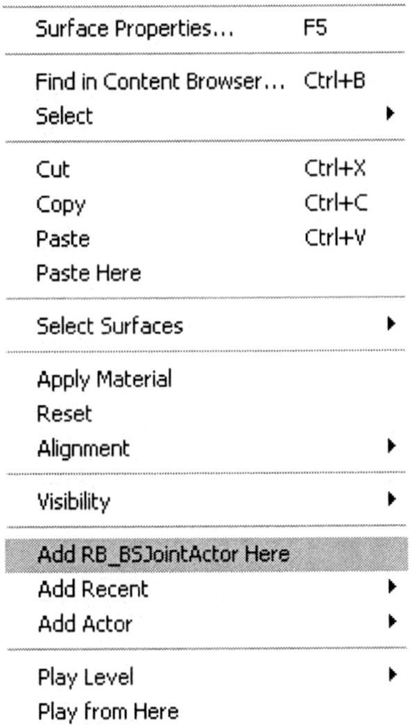

Surface Properties...	F5
Find in Content Browser...	Ctrl+B
Select	▶
Cut	Ctrl+X
Copy	Ctrl+C
Paste	Ctrl+V
Paste Here	
Select Surfaces	▶
Apply Material	
Reset	
Alignment	▶
Visibility	▶
Add RB_BSJointActor Here	
Add Recent	▶
Add Actor	▶
Play Level	▶
Play from Here	

Figure 4–19. *Adding a Ball and Socket Physics Constraint*

The constraint should appear in the level. See Figure 4–20.

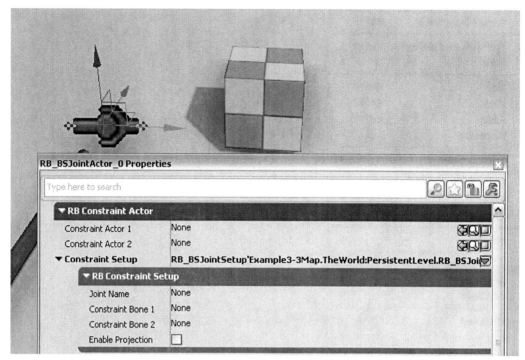

Figure 4–20. *Physics Constraint and Properties*

There are two key properties under the RB_Constraint Actor category. The Constraint Actor 1 and Constraint Actor 2 properties are the actors to bind together with this physics constraint. Under the RB_Constraint Setup category, Constraint Bone 1 refers to the bone from the first actor (if any) to constrain and the Constraint Bone 2 refers to the bone from the second actor (if any) to constrain. Thus, you can constrain a static mesh (KActor) to a skeletal Mesh (KAsset) using one of the skeletal mesh's bones. This is actually what we are going to do.

1. First arrange a cube, one end of the wire, and the constraint as in the following. See Figure 4–21.

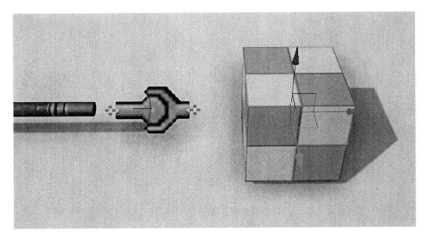

Figure 4–21. *Connecting the Cube to one end of the Wire*

2. Then move the wire, constraint and cube so that they are close together but not overlapping. The reason for this is if you overlap them too much the collision areas of both objects with overlap and the physics engine will try to fix this situation with attempting to push them apart resulting in weird behavior.

3. Then double-click on the constraint to bring up its properties. Next you need to set the lock on the upper right hand side of the properties window so that you can select an actor in the viewport and keep the properties windows open and on top. See Figure 4–22.

Figure 4–22. *Click on the Lock Icon to keep window open and on top*

4. After clicking the lock icon the graphic should change from an unlocked image to one that is locked. See Figure 4–23.

Figure 4–23. *Properties window is now locked*

5. Now you can easily click on the wire and set this as Constraint Actor 1. Click on the cube and set this as Constraint Actor 2. The Constraint Bone 1 will be either Bone01 or Bone12 depending on the wire's orientation. After setting the bone you should see a line going from the constraint to the actual bone in the wire that it is now constrained to. If this bone is not at the end of the wire that is closest to the cube then you need to change the bone name to Bone01. See Figure 4–24.

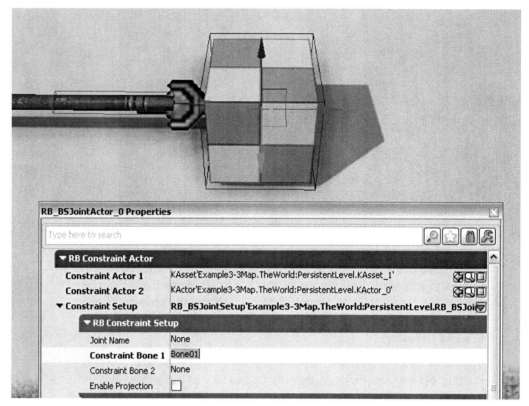

Figure 4–24. *Constraint binding a KAsset (Bone1 at End of Wire) with a Kactor (Cube)*

6.   After properly setting the constraint properties you need to slide the end of the wire, constraint, and the cube closer together to make it look as if they are attached. You may need to turn off the grid snapping feature of the editor in order to get a good fit between the objects. Grid snapping is a feature that allows the user to move an object only in specified increments. For our example, uncheck the Grid Snapping checkbox (see Figure 4–25).

Figure 4–25. *Turning Grid Snapping on/off*

After placing the cube and the wire closer together it should look something like Figure 4–26.

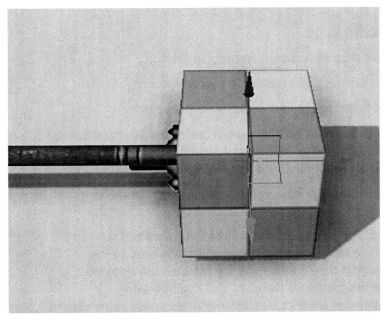

Figure 4–26. *Constrained Wire and Cube*

7. Next, you need to set up the constraints for the sphere and the other end of the wire using the same method as for the cube. The final result should look like Figure 4–27.

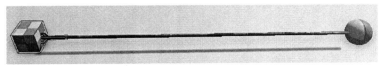

Figure 4–27. *Sphere and Cube constrained to opposite ends of the Wire.*

8. Now save the level and exit the Unreal Editor.

Changing the Unreal Script

The next thing you need to do is increase the value of the force applied to an object when you click on it. Open the ExampleCh42PC.uc file in the ExampleCh42 directory and change the line in the function SwipeZoneCallback() to increase the impulse magnitude.

```
ImpulseMag = 500;
```

Now you are ready to run the game.

Running the new Game Type

Follow these steps to run the game and see what you've created:

1.   Bring up the Unreal Frontend and recompile your script code.

2.   Start up the Unreal Editor and load in the level for this exercise.

3.   Set the game type to ExampleCh42Game. Select **View ➤ World Properties** to bring up the World Properties window and set the Default Game Type to ExampleCh42Game under the Game Type category.

4.   Run the game on the mobile previewer by selecting **Play ➤ On Mobile Previewer.**

5.   Click on the sphere. You should see the sphere fly upward and forward while at the same time being attached to one end of the wire. As the sphere hits the ground it should also move the cube as well since the cube is attached to the sphere via the wire. See Figure 4–28.

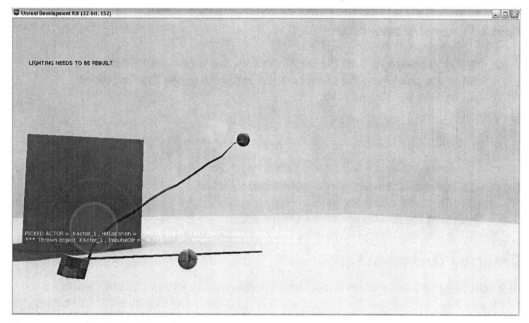

Figure 4–28. *Using Physics Constraints to bind together a Sphere, Cube and a Wire*

Collisions

This section covers collisions. First an overview of collisions in the UDK is given, followed by two hands-on examples. In the first example, you create a custom KActor collision object that is able to detect when another object collides with it. The second example shows how to make this custom object explode and disappear when hit hard enough.

Collision Overview

This section will explain how you would set up and handle collisions for a physics object. For our example, we will use a new class called RigidBodyCube that is derived from a KActor class.

```
class RigidBodyCube extends KActor
placeable;
```

The RigidBodyCollision() function is declared in the Actor class and will be overridden here. This function will process collisions for this object.

```
event RigidBodyCollision(PrimitiveComponent HitComponent,
                         PrimitiveComponent OtherComponent,
                         const out CollisionImpactData RigidCollisionData,
                         int ContactIndex)
{
    // Process Collision Here
}
```

This function is called under certain circumstances when a PrimitiveComponent that is owned by this class has

- bNotifyRigidBodyCollision = true

- ScriptRigidBodyCollisionThreshold is > 0

- Is involved in a physics collision where the relative velocities between the two objects exceed the ScriptRigidBodyCollisionThreshold value.

In the defaultproperties section, the 3D static mesh that represents this class is created through defining a StaticMeshComponent called RigidBodyCubeMesh and adding it to this class's Component array.

```
defaultproperties
{
    Begin Object Class=StaticMeshComponent Name=RigidBodyCubeMesh
        StaticMesh=StaticMesh'EngineMeshes.Cube'

        CollideActors=true
        BlockActors=true
        BlockRigidBody=true

        bNotifyRigidBodyCollision=true
        ScriptRigidBodyCollisionThreshold=0.001
        RBChannel=RBCC_GameplayPhysics
```

```
            RBCollideWithChannels=(Default=true,
                                   BlockingVolume=true,
                                   GameplayPhysics=true,
                                   EffectPhysics=true)
        End Object
    StaticMeshComponent=RigidBodyCubeMesh
    Components.Add(RigidBodyCubeMesh)
    CollisionComponent = RigidBodyCubeMesh

    bWakeOnLevelStart = true

    Physics = PHYS_RigidBody
    BlockRigidBody = true
    bBlockActors = true
    bCollideActors = true
}
```

The Component array holds items that are attached to this class object's location and rotation. The actual 3D static mesh that is used to represent this class is defined in the StaticMesh variable that is set equal to a Cube. The StaticMeshComponent of the KActor is also set to the RigidBodyCubeMesh. The CollisionComponent which points to the collision mesh used for colliding this object against other objects also is set to the RigidBodyCubeMesh.

The following lists the key variables that must be set to produce rigid body collisions for this class and for components within this class:

- The CollideActors variable must be set to true so that this object will be considered for collisions.

- The BlockActors variable should be set to True so the Player will be blocked from moving through this object.

- The BlockRigidBody variable must be set to True to have this object collide with other objects that use the Novodex physics engine.

- The bNotifyRigidBodyCollision variable must be set to true and the ScriptRigidBodyCollisionThreshold variable must be > 0 to have the RigidBodyCollision() function called for collision processing.

- The variable RBChannel should be set to RBCC_GameplayPhysics which indicates what type of object this is with respect to a rigid body physics collision. The RBCollideWithChannels variable indicates what other kinds of objects can collide with this one.

- The variable bWakeOnLevelStart is set to true to indicate that this object's physics simulation should begin when the level starts up.

- The Physics variable of this object is set to PHYS_RigidBody to indicate that Rigid Body physics simulation using the Novodex physics engine should be performed on this object.

- The variable BlockRigidBody in the KActor class is set to true to indicate that objects of this class will collide with other Rigid Bodies.

- The variable bBlockActors in the KActor class is set to true to indicate that objects of this class will block a player from moving through it.

- The variable bCollideActors in the KActor class is set to true to indicate that objects of this class are enabled for collision detection.

Next, let's see how the above variables are used in a real hands-on example.

Hands-on Example: Creating a Collision Object and Putting It in a Level

In this tutorial you will creating a new class RigidBodyCube that will be a KActor rigid body and that will be placeable in a level using the Unreal Editor. An object of the RigidBodyCube class will be able to tell when it is hit. When hit the function RigidBodyCollision() will be called and code can be added to handle the event.

Creating the Unreal Script

The first thing we need to do is create the code for RigidBodyCube object as well as the other classes, such as the game type, and player controller, and compile it. We need to do this in order to put this new class into the UDK system where the Unreal Editor will have access to it.

Create a new directory for your code at Development\Src\ ExampleCh43\Classes under your UDK installation directory. Then, as previously, you will define the game type and create the player controller. Finally, you define the RigidBodyCube class.

Custom Game Type

First create the class that defines the type of game the player will be playing and put it in a new file ExampleCh43Game.uc. See Listing 4–9.

Listing 4–9. *Game type*

```
class ExampleCh43Game extends FrameworkGame;

event OnEngineHasLoaded()
{
    WorldInfo.Game.Broadcast(self," ExampleCh43Game Type Active - Engine Has Loaded
!!!!");
}

function bool PreventDeath(Pawn KilledPawn, Controller Killer, class<DamageType>
DamageType, vector HitLocation)
{
    return true;
}

static event class<GameInfo> SetGameType(string MapName, string Options, string Portal)
{
    return super.SetGameType(MapName, Options, Portal);
```

```
}

defaultproperties
{

    PlayerControllerClass=class'ExampleCh43.ExampleCh43PC'

    DefaultPawnClass=class'UDKBase.SimplePawn'
    HUDType=class'UDKBase.UDKHUD'

    bRestartLevel=false
    bWaitingToStartMatch=true
    bDelayedStart=false
}
```

Custom Player Controller

Next, you need to create the custom player controller. Create a new file called
ExampleCh43PC.uc using the code in Listing 4–10.

Listing 4–10. *Player controller*

```
class ExampleCh43PC  extends SimplePC;

var float PickDistance;

function ApplyForceRigidBody(Actor SelectedActor, Vector ImpulseDir,float ImpulseMag,
Vector HitLocation)
{
    if (SelectedActor.IsA('KActor'))
    {
        WorldInfo.Game.Broadcast(self,"*** Thrown object " @ SelectedActor @
                                    ", ImpulseDir = " @ ImpulseDir @
                                    ", ImpulseMag = " @ ImpulseMag @
                                    ", HitLocation = " @ HitLocation);
        KActor(SelectedActor).ApplyImpulse(ImpulseDir,ImpulseMag, HitLocation);
    }
    else
    if (SelectedActor.IsA('KAsset'))
    {
        WorldInfo.Game.Broadcast(self,"*** Thrown object " @ SelectedActor @
                                    ", ImpulseDir = " @ ImpulseDir @
                                    ", ImpulseMag = " @ ImpulseMag @
                                    ", HitLocation = " @ HitLocation);
        KAsset(SelectedActor).SkeletalMeshComponent.AddImpulse(ImpulseDir* ImpulseMag,
,'Bone06');
    }
    else
    {
        WorldInfo.Game.Broadcast(self,"!!!ERROR Selected Actor " @ SelectedActor @
                                    " is not a KActor or KAsset, you can not
apply an impulse to this object!!!");
    }
}
```

```
function Actor PickActor(Vector2D PickLocation, out Vector HitLocation, out TraceHitInfo
HitInfo)
{
    local Vector TouchOrigin, TouchDir;
    local Vector HitNormal;
    local Actor PickedActor;
    local vector Extent;

    //Transform absolute screen coordinates to relative coordinates

    PickLocation.X = PickLocation.X / ViewportSize.X;

    PickLocation.Y = PickLocation.Y / ViewportSize.Y;
        //Transform to world coordinates to get pick ray
    LocalPlayer(Player).Deproject(PickLocation, TouchOrigin, TouchDir);
        //Perform trace to find touched actor    Extent = vect(0,0,0);
    PickedActor = Trace(HitLocation,
                    HitNormal,
                    TouchOrigin + (TouchDir * PickDistance),
                    TouchOrigin,
                    True,
                    Extent,
                    HitInfo);

        //Return the touched actor for good measure
        return PickedActor;
}
function bool SwipeZoneCallback(MobileInputZone Zone,
                        float DeltaTime,
                        int Handle,
                        EZoneTouchEvent EventType,
                        Vector2D TouchLocation)
{
    local bool retval;

    local Actor PickedActor;
    local  Vector HitLocation;
    local TraceHitInfo HitInfo;

    // Variables for physics
    Local Vector ImpulseDir;
    Local float ImpulseMag;

    Local float KickAngle;

    // Constants defined in Object.uc
    // const Pi = 3.1415926535897932;
    // const RadToDeg = 57.295779513082321600;      // 180 / Pi
    // const DegToRad = 0.017453292519943296;       // Pi / 180
    // const UnrRotToRad = 0.00009587379924285;     // Pi / 32768
    // const RadToUnrRot = 10430.3783504704527;     // 32768 / Pi
    // const DegToUnrRot = 182.0444;
    // const UnrRotToDeg = 0.00549316540360483;

    retval = true;        if (EventType == ZoneEvent_Touch)
    {
```

```
            // If screen touched then pick actor
            PickedActor = PickActor(TouchLocation,HitLocation,HitInfo);

            WorldInfo.Game.Broadcast(self,"PICKED ACTOR = "
                                    @ PickedActor @ ", HitLocation = "
                                    @ HitLocation @ ", Zone Touched = "
                                    @ Zone);

        KickAngle = 15 * DegToRad;
        ImpulseDir = (Normal(Vector(Pawn.Rotation)) * cos(KickAngle)) + (vect(0,0,1) *
sin(KickAngle));

            ImpulseMag = 500;
            ApplyForceRigidBody(PickedActor,ImpulseDir,ImpulseMag,HitLocation);
        }
        else
        if(EventType == ZoneEvent_Update)
        {
        }
        else
        if (EventType == ZoneEvent_UnTouch)
        {
        }
        return retval;
    }

function SetupZones()
{
    Super.SetupZones();

    // If we have a game class, configure the zones
    if (MPI != None && WorldInfo.GRI.GameClass != none)
    {
        LocalPlayer(Player).ViewportClient.GetViewportSize(ViewportSize);
if (FreeLookZone != none)
        {
            FreeLookZone.OnProcessInputDelegate = SwipeZoneCallback;         }
    }
}

defaultproperties
{
    PickDistance = 10000;
}
```

Most of the code is the same as the previous example in Listing 4–8. However, there are some new elements.

```
KickAngle = 15 * DegToRad;
```

Kickangle is the angle that the force is applied to the object measured from the horizontal and is set to 15 degrees.

ImpulseDir is a vector that represents the direction of the force that will be applied to the object. The ImpulseDir is composed of two parts the forward vector component and the vertical vector component that when added together produces the final direction of the force. The forward component of the direction is calculated by multiplying the normalized vector representing the direction the player's pawn is facing by the cosine of the KickAngle. The vertical component is calculated by multiplying the Z axis unit vector by the sine of the KickAngle.

> **NOTE:** Basically, we figure out the horizontal and vertical components of the ImpulseDir vector on a 2D plane and then project them onto the 3D world by multiplying each component by horizontal and vertical 3D unit vectors. Please refer to Chapter 8 for more information on vectors, sine, cosine, etc as well as a detailed explanation of the mathematics involved in this example.

This gives the forward and vertical components a range of 0 to 1. If the KickAngle is 0 then the cosine of this angle is 1 and the sine of this angle is 0. This would make the direction all in the forward direction and none in the vertical direction as expected. If the KickAngle is 90 degrees or PI/2 then the cosine of the angle would be 0 and the sine of the angle would be 1. This would make the forward component 0 and would maximize the vertical direction.

```
ImpulseDir = (Normal(Vector(Pawn.Rotation)) * cos(KickAngle)) + (vect(0,0,1) *
sin(KickAngle));
```

The other code in Listing 4–10 was explained previously in the first Hands-on Example of this chapter.

The RigidBodyCube Class

The next class you will need to create is the RigidBodyCube class. Create a new file called RigidBodyCube.uc and enter the following code into it and then save the file. Declare the new RigidBodyCube class as follows. The placeable option at the end of the class indicates that this class is defined as placeable. That means that using the Unreal Editor you can select this class from the Actor Classes tab and right-click on the level to place an object of this type in the actual game level. The new RigidBodyCube class is declared as a subclass of KActor. See Listing 4–11.

Listing 4–11. *RigidBodyCube class*

```
class RigidBodyCube extends KActor
placeable;
event RigidBodyCollision(PrimitiveComponent HitComponent,
                         PrimitiveComponent OtherComponent,
                         const out CollisionImpactData RigidCollisionData,
                         int ContactIndex)
{
WorldInfo.Game.Broadcast(self,"RigidBodyCube COLLISION!!!! - " @ self @
                          ", HitComponent =  " @ Hitcomponent @
                          " Has Collided with " @ OtherComponent @
                          " With Force " @
VSize(RigidCollisionData.TotalNormalForceVector));
}
defaultproperties
{
```

```
            Begin Object Class=StaticMeshComponent Name=RigidBodyCubeMesh
            StaticMesh=StaticMesh'EngineMeshes.Cube'

            CollideActors=true
            BlockActors=true
            BlockRigidBody=true

            bNotifyRigidBodyCollision=true
            ScriptRigidBodyCollisionThreshold=0.001
            RBChannel=RBCC_GameplayPhysics
            RBCollideWithChannels=(Default=true,
                                    BlockingVolume=true,
                                    GameplayPhysics=true,
                                    EffectPhysics=true)
        End Object
        StaticMeshComponent=RigidBodyCubeMesh
        Components.Add(RigidBodyCubeMesh)

        CollisionComponent = RigidBodyCubeMesh
        bWakeOnLevelStart = true

        bEdShouldSnap = false


        Physics = PHYS_RigidBody
        BlockRigidBody = true
        bBlockActors = true
        bCollideActors = true
}
```

The variable bEdShouldSnap is set to false to indicate that this object by default should not use grid snapping while in the editor. The rest of the code in the default properties block was explained in the collision overview section that was presented before this example.

Game Type Setup

Now we need to set up our new game type and compile our new code. In your UDKGame\Config directory change Mobile-UDKGame.ini and UDKEngine.ini to compile our new code.

```
Mobile-UDKGame.ini
[ExampleCh43.ExampleCh43Game]
RequiredMobileInputConfigs=(GroupName="UberGroup",RequireZoneNames=("UberStickMoveZone",
"UberStickLookZone","UberLookZone"))
UDKEngine.ini
[UnrealEd.EditorEngine]
ModEditPackages= ExampleCh43
```

Now bring up the Unreal Frontend and compile the code.

Setting up the Level

The next thing to do is to bring up the Unreal Editor so you can set up the level.

1. First of all you need to load in your level from that last example and save it as a different map for this exercise.

2. Go to the Actor Classes tab and under the **Physics ➤ Kactor** category and select the new `RigidBodyCube` class you just created. See Figure 4–29.

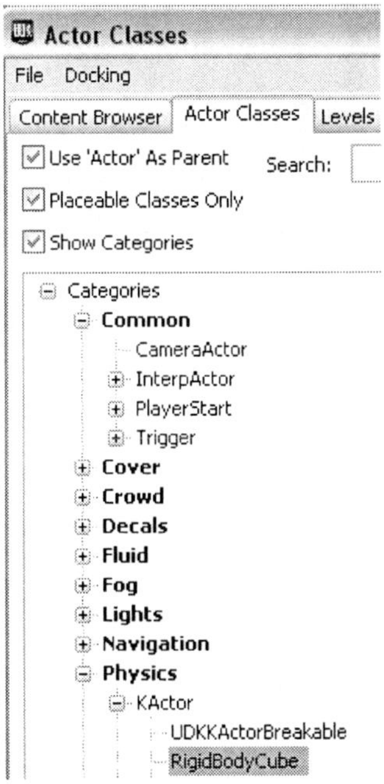

Figure 4–29. *Selecting your new RigidBodyCube class from the Actor Classes Browser*

3. Right-click on an empty area in the level and select Add RigidBodyCube Here to add the object to your level. Double-click on the object to bring up its properties. See Figure 4–30.

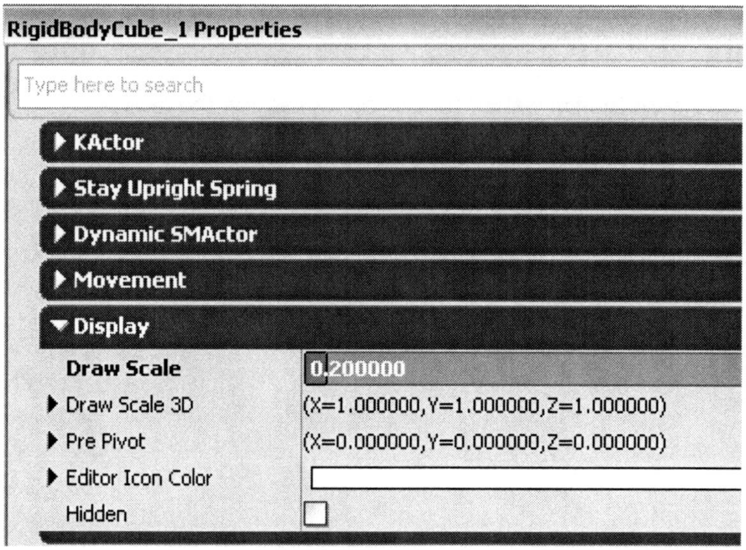

RigidBodyCube_1 Properties

Type here to search

▶ **KActor**

▶ **Stay Upright Spring**

▶ **Dynamic SMActor**

▶ **Movement**

▼ **Display**

Draw Scale	0.200000
▶ Draw Scale 3D	(X=1.000000,Y=1.000000,Z=1.000000)
▶ Pre Pivot	(X=0.000000,Y=0.000000,Z=0.000000)
▶ Editor Icon Color	
Hidden	☐

Figure 4–30. *Properties of new class RigidBodyCube*

4. Change the Draw Scale property under the Display category to .20 and close out the properties window.

5. Next you need to create a wall of blocks using this new class in the center of the arena. To help you along, selecting a block and then holding down the Alt key while dragging the transformation widget will allow you to simultaneously create a new copy of this object and drag that copy of the object using the transformation widget. Holding down the Ctrl key and clicking on multiple objects will allow you to select multiple objects for movement or copying using the Alt key technique. Also, make copies of the Spheres and place them around this wall of blocks, as in Figure 4–31.

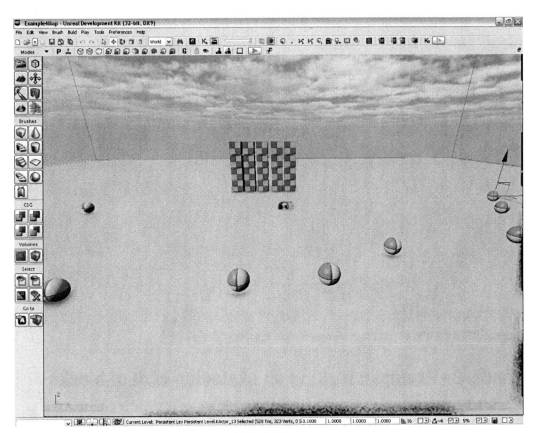

Figure 4–31. *A wall made of our custom class RigidBodyCube*

Running the Game Type

Finally, we are ready to try out our game. Change the level's default game type to ExampleCh43Game and start the game up on the mobile previewer.

Try moving around the wall and kicking balls into it. When the ball hits the wall a message should appear stating that there was a RigidBodyCube collision. See Figure 4–32.

Figure 4–32. *Ball hitting a block made of our new class RigidBodyCube*

Hands-On Example: Making an exploding wall of blocks

This tutorial will build upon the last tutorial. Now what we need to do is take that wall of blocks and make them explode when you hit them with another object hard enough. In order to do this we need to change the code in the RigidBodyCube class.

Just under the class declaration add in the following variables. The ExplosionTemplate refers to the particle system that will be used for the explosion of a RigidBodyCube. You can search for particle systems in the Content Browser by checking the box under the Object **Type ➤ Favorites** heading and selecting "Mobile Game" under Packages. The Explosion variable holds a reference to a new emitter that is created using the SpawnEmitter() function.

```
Var ParticleSystem ExplosionTemplate;
Var ParticleSystemComponent Explosion;
```

For this example, we have decided to "destroy" the block by moving it out of the player's view and turning off Rigid Body physics for this object to save processing resources. This way we can easily add in more information later if needed such as the time this block was destroyed, what object destroyed it, and so on. The OutOfViewLocation variable holds the location in the world where destroyed blocks are moved to.

```
Var vector OutOfViewLocation;
```

The MinimumForceToExplode variable is the minimum force it would take to destroy a RigidBodyCube class object. bDestroyed is set to true if the RigidBodyCube is destroyed.

```
Var float MinimumForceToExplode;
Var bool bDestroyed;
```

In the defaultproperties section add in the default values of the following variables

```
MinimumForceToExplode = 370;
bDestroyed = false
OutOfViewLocation = (X = 0, Y = 0, Z = -5000)
ExplosionTemplate = ParticleSystem'Castle_Assets.FX.P_FX_Fire_SubUV_01'
```

For the ExplosionTemplate default value you can actually view this system from within Unreal Cascade. Search for particle systems using the search term "fx_fire" in the "UDKGame" package and you should see 1 particle system asset. Double-click on this asset to bring it up in Unreal Cascade. See Figure 4–33

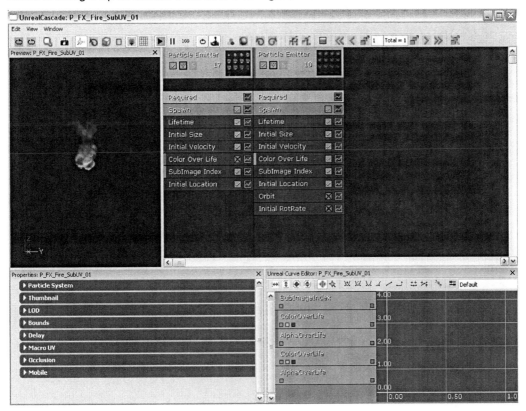

Figure 4–33. *Our particle system used for explosions viewed in Unreal Cascade*

You also need to change the RigidBodyCollision() function to the new function that follows. What this function does is first test to see if collision force between this object and the object that it collided into is equal to or greater than the minimum force needed to destroy this object. If it is then the object is destroyed. First a new explosion is created using a particle emitter that is spawned from a pool of particle emitters. Next, this object is moved to a location out of the player's view, its physics state is set to none and its destroyed variable is set to true.

```
event RigidBodyCollision(PrimitiveComponent HitComponent,
                         PrimitiveComponent OtherComponent,
                         const out CollisionImpactData RigidCollisionData,
                         int ContactIndex)
{
    local vector ExplosionLocation;
    local float CollisionForce;

    WorldInfo.Game.Broadcast(self,"RigidBodyCube COLLISION!!!! - " @ self @
                                    ", HitComponent =  " @ Hitcomponent @
                                    " Has Collided with " @ OtherComponent @
                                    " With FOrce " @
VSize(RigidCollisionData.TotalNormalForceVector));

    CollisionForce = VSize(RigidCollisionData.TotalNormalForceVector);

    if (CollisionForce >= MinimumForceToExplode)
    {
        // Spawn Explosion Emitter
        ExplosionLocation = HitComponent.Bounds.Origin;
        Explosion = WorldInfo.MyEmitterPool.SpawnEmitter(ExplosionTemplate,
ExplosionLocation);

        // Object has been Destroyed
        bDestroyed = true;

        // Move Rigid Body out of view
        HitComponent.SetRBPosition(OutOfViewLocation);
        SetPhysics(Phys_None);
    }
}
```

Recompile this code and launch the game. Kick some objects into the wall. See Figure 4–34.

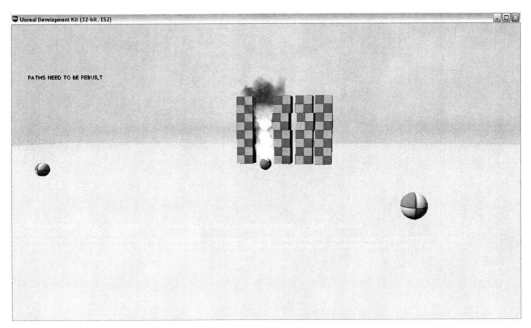

Figure 4–34. *Kicking objects into wall formed by exploding RigidBodyCubes*

Summary

In this chapter we covered the UDK physics system. We discussed collision meshes and how you can create your own through a 3d modeling program like Blender. We showed you how to create both KActors from static meshes and KAssets from skeletal meshes and how to apply forces to each type of object. Then we showed you how to use physics constraints to tie together KActors and KAssets so that a force applied to one of these objects will affect all of them. Next we demonstrated how to create a new class that was a placeable rigid body that is able to react to collisions. Building on that example we added code to make that new class explode when it collides with another object.

Chapter 5

UDK Bots

In this chapter we will cover UDK bots. Bots are basically computer-controlled enemies. They are important because, unless the game is a completely multiplayer, you will generally need some bots to make the game interesting and challenging.

First an overview of bots is given. This is followed by a discussion of bot Artificial Intelligence path finding and the different methods that the UDK uses which are pathnodes and navigation meshes. Finally, using weapons with bots is covered along with how players and bots can take damage from their weapons. Hands-on examples are given to illustrate these concepts including:

- ▓ How to create a bot and have it follow the player using Pathnodes
- ▓ How to create a bot and have it follow the player using Navmesh
- ▓ How to move a bot to a point in the world specified by the Player
- ▓ How to equip a bot with a weapon
- ▓ How a bot and a player can take damage from a weapon

UDK Bot Overview

A UDK bot is basically a 3D animated object, or "robot", with built-in artificial intelligence features that allow for such things like finding a path to another object in the game world and then being able to move to that object along that path. For example, let's say you are in control of a squad of computer-controlled soldiers or bots. You can indicate the location that you want the bots to move to by touching the screen on your iOS device. The bots then calculate the path to that location and in the process avoid obstacles that would block their way. The code to find this path is already built into the base UDK code and is what we will discuss in this chapter. Other things, such as when to fire weapons and who or what to fire at under what circumstances, must be programmed separately.

There are certain classes within the UDK base code and functions within those classes that must be used in order to create a working bot. In order to create a bot with custom user-defined behavior, a custom bot controller must be created. Bot controllers are similar to player controllers except that there will be no player input in determining a bot's behavior. Think of the controller as the bot's brain. Once a custom bot controller has been created then the controller must possess the bot's pawn in order to connect the bot's brain which is the controller to the bot's body which is the bot's pawn. The way we connect the two is simple. We use the Possess() function located in the bot controller to connect the brain to the body. This is covered in detail in a later section in this chapter.

Bot Related Classes

The UDK has a couple of built-in classes that handle bots. They are the `AIController` class and the `UDKBot` class. The definitions of these classes are as follows.

```
class AIController extends Controller
    native(AI);
```

```
class UDKBot extends AIController
    native;
```

Note that both classes are defined as native which means that part of the class is implemented in C/C++ instead of UnrealScript. Native classes should not be altered. Native classes have a portion of their code implemented elsewhere in C/C++ and are not designed to be altered by the UDK user. In order to create a custom bot controller we must derive a new class from the `UDKBot` class. The following declares a new custom class called `BotCustomController` that derives from the `UDKBot` class.

```
class BotCustomController extends UDKBot;
```

It is in this new custom bot controller class that code can be placed to give the bot custom behavior. This new controller class will inherit the built in pathfinding abilities of the Controller class. The Controller class is the base class for controllers.

Key Bot Related Functions

There are some key functions that are essential to basic bot AI.

- LatentWhatToDoNext() – This function is declared in a state and is used to transition to the WhatToDoNext() function. The importance of using this function is that game time passes at least one clock tick before the actual bot decision making code in ExecuteWhatToDoNext() is executed. This prevents a critical timing error from occurring. See the example below.

  ```
  auto state Initial
  {
      Begin:
      LatentWhatToDoNext();
  }
  ```

- WhatToDoNext() – This function is called by LatentWhatToDoNext() and calls ExecuteWhatToDoNext() on the next game tick if the DecisionComponent.bTriggered is set to true. See the following example.

```
event WhatToDoNext()
{
    DecisionComponent.bTriggered = true;
}
```

- ExecuteWhatToDoNext() – This function is the main decision making function for your bot. It is in this function that your bot will decide which state to transition to based on the current state it is in and other programmer defined factors.

  The following is example code from a bot that basically is designed to loop continuously in the FollowTarget state forever. If the bot is in the Initial state then it goes into the FollowTarget state. Otherwise if it is in the FollowTarget state it goes back into the FollowTarget state.

```
protected event ExecuteWhatToDoNext()
{
    if (IsInState('Initial'))
    {
        GotoState('FollowTarget', 'Begin');
    }
    else
    {
        GotoState('FollowTarget', 'Begin');
    }
}
```

The bottom line is that these functions form the basic decision making loop that is needed for the bot AI. At the end of each state block the following process occurs:

1. The LatentWhatToDoNext() function is called.

2. It in turn calls the WhatToDoNext() function.

3. Finally, WhatToDoNext() then calls the ExecuteWhatToDoNext() function.

The ExecuteWhatToDoNext() function is the main decision making function for the bot where the bot can be put into a different state through the GotoState() function.

Possession

In terms of the AI controller there are several important functions. Before the bot can control its pawn you will need to assign the pawn to the controller. You do this through the Possess() function that is declared in the Controller class. The Possess() function takes a reference to a Pawn that is to be assigned to this controller as the first parameter and the second parameter is true if this involves a vehicle transition. The PossessedBy() function of the Pawn is also called. The function declaration is as seen below.

```
Possess(Pawn inPawn, bool bVehicleTransition)
```

The UnPossess() function is called to release the Pawn from the controller and the pawn's UnPossessed() function is also called. See Listing 5–1.

Listing 5–1. *Spawning and Possessing a Bot*

```
Var Controller BotController;
Var Pawn BotPawn;

function SpawningBot(Vector SpawnLocation)
{
    BotController = Spawn(class'BotCoverController',,,SpawnLocation);
    BotPawn = Spawn(class'BotCoverPawn',,,SpawnLocation);
    BotController.Possess(BotPawn,false);
}
```

The code in Listing 5–1 dynamically creates a new controller and a new pawn using the Spawn() function at SpawnLocation in the 3d world. The pawn is then assigned to the controller using the Possess() function.

Path Finding

Path finding is the process of a computer controlled bot determining the path from its current location to a target destination location in the game world. In this process obstacles must be taken into account and avoided. There are two ways that the UDK can handle this. One is through the use of path nodes and the other is through the use of a navigation mesh.

Path Nodes

In order to use the path nodes method of path finding you must place path nodes using the Unreal Editor on areas in the level that your bot will have access to. If an area has no path nodes then the bot may not be able to walk through that area.

The following Figure 5–1 illustrates how to set up a level to use pathnodes. The key here is that all the areas you want a bot to have access to must be reachable directly or indirectly from a network of pathnodes. If an area is blocked off by an obstacle and there is no pathnode to that area then the bot will not be able to go to that area. Blocking off parts of your game world from bots might actually be preferred if you have a special area in your game that only the player should be allowed access to.

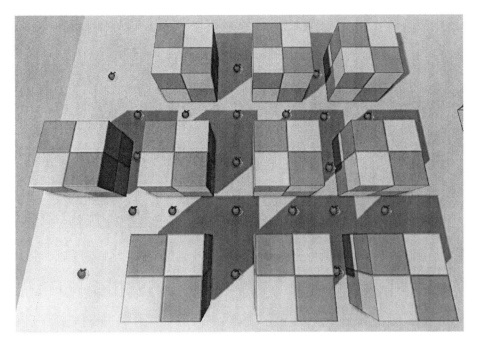

Figure 5–1. *Pathfinding by pathnodes*

Navigation Mesh

In order to use the navigation mesh you must put a pylon just above the area you want the bot to be able to navigate using the Unreal Editor.

One advantage of using a navigation mesh is that it automatically calculates all available paths around obstacles unlike the path nodes method where you need to manually put path nodes around the obstacles to ensure that the bot is able to walk through that area. Also, when a game level changes all you need to do if you use the navigation mesh method is to rebuild the AI Paths. With the path node method you may need to rearrange your path nodes and perhaps add more path nodes manually to adjust for the changes in the level.

The Figure 5–2 illustrates the use of the navigation mesh for pathfinding the same area as in Figure 5–1. The graphic with the P is the pylon and the screen capture was performed after the AI paths were built. The lines you see in the level are part of the navigation mesh.

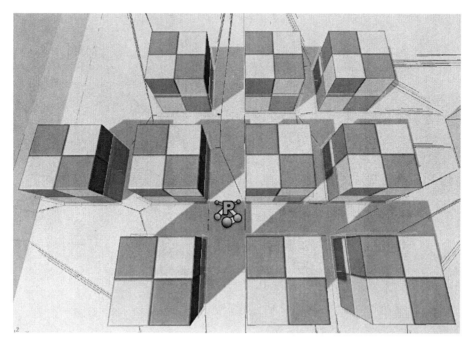

Figure 5–2. *Pathfinding by Navigation Mesh*

Hands-On Example: Creating a bot and having it follow you using Path Nodes.

In this example we will create a new level in the Unreal Editor full of obstacles. We will then place path nodes in the level so as to provide a path for our bot through these obstacles. We will then give the bot the ability to follow the player as the player walks around the level. The bot will continue to follow the player and avoid the obstacles using the path node method of path finding. In terms of bot movement navigation meshes can produce smoother more natural movement around corners and around obstacles than pathnodes.

In this example, we create a new game type, a player controller, player pawn, player weapon, player weapon projectile, weapon inventory manager a controller, and a pawn for our bot. For our player pawn we will use a third-person viewpoint. For those who need a review of vectors and trigonometry please see Chapter 8. There is also a detailed section in Chapter 8 that explains the math behind the third person camera positioning.

Creating the Level

The first thing to do is to create the level with the obstacles.

1. Open the Unreal Editor and select the Content Browser.

2. First we need obstacles. What we need is a static mesh with a collision model to place into the level. Type **Cube** into the search box and check the Static Meshes checkbox under the Object Type heading on the top part of the Content Browser.

3. A static mesh called Cube should appear in the preview pane of the Content Browser. Select the Cube by clicking on it.

4. Find an empty space on the level and add the Cube static mesh to the level by right-clicking and selecting the Add Static Mesh option.

5. Repeat step 4 until there are a significant number of Cubes in the level.

6. Pick a cube and place pathnodes all around it. Right-click on the area you want to add a path node to and select **Add Actor ➤ Add Path Node** to add the path node. See Figure 5–3.

7. Next you need to add path nodes to all the areas between the Cubes and other areas that you want your bot have access to. Repeat step 6 for all the cubes in the level.

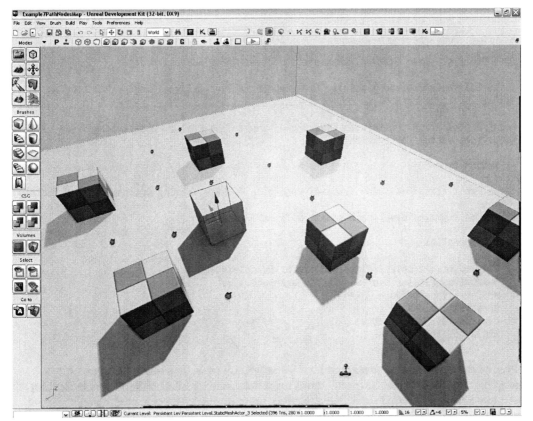

Figure 5–3. *Creating a level with Cube static meshes and path nodes*

8. You now need to build the AI paths for this level by selecting **Build** ➤ **AI Paths** from the Unreal Editor menu. All the path nodes are now connected into one single network. You don't need to add the pathnodes in any specific order.

9. Once the AI has been successfully built then you can save your level.

10. Try to run this level on the Mobile Game Previewer by selecting **Play** ➤ **On Mobile Previewer**. The level should appear without the pathnode graphics. The pathnodes are only visible in the editor and not the actual game level.

Creating the Game Type

Next, we need to start creating the code for this example. In the default source directory C:\UDK\UDK-2011-06\Development\Src, create a new directory called ExampleCh5 and under that create a new directory called Classes. You will put all your UnrealScript code into this new Classes directory.

Enter the following code (Listing 5–2) in a new file called ExampleCh5Game.uc and save the file. We will build examples using this game type for all the examples in this chapter.

Listing 5–2. *Game Type class for Chapter 5*

```
class ExampleCh5Game extends FrameworkGame;event OnEngineHasLoaded()
{
    WorldInfo.Game.Broadcast(self,"ExampleCh5Game Type Active - Engine Has Loaded
!!!!");
}
function bool PreventDeath(Pawn KilledPawn, Controller Killer, class<DamageType>
DamageType, vector HitLocation)
{
    return true;
}
static event class<GameInfo> SetGameType(string MapName, string Options, string Portal)
{
    return super.SetGameType(MapName, Options, Portal);
}
defaultproperties
{
    PlayerControllerClass=class'ExampleCh5.ExampleCh5PC'
    DefaultPawnClass=class'ExampleCh5.JazzPawnDamage'
    HUDType=class'UDKBase.UDKHUD'
    bRestartLevel=false
    bWaitingToStartMatch=true
    bDelayedStart=false
}
```

Most of the above code should be familiar to you by now. The key differences have been highlighted. When the game starts up a message should be displayed indicating that the new game type ExampleCh5Game has been started. There is also a new PlayerControllerClass and DefaultPawnClass specified.

Creating the Player Controller and Player Pawn

Next, we need to create a custom player pawn which is called JazzPawnDamage as shown in Listing 5–3.

The view of this pawn is the third person as defined by the CalcCamera() function. If you need a more detailed explanation of the math involved please check out Chapter 8. This pawn is called JazzPawnDamage because later in this chapter we will add the ability of this pawn to process damage through the addition of a TakeDamage() function. Also refer to Chapter 3 if you need a review of weapons and pawns.

Listing 5–3. *JazzPawnDamage custom player pawn.*

```
class JazzPawnDamage extends SimplePawn;

var float CamOffsetDistance;
var int CamAngle;
var Inventory MainGun;
var vector InitialLocation;

simulated singular event Rotator GetBaseAimRotation()
{
    local rotator TempRot;

    TempRot = Rotation;
    TempRot.Pitch = 0;
    SetRotation(TempRot);
    return TempRot;
}
function AddGunToSocket(Name SocketName)
{
    local Vector SocketLocation;
    local Rotator SocketRotation;
    if (Mesh != None)
    {
        if (Mesh.GetSocketByName(SocketName) != None)
        {
            Mesh.GetSocketWorldLocationAndRotation(SocketName, SocketLocation,
SocketRotation);
            MainGun.SetRotation(SocketRotation);
            MainGun.SetBase(Self,, Mesh, SocketName);
        }
        else
        {
            WorldInfo.Game.Broadcast(self,"!!!!!!SOCKET NAME NOT FOUND!!!!!");
        }
    }
    else
    {
        WorldInfo.Game.Broadcast(self,"!!!!!!MESH NOT FOUND!!!!!");
    }
}
function AddDefaultInventory()
{
    MainGun = InvManager.CreateInventory(class'JazzWeaponDamage');
```

```
        MainGun.SetHidden(false);
        AddGunToSocket('Weapon_R');
        Weapon(MainGun).FireOffset = vect(0,0,-70);
    }
    simulated function bool CalcCamera( float fDeltaTime, out vector out_CamLoc, out rotator
    out_CamRot, out float out_FOV )
    {
        local vector BackVector;
        local vector UpVector;

        local float  CamDistanceHorizontal;
        local float  CamDistanceVertical;

        // Set Camera Location
        CamDistanceHorizontal = CamOffsetDistance * cos(CamAngle * UnrRotToRad);
        CamDistanceVertical   = CamOffsetDistance * sin(CamAngle * UnrRotToRad);

        BackVector = -Normal(Vector(Rotation)) * CamDistanceHorizontal;
        UpVector   =  vect(0,0,1) * CamDistanceVertical;

        out_CamLoc = Location + BackVector + UpVector;

        // Set Camera Rotation
        out_CamRot.pitch = -CamAngle;
        out_CamRot.yaw   = Rotation.yaw;
        out_CamRot.roll  = Rotation.roll;

        return true;
    }
    defaultproperties
    {
        Begin Object Class=SkeletalMeshComponent Name=JazzMesh
            SkeletalMesh=SkeletalMesh'KismetGame_Assets.Anims.SK_Jazz'
            AnimSets(0)=AnimSet'KismetGame_Assets.Anims.SK_Jazz_Anims'
            AnimTreeTemplate=AnimTree'KismetGame_Assets.Anims.Jazz_AnimTree'
            BlockRigidBody=true
            CollideActors=true
        End Object
        Mesh = JazzMesh; // Set The mesh for this object
        Components.Add(JazzMesh); // Attach this mesh to this Actor

        CamAngle=3000;
        CamOffsetDistance= 484.0
        InventoryManagerClass=class'ExampleCh5.WeaponsCh5IM1'
    }
```

Most of the code should be familiar to you with key changes highlighted in bold type.
InitialLocation holds the starting location of the player's pawn and is used to reset the
player to its starting location when the player dies. This is needed later in this chapter
where we show you how the player and the bot can both take damage from each other's
weapons.

Next, we need to create a player controller for this example. The player controller is
shown in Listing 5–4. The main difference between this player controller and others in
past examples is that this one spawns a bot right above the player's starting location.

Listing 5–4. *The ExampleCh5PC Player Controller*

```
class ExampleCh5PC extends SimplePC;

var Controller FollowBot;
Var Pawn FollowPawn;
var bool BotSpawned;
var Actor BotTarget;

function SpawnBot(Vector SpawnLocation)
{
    SpawnLocation.z = SpawnLocation.z + 500;
    FollowBot = Spawn(class'BotController',,,SpawnLocation);
    FollowPawn = Spawn(class'BotPawn',,,SpawnLocation);
    FollowBot.Possess(FollowPawn,false);

    BotController(FollowBot).CurrentGoal = Pawn;
    BotPawn(Followpawn).InitialLocation = SpawnLocation;
    FollowPawn.SetPhysics(PHYS_Falling);

    BotSpawned = true;
}
function bool SwipeZoneCallback(MobileInputZone Zone,
                               float DeltaTime,
                               int Handle,
                               EZoneTouchEvent EventType,
                               Vector2D TouchLocation)
{
    local bool retval;

    retval = true;

    if (EventType == ZoneEvent_Touch)
    {
        WorldInfo.Game.Broadcast(self,"You touched the screen at = "
                                 @ TouchLocation.x @ " , "
                                 @ TouchLocation.y @ ", Zone Touched = "
                                 @ Zone);
    // Start Firing pawn's weapon
    StartFire(0);
    }
    else
    if(EventType == ZoneEvent_Update)
    {
    }
    else
    if (EventType == ZoneEvent_UnTouch)
    {
    // Stop Firing Pawn's weapon
    StopFire(0);
    }
    return retval;
}
function SetupZones()
{
    Super.SetupZones();
    // If we have a game class, configure the zones
```

```
        if (MPI != None && WorldInfo.GRI.GameClass != none)
        {
            LocalPlayer(Player).ViewportClient.GetViewportSize(ViewportSize);
            if (FreeLookZone != none)
            {
                FreeLookZone.OnProcessInputDelegate = SwipeZoneCallback;
            }
        }
    }
}
function PlayerTick(float DeltaTime)
{
    Super.PlayerTick(DeltaTime);
    if (!BotSpawned)
    {
        SpawnBot(Pawn.Location);
        BotSpawned = true;
        JazzPawnDamage(Pawn).InitialLocation = Pawn.Location;
    }
}
defaultproperties
{
    BotSpawned=false
}
```

The main additions to this player controller from previous examples are the SpawnBot()
function that dynamically creates a new bot and the PlayerTick() function which is
used to call the SpawnBot() function when the player first begins the level.

The SpawnBot() function creates a bot above the spawn location input. It creates a new
BotController and new BotPawn and has the BotController possess the BotPawn which
activates the bot AI. The Actor that the bot follows around is set to the player's pawn in
this function. The initial location of the bot's pawn is also saved. The physics model of
the bot's pawn is also set to PHYS_Falling which makes the pawn fall to the ground
from its spawn point high in the air.

The PlayerTick() function is called continuously throughout the game as long as the
player is alive. Here, if this is the first time this function is called then we create our bot
and save the initial location of the Player.

Creating the Player Weapon, Weapon Inventory Manager, and Projectile

Next we need to create a new weapon class called JazzWeaponDamage. See Listing 5–5.
We have discussed weapons before in Chapter 3. This weapon is called
JazzWeaponDamage because later in this chapter will add code to this weapon's projectile
class to cause damage to what it hits.

The actual graphic of this weapon is set in the SkeletalMesh variable. The general
category of ammunition this weapon fires is EWFT_Projectile which launches another 3d
mesh object that you can actually see. The variable FireInterval is the time in seconds
between projectile firings.

Listing 5–5. *JazzWeaponDamage class*

```
class JazzWeaponDamage extends Weapon;

defaultproperties
{
    Begin Object Class=SkeletalMeshComponent Name=FirstPersonMesh
        SkeletalMesh=SkeletalMesh'KismetGame_Assets.Anims.SK_JazzGun'
    End Object
    Mesh=FirstPersonMesh
    Components.Add(FirstPersonMesh);

    Begin Object Class=SkeletalMeshComponent Name=PickupMesh
        SkeletalMesh=SkeletalMesh'KismetGame_Assets.Anims.SK_JazzGun'
    End Object
    DroppedPickupMesh=PickupMesh
    PickupFactoryMesh=PickupMesh

    WeaponFireTypes(0)=EWFT_Projectile
    WeaponFireTypes(1)=EWFT_NONE

    WeaponProjectiles(0)=class'JazzBulletDamage'
    WeaponProjectiles(1)=class'JazzBulletDamage'

    FiringStatesArray(0)=WeaponFiring
    FireInterval(0)=0.25
    Spread(0)=0
}
```

Most of this weapon code should look familiar to you. The main change is that this weapon code uses a custom projectile called JazzBulletDamage. See Listing 5–6.

Listing 5–6. *JazzBulletDamage projectile class*

```
class JazzBulletDamage extends Projectile;

simulated function Explode(vector HitLocation, vector HitNormal)
{
}
function Init( Vector Direction )
{
    local vector NewDir;
    NewDir = Normal(Vector(InstigatorController.Pawn.Rotation));
    Velocity = Speed * NewDir;
}
defaultproperties
{
    Begin Object Class=StaticMeshComponent Name=Bullet
        StaticMesh=StaticMesh'EngineMeshes.Sphere'
        Scale3D=(X=0.050000,Y=0.050000,Z=0.05000)
    End Object
    Components.Add(Bullet)

    Begin Object Class=ParticleSystemComponent  Name=BulletTrail
        Template=ParticleSystem'Castle_Assets.FX.P_FX_Fire_SubUV_01'
    End Object
    Components.Add(BulletTrail)
```

```
    MaxSpeed=+05000.000000
    Speed=+05000.000000
}
```

This code should also look familiar. This projectile class is basically the same as one in Chapter 3 that uses spheres as projectiles. Please refer to the Figure 3-5 in Chapter 3 for a visual of this kind of projectile.

This class will need to be modified in order to give damage to the object it hits. We do that later in this chapter in the example of how the player and bot give and take damage. We introduce it here to provide a good foundation to start on.

Finally, there is the inventory manager class. See Listing 5–7.

Listing 5–7. *WeaponsCh5IM1 class to manage weapon inventory*

```
class WeaponsCh5IM1 extends InventoryManager;

defaultproperties
{
    PendingFire(0)=0
    PendingFire(1)=0
}
```

Creating the Bot Controller and Bot Pawn

Next, we need to create the pawn for our bot. See Listing 5–8 below. This class is basically the same as pawns covered in Chapter 3, but with a collision component added. Again we are using the Jazz Jackrabbit 3d skeletal mesh asset for the bot's physical presence in the game.

Listing 5–8. *BotPawn class*

```
class BotPawn extends SimplePawn;

var vector InitialLocation;

defaultproperties
{
    // Jazz Mesh Object
    Begin Object Class=SkeletalMeshComponent Name=JazzMesh
        SkeletalMesh=SkeletalMesh'KismetGame_Assets.Anims.SK_Jazz'
        AnimSets(0)=AnimSet'KismetGame_Assets.Anims.SK_Jazz_Anims'
        AnimTreeTemplate=AnimTree'KismetGame_Assets.Anims.Jazz_AnimTree'
        BlockRigidBody=true
        CollideActors=true
    End Object
    Mesh = JazzMesh;
    Components.Add(JazzMesh);

    // Collision Component for This actor
    Begin Object Class=CylinderComponent NAME=CollisionCylinder2
        CollideActors=true
        CollisionRadius=+25.000000
        CollisionHeight=+60.000000
    End Object
```

```
    CollisionComponent=CollisionCylinder2
    CylinderComponent=CollisionCylinder2
    Components.Add(CollisionCylinder2)
}
```

This pawn is represented by the Jazz Jackrabbit skeletal mesh like in previous examples. The main difference here is the addition of the collision cylinder that is defined by the `CylinderComponent` class and named `CollisionCylinder2`. This cylinder is set as the `CollisionComponent` of this Pawn as well as being attached to this pawn by way of being added to the `Components` array. Creating this collision component and attaching it to the bot's pawn is essential for path finding to work. Figure 5–4 shows the difference between the bot's pawn collision cylinder which is 60 units in height shown on the left and the player's pawn collision cylinder which by default is 44.

> **NOTE:** Experimentally I found that for the navigation mesh method of pathfinding we may need the taller collision cylinder. The default height for a collision cylinder for a Pawn is set to 78 units of height. Since our Jazz JackRabbit asset is much shorter than this about half the size we may need to create a taller collision cylinder in order for the navigation mesh method to work correctly.

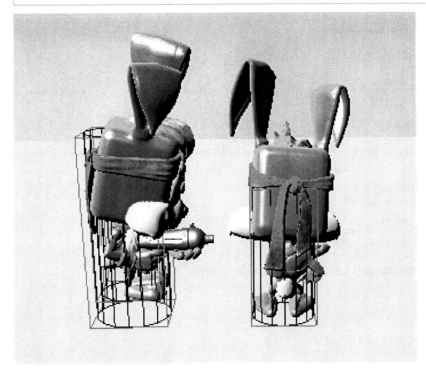

Figure 5–4. *Collision cylinder for bot pawn and player pawn*

Now, we need to create the BotController class. This class controls the bot's pawn and contains the bot's artificial intelligence. See Listing 5–9.

The key part of this class involves the actual pathfinding code located in the FollowTarget state. The critical steps to path finding using path nodes are as follows:

1. If the bot has a valid goal then the FindPathToward() function attempts to find a path to this goal using the path node network in the level and saves the first node in this path to the variable TempGoal.

2. If the bot can reach the goal directly without having to go around an obstacle then the MoveTo() function is called to move the bot directly to the location of the goal. The MoveTo() function does no path finding.

3. If not then the bot must move toward the temporary actor generated by the FindPathToward() function in step 1 that it can reach directly via the MoveToward() function. The MoveToward() function moves the bot toward the actor saved in the TempGoal variable.

4. If there is no valid path generated from the FindPathToward() function then an error is generated.

Listing 5–9. *BotController class*

```
class BotController extends UDKBot;

var Actor CurrentGoal;
var Vector TempDest;
var float FollowDistance;
var Actor TempGoal;

// Path Nodes
state FollowTarget
{
    Begin:

    // Move Bot to Target
    if (CurrentGoal != None)
    {
        TempGoal = FindPathToward(CurrentGoal);
        if (ActorReachable(CurrentGoal))
        {
            MoveTo(CurrentGoal.Location, ,FollowDistance);
        }
        else
        if (TempGoal != None)
        {
            MoveToward(TempGoal);
        }
        else
        {
            //give up because the nav mesh failed to find a path
            `warn("PATCHNODES failed to find a path!");
```

```
            WorldInfo.Game.Broadcast(self,"PATHNODES failed to find a path!, CurrentGoal
= " @ CurrentGoal);
            MoveTo(Pawn.Location);
        }
    }
    LatentWhatToDoNext();
}

auto state Initial
{
    Begin:
    LatentWhatToDoNext();
}

event WhatToDoNext()
{
    DecisionComponent.bTriggered = true;
}

protected event ExecuteWhatToDoNext()
{
    if (IsInState('Initial'))
    {
        GotoState('FollowTarget', 'Begin');
    }
    else
    {
        GotoState('FollowTarget', 'Begin');
    }
}
defaultproperties
{
    CurrentGoal = None;
    FollowDistance = 700;
}
```

Configuring the new Game Type

Next, we need to configure this new game type for compilation and playing on the mobile previewer. In order to configure this for compilation we need to add in the following line to the UDKEngine.ini configuration file located at C:\UDK\UDK-2011-06\UDKGame\Config if you are using the June 2011 UDK. If you are using a different UDK version then your base directory will be different.

UDKEngine.ini

```
[UnrealEd.EditorEngine]
ModEditPackages=ExampleCh5
```

In order to configure this new game type to play correctly with the mobile input controls on the mobile previewer we need to add in the following lines to the Mobile-UDKGame.ini file in the same directory.

Mobile-UDKGame.ini
[ExampleCh5.ExampleCh5Game]

RequiredMobileInputConfigs=(GroupName="UberGroup",RequireZoneNames=("UberStickMoveZone",
"UberStickLookZone","UberLookZone"))

Bring up the Unreal Frontend and compile your scripts.

Running the new Game Type

After a successful compilation bring up the Unreal Editor and load in your level that you
created for this example. Set your game type to ExampleCh5Game by selecting **View ➤
World Properties** from the main menu to bring up the World Properties window and then
selecting this game type as the Default Game Type under the Game Type category. You
should see something like in Figure 5–5.

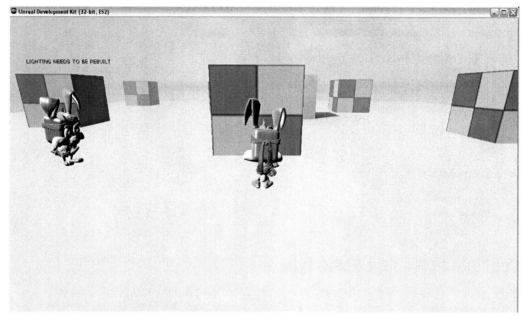

Figure 5–5. *Bot following the player around via path nodes*

The bot should now follow you around the level using the path node method of path
finding.

Hands-On Example: Creating a bot and having it follow you using a Navigation Mesh

In this example we will demonstrate how a bot can use a navigation mesh as a
pathfinding method. The two key elements in creating a bot that uses a navigation mesh

are creating a navigation mesh on the level and a bot controller that uses the navigation mesh to move around the level. In this hands-on example, we show you how to do both.

For this example, you can reuse much of the code from the pathnode example, so we will refer you back to the relevant listings in the preceding section instead of repeating all the code here.

Creating a Level

Load in the level you created in the previous example and save it as a new map such as **Example5–2NavMeshMap** to indicate that this map will use navigation mesh. Now, it's time to start making some changes to our new map.

1. Delete all the path nodes that you added previously to the level. To delete the node you can click on it and press the Delete key.

2. Now place a pylon at the center of your level by right-clicking and selecting Add **Actor** ➤ **Add Pylon**. Make sure the Pylon is just above the surface of the level and is not inside another object.

3. Select **Build** ➤ AI paths from the main Unreal Editor menu to build the new AI paths using the navigation mesh method. The resulting navigation mesh that is generated should look similar to Figure 5–6.

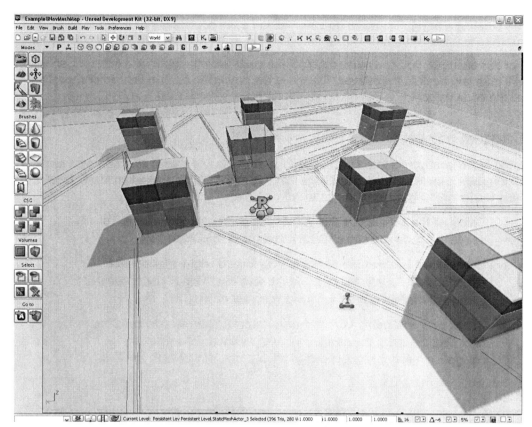

Figure 5–6. *A level using a navigation mesh*

4. Save the map.

Creating the Pieces of the Game

As indicated above, many parts of this example use the same code as in the pathnode example. Follow the same steps you did in that example. Here is the specific sequence and relevant code listings:

1. Create the game type (see Listing 5–2).

2. Create the player's pawn (see Listing 5–3).

3. Create the player controller (see Listing 5–4).

4. Create the player weapon, the weapon inventory manager, and the projectile (see Listing 5–5).

5. Create the pawn for the bot (see Listing 5–6).

Creating the BotController

Next, we need to create the controller for our bot. This is the class in which we will implement the navigation mesh pathfinding method. In this section, we'll look at the general navigation mesh method and then go through the relevant code step by step.

Navigation Mesh Method

The function GeneratePathTo() actually generates a path to an Actor using the navigation mesh method of pathfinding. The FollowTarget state uses this function to help implement the behavior of following the player around the level.

In the FollowTarget state the general path finding method is:

1. If there is a valid goal (a valid Actor which to move toward), then generate a path to that goal using the navigation mesh method.

2. If a path is found to that location, then check to see if the goal is directly accessible.

> **NOTE:** If a location is directly accessible then we actually don't use any pathfinding at all but use the MoveTo() function that moves the Pawn to a location directly.

3. If it is directly accessible, then use the MoveTo() function to move the bot to that location.

4. If the goal is not directly accessible, then move to an intermediate point that was found using the navigation mesh path finding method in Step 1.

5. If a path is not found in step 1, then output an error message. This message is displayed in the mobile previewer for debugging purposes.

The above steps are repeated as long as the bot remains in the FollowTarget state. Eventually, the goal actor will be reachable directly but if it is not then intermediate points determined by the navigation mesh pathfinding method will be used.

The intermediate points are retrieved from the NavigationHandle variable through the GetNextMoveLocation() function. Then MoveTo() is called to move the bot to this intermediate point which will be directly reachable.

For the navigation mesh method most of the pathfinding is done through the Navigationhandle class.

Implementing a Navigation Mesh

The code in this section is a complete listing of how you would implement a navigation mesh in the bot's controller. You can also refer to the downloadable source code for this book. The code listings in this section are presented sequentially.

The GeneratePathTo() function uses the navigation mesh method implemented in the NavigationHandle variable to find a path to the input Goal Actor variable from the current location of the bot's pawn. See Listing 5–10.

Listing 5–10. *The GeneratePathTo function for the Navigation Mesh*

```
class BotController extends UDKBot;

var Actor CurrentGoal;
var Vector TempDest;
var float FollowDistance;
var Actor TempGoal;
event bool GeneratePathTo(Actor Goal, optional float WithinDistance, optional bool
bAllowPartialPath)
{
    if( NavigationHandle == None )
    return FALSE;

    // Clear cache and constraints (ignore recycling for the moment)
    NavigationHandle.PathConstraintList = none;
    NavigationHandle.PathGoalList = none;

    class'NavMeshPath_Toward'.static.TowardGoal( NavigationHandle, Goal );
    class'NavMeshGoal_At'.static.AtActor( NavigationHandle, Goal, WithinDistance,
bAllowPartialPath );

    return NavigationHandle.FindPath();
}
```

First we make sure that there is a valid NavigationHandle and return false if not. Then we clear any old path information that may be cached and clear any path constraints that may limit our path choices. We then find the actual path to the Goal.

The previous listing concentrated on the GeneratePathTo() function which does the actual navigation mesh pathfinding. Listing 5–11 is the rest of the bot's controller code and uses this function for pathfinding.

Listing 5–11. *The remaining controller code for the bot*

```
state FollowTarget
{
    Begin:
    WorldInfo.Game.Broadcast(self,"BotController-USING NAVMESH FOR FOLLOWTARGET STATE");

    // Move Bot to Target
    if (CurrentGoal != None)
    {
        if(GeneratePathTo(CurrentGoal))
```

```
        {
            NavigationHandle.SetFinalDestination(CurrentGoal.Location);

            if( NavigationHandle.ActorReachable(CurrentGoal) )
            {
                // then move directly to the actor
                MoveTo(CurrentGoal.Location, ,FollowDistance);
            }
            else
            {
                // move to the first node on the path
                if( NavigationHandle.GetNextMoveLocation(TempDest,
Pawn.GetCollisionRadius()) )
                {
                    // suggest move preparation will return TRUE when the edge's
                    // logic is getting the bot to the edge point
                    // FALSE if we should run there ourselves
                    if (!NavigationHandle.SuggestMovePreparation(TempDest,self))
                    {
                        MoveTo(TempDest);
                    }
                }
            }
        }
        else
        {
            //give up because the nav mesh failed to find a path
            `warn("FindNavMeshPath failed to find a path!");
            WorldInfo.Game.Broadcast(self,"FindNavMeshPath failed to find a path!,
CurrentGoal = " @ CurrentGoal);
            MoveTo(Pawn.Location);
        }
    }
    LatentWhatToDoNext();
}
auto state Initial
{
    Begin:
    LatentWhatToDoNext();
}
event WhatToDoNext()
{
    DecisionComponent.bTriggered = true;
}
protected event ExecuteWhatToDoNext()
{
    if (IsInState('Initial'))
    {
        GotoState('FollowTarget', 'Begin');
    }
    else
    {
        GotoState('FollowTarget', 'Begin');
    }
}
```

```
defaultproperties
{
    CurrentGoal = None;
    FollowDistance = 700;
}
```

The key parts of this listing:

- The FollowTarget state implements the bot's pathfinding behavior explained at the beginning of this section.

- The Initial state is the state the bot starts out in. The auto keyword sets this state as the default state when the bot controller is first created.

- The WhatToDoNext() function is called from within the LatentWhatToDoNext() function. If DecisionComponent.bTriggered is set to true then then the ExecuteWhatToDoNext() function is called next.

- The ExecuteWhatToDoNext() function is the main decision making block for the bot's AI. Here we can test for conditions and move to different states based on these conditions.

The main differences between this version of the BotController and the version in the pathnode example are that the old path nodes pathfinding code has been deleted, and the functions GeneratePathTo() and FollowTarget() have been added. The new FollowTarget() function that contains navigation mesh pathfinding code replaces the old FollowTarget() function.

Configuring the Game Type

Configuring this game type for this example is the same as for the previous example. Please refer to the previous example to configure this game type if you haven't already.

Running the Game

Make sure to compile your source code using the Unreal Frontend. After a successful compilation bring up the Unreal Editor. Load in your level map that is set up for the navigation mesh path finding method. Double-check the game type is set to ExampleCh5Game and run the game on the mobile previewer. You should be able to move around the obstacles and have the bot follow you around. See Figure 5–7.

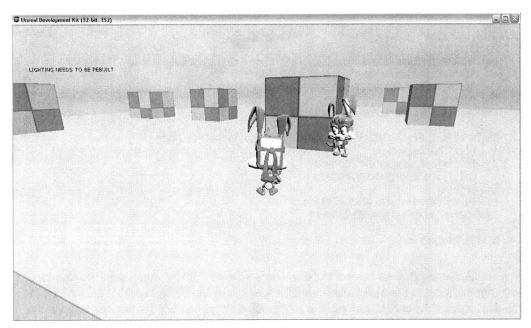

Figure 5–7. *Using the navigation mesh for path finding*

Hands-On Example: Moving a Bot to a point in the world specified by the Player

In this example we will add the ability of the player to touch the screen and have the bot move to that location in the game level. In addition a sphere will be displayed at the location the player touches as an indicator of where the bot should move to.

The concepts in this chapter can be applied to both the pathnode and navigation mesh methods of pathfinding. First a botmarker which is basically a 3d mesh asset will be created in the game world. We then move the bot toward this asset using a path finding method.

Creating the BotMarker

First we need to create a new class for the bot marker that will represent the bot's goal location. See Listing 5–12.

Listing 5–12. *Creating the BotMarker Class*

```
class BotMarker extends Actor;

event Touch(Actor Other, PrimitiveComponent OtherComp, vector HitLocation, vector
HitNormal)
{
    //WorldInfo.Game.Broadcast(self,"BotMarker Has Been Touched");
}
```

```
defaultproperties
{
    Begin Object Class=StaticMeshComponent Name=StaticMeshComponent0
        StaticMesh=StaticMesh'EngineMeshes.Sphere'
        Scale3D=(X=0.250000,Y=0.250000,Z=0.25000)
    End Object
    Components.Add(StaticMeshComponent0)

    Begin Object Class=CylinderComponent NAME=CollisionCylinder
        CollideActors=true
        CollisionRadius=+0040.000000
        CollisionHeight=+0040.000000
    End Object
    CollisionComponent=CollisionCylinder
    Components.Add(CollisionCylinder)

    bCollideActors=true
}
```

The BotMarker's physical appearance will be a sphere. The 3d mesh asset to use for this marker is set in the `StaticMesh` variable located in the `defaultproperties` block in the `StaticMeshComponent0` object. It is also scaled down to 25% its original size via the `Scale3D` variable.

Adding to the Player Controller

Next, you need to add some code to the player controller. What is added are the `PickActor()` and the `ExecuteBotMoveCommand()` functions. The purpose of these functions is to allow the player to touch a location in the game world and have a bot move to that location.

The process of directing the bot to where the user has touched is as follows:

1.   When the user touches the iOS screen, the `PickActor()` function is called to determine the `HitLocation` in the 3d game world that the user's touch points to.

2.   The `ExecuteBotMoveCommand()` function is then called to execute the bot's move to this touched location. First the bot marker is created if one does not already exist. Then it is placed at the location of the user's touch in the game world. Next, the `CurrentGoal` of the bot is set to the bot marker. This will now make the bot follow a path toward where the user has touched. The bot will now instead of following the player it will go to the marker.

Listing 5–13 provides the full code for the modified player controller including the old code. The new code is highlighted in bold.

Listing 5–13. *The Modified ExampleCh5PC class*

```
class ExampleCh5PC extends SimplePC;

var Controller FollowBot;
Var Pawn FollowPawn;
var bool BotSpawned;
var Actor BotTarget;

var float PickDistance;

function Actor PickActor(Vector2D PickLocation, out Vector HitLocation, out TraceHitInfo
HitInfo)
{
    local Vector TouchOrigin, TouchDir;
    local Vector HitNormal;
    local Actor  PickedActor;
    local vector Extent;

    //Transform absolute screen coordinates to relative coordinates
    PickLocation.X = PickLocation.X / ViewportSize.X;
    PickLocation.Y = PickLocation.Y / ViewportSize.Y;

    //Transform to world coordinates to get pick ray
    LocalPlayer(Player).Deproject(PickLocation, TouchOrigin, TouchDir);

    //Perform trace to find touched actor
    Extent = vect(0,0,0);
    PickedActor = Trace(HitLocation,
                        HitNormal,
                        TouchOrigin + (TouchDir * PickDistance),
                        TouchOrigin,
                        True,
                        Extent,
                        HitInfo);

    //Return the touched actor for good measure
    return PickedActor;
}
reliable server function ExecuteBotMoveCommand(Vector HitLocation)
{
    // 1. Set AttackMove Target Marker
    Hitlocation.z += 50; // Add offset to help bot navigate to point
    If (BotTarget == None)
    {
        WorldInfo.Game.Broadcast(None,"Creating New Move Marker!!!!!!!!");
        BotTarget = Spawn(class'BotMarker',,,HitLocation);
    }
    else
    {
        BotTarget.SetLocation(HitLocation);
    }
    // 2. Send Move Command to bot along with target location
    BotController(FollowBot).CurrentGoal = BotTarget;
    BotController(FollowBot).FollowDistance = 75;
```

```
}
function SpawnBot(Vector SpawnLocation)
{
    SpawnLocation.z = SpawnLocation.z + 500;

    FollowBot = Spawn(class'BotController',,,SpawnLocation);
    FollowPawn = Spawn(class'BotPawn',,,SpawnLocation);
    FollowBot.Possess(FollowPawn,false);

    BotController(FollowBot).CurrentGoal = Pawn;
    BotPawn(Followpawn).InitialLocation = SpawnLocation;
    FollowPawn.SetPhysics(PHYS_Falling);
    BotSpawned = true;
}

function bool SwipeZoneCallback(MobileInputZone Zone,
                               float DeltaTime,
                               int Handle,
                               EZoneTouchEvent EventType,
                               Vector2D TouchLocation)
{
    local bool retval;

    local Vector HitLocation;
    local TraceHitInfo HitInfo;

    retval = true;

    if (EventType == ZoneEvent_Touch)
    {
        WorldInfo.Game.Broadcast(self,"You touched the screen at = "
                                 @ TouchLocation.x @ " , "
                                 @ TouchLocation.y @ ", Zone Touched = "
                                 @ Zone);
        // Start Firing pawn's weapon
        StartFire(0);

        // Code for Setting Bot WayPoint
        PickActor(TouchLocation, HitLocation, HitInfo);
        ExecuteBotMoveCommand(HitLocation);
    }
    else
    if(EventType == ZoneEvent_Update)
    {
    }
    else
    if (EventType == ZoneEvent_UnTouch)
    {
        // Stop Firing Pawn's weapon
        StopFire(0);
    }
    return retval;
}

function SetupZones()
{
    Super.SetupZones();
```

```
        // If we have a game class, configure the zones
        if (MPI != None && WorldInfo.GRI.GameClass != none)
        {
            LocalPlayer(Player).ViewportClient.GetViewportSize(ViewportSize);
            if (FreeLookZone != none)
            {
                FreeLookZone.OnProcessInputDelegate = SwipeZoneCallback;
            }
        }
    }
}

function PlayerTick(float DeltaTime)
{
    Super.PlayerTick(DeltaTime);
    if (!BotSpawned)
    {
        SpawnBot(Pawn.Location);
        BotSpawned = true;
        JazzPawnDamage(Pawn).InitialLocation = Pawn.Location;
    }
}
defaultproperties
{
    BotSpawned=false
    PickDistance = 10000
}
```

Note that enabling the ability for the player to direct bots like in this example can be useful in many situations in which the player needs to coordinate the behavior of multiple bots. For example, it would be applicable to a game where the player is a squad leader and controls the actions of soldiers (bots) in his unit. The player would direct the bots to perform various actions such as attack a specific target.

Running the Game

Bring up the Unreal Frontend and compile your code. Next, bring up the Unreal Editor and load in the level map with the navigation mesh. Run the game on the mobile previewer. The bot should follow you around by default. Click on an empty area where the bot can walk to and the sphere BotMarker should appear there. The bot should then walk to this sphere. See Figure 5–8.

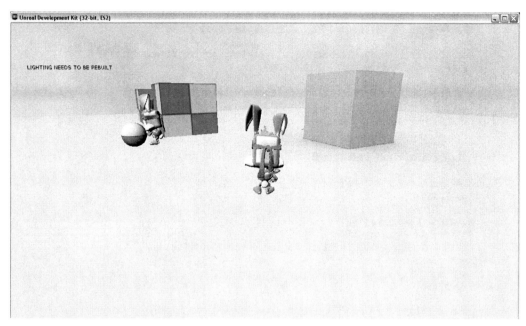

Figure 5–8. *Directing your bot to the marker which is indicated by a sphere*

Hands-On Example: Equipping your bot with a weapon and Taking Damage

In this example, we will again build on the previous examples and equip the bot with a working weapon and modify the code so that both the player and bot can take damage from each other's weapons.

Modifying the Bot's Pawn to Add a Weapon

We must add code to the bot's pawn BotPawn to add a weapon. See Listing 5–14. The code in bold is the new code.

The code for adding a weapon to the bot should look familiar from the sections on Weapons in Chapter 3. You add weapons to a bot by adding it to the bot's pawn. This is exactly the same as adding a weapon to a pawn owned by a player. The AddGunToSocket() function attaches the weapon mesh to the pawn. The AddDefaultInventory() function creates the weapon and adds it into the pawn's inventory. We have also added the variable JazzHitSound that holds a sound effect that is played when the bot is hit.

The function that processes damage to this pawn and adjusts the bot's health is TakeDamage(). TakeDamage() also resets the bot's position to the bot's start position if the bot's health becomes less than or equal to 0. The bot's health is then restored to 100.

Listing 5–14. *Modifying the BotPawn class*

```
class BotPawn extends SimplePawn;

var Inventory MainGun;
var SoundCue JazzHitSound;
var vector InitialLocation;

event TakeDamage(int Damage, Controller InstigatedBy, vector HitLocation, vector
Momentum, class<DamageType> DamageType, optional TraceHitInfo HitInfo, optional Actor
DamageCauser)
{
    PlaySound(JazzHitSound);
    Health = Health - Damage;
    WorldInfo.Game.Broadcast(self,self @ " Has Taken Damage IN TAKEDAMAGE, HEALTH = " @
Health);

    if (Health <= 0)
    {
        SetLocation(InitialLocation);
        SetPhysics(PHYS_Falling);
        Health = 100;
    }
}

function AddGunToSocket(Name SocketName)
{
    local Vector SocketLocation;
    local Rotator SocketRotation;

    if (Mesh != None)
    {
        if (Mesh.GetSocketByName(SocketName) != None)
        {
            Mesh.GetSocketWorldLocationAndRotation(SocketName, SocketLocation,
SocketRotation);
            MainGun.SetRotation(SocketRotation);
            MainGun.SetBase(Self,, Mesh, SocketName);
        }
        else
        {
            WorldInfo.Game.Broadcast(self,"!!!!!!SOCKET NAME NOT FOUND!!!!!");
        }
    }
    else
    {
        WorldInfo.Game.Broadcast(self,"!!!!!!MESH NOT FOUND!!!!!");
    }
}

function AddDefaultInventory()
{
    MainGun = InvManager.CreateInventory(class'JazzWeapon2Damage');
    MainGun.SetHidden(false);
```

```
        AddGunToSocket('Weapon_R');
        Weapon(MainGun).FireOffset = vect(0,13,-70);
}

defaultproperties
{
    // Jazz Mesh Object
    Begin Object Class=SkeletalMeshComponent Name=JazzMesh
        SkeletalMesh=SkeletalMesh'KismetGame_Assets.Anims.SK_Jazz'
        AnimSets(0)=AnimSet'KismetGame_Assets.Anims.SK_Jazz_Anims'
        AnimTreeTemplate=AnimTree'KismetGame_Assets.Anims.Jazz_AnimTree'
        BlockRigidBody=true
        CollideActors=true
    End Object
    Mesh = JazzMesh;
    Components.Add(JazzMesh);

    // Collision Component for This actor
    Begin Object Class=CylinderComponent NAME=CollisionCylinder2
        CollideActors=true
        CollisionRadius=+25.000000
        CollisionHeight=+60.000000 //Nav Mesh
    End Object
    CollisionComponent=CollisionCylinder2
    CylinderComponent=CollisionCylinder2
    Components.Add(CollisionCylinder2)

    JazzHitSound = SoundCue'KismetGame_Assets.Sounds.Jazz_Death_Cue'
    InventoryManagerClass=class'ExampleCh5.WeaponsCh5IM1'
}
```

Creating the Bot's Weapon and Projectile

Next, we need to create the bot's weapon which is JazzWeapon2Damage. See Listing 5–15.

Listing 5–15. *Creating the JazzWeapon2Damage class*

```
class JazzWeapon2Damage extends Weapon;

defaultproperties
{
    Begin Object Class=SkeletalMeshComponent Name=FirstPersonMesh
        SkeletalMesh=SkeletalMesh'KismetGame_Assets.Anims.SK_JazzGun'
    End Object
    Mesh=FirstPersonMesh
    Components.Add(FirstPersonMesh);

    Begin Object Class=SkeletalMeshComponent Name=PickupMesh
        SkeletalMesh=SkeletalMesh'KismetGame_Assets.Anims.SK_JazzGun'
    End Object
    DroppedPickupMesh=PickupMesh
    PickupFactoryMesh=PickupMesh

    WeaponFireTypes(0)=EWFT_Projectile
    WeaponFireTypes(1)=EWFT_NONE
```

```
WeaponProjectiles(0)=class'JazzBullet2Damage'
WeaponProjectiles(1)=class'JazzBullet2Damage'

FiringStatesArray(0)=WeaponFiring
FireInterval(0)=0.25
Spread(0)=0
}
```

This new class uses the custom projectiles of class JazzBullet2Damage which is shown in Listing 5–16.

Listing 5–16. *JazzBullet2Damage projectile class*

```
class JazzBullet2Damage extends Projectile;

simulated singular event Touch(Actor Other, PrimitiveComponent OtherComp, vector
HitLocation, vector HitNormal)
{
    Other.TakeDamage(33, InstigatorController, HitLocation, -HitNormal, None);
}

simulated function Explode(vector HitLocation, vector HitNormal)
{
    SetPhysics(Phys_Falling);
}

function Init( Vector Direction )
{
    super.Init(Direction);
    RandSpin(90000);
}

defaultproperties
{
    Begin Object Class=StaticMeshComponent Name=Bullet
        StaticMesh=StaticMesh'Castle_Assets.Meshes.SM_RiverRock_01'
        Scale3D=(X=0.300000,Y=0.30000,Z=0.3000)
    End Object
    Components.Add(Bullet)

    Begin Object Class=ParticleSystemComponent  Name=BulletTrail
        Template=ParticleSystem'Castle_Assets.FX.P_FX_Fire_SubUV_01'
    End Object
    Components.Add(BulletTrail)

    MaxSpeed=+05000.000000
    Speed=+05000.000000
}
```

The new function introduced here is the Touch() function which is called whenever this actor touches another actor. In this function the projectile calls the TakeDamage() function of the object it hits.

The other key elements in this code:

- ▨ The SetPhysics() function sets the physics model of this projectile to Phys_Falling in which objects fall realistically according to gravity.

- The StaticMesh variable refers to the 3d mesh to be used as the projectile graphic.

- The Scale3D variable sizes the StaticMesh with 1.0 representing normal size.

- The Template variable holds what type of particle emitter to attach to the projectile. Currently it is set to a fire emitter with gives the impression that the projectile is on fire.

- The MaxSpeed variable sets the maximum speed the projectile will move. Set MaxSpeed to 0 for no limit on projectile speed.

- The Speed variable sets the initial speed of the projectile

Modifying the Player Controller

Next, we need to add in the following code that is in bold for the player controller ExampleCh5PC (see Listing 5–17). The new code will add in the weapon to the bot's pawn and fire the bot's weapon when the player touches the screen. For a full listing for the player controller please download the full source code.

Listing 5–17. *Adding in code to ExampleCh5PC*

```
function SpawnBot(Vector SpawnLocation)
{
    SpawnLocation.z = SpawnLocation.z + 500;
    FollowBot = Spawn(class'BotController',,,SpawnLocation);
    FollowPawn = Spawn(class'BotPawn',,,SpawnLocation);
    FollowBot.Possess(FollowPawn,false);
    BotController(FollowBot).CurrentGoal = Pawn;
    Botpawn(FollowPawn).AddDefaultInventory();
    BotPawn(Followpawn).InitialLocation = SpawnLocation;
    FollowPawn.SetPhysics(PHYS_Falling);
    BotSpawned = true;
}

function bool SwipeZoneCallback(MobileInputZone Zone,
                                float DeltaTime,
                                int Handle,
                                EZoneTouchEvent EventType,
                                Vector2D TouchLocation)
{
    local bool retval;
    local Vector HitLocation;
    local TraceHitInfo HitInfo;

    retval = true;
    if (EventType == ZoneEvent_Touch)
    {
        WorldInfo.Game.Broadcast(self,"You touched the screen at = "
                                 @ TouchLocation.x @ " , "
                                 @ TouchLocation.y @ ", Zone Touched = "
                                 @ Zone);
```

```
            // Start Firing pawn's weapon
            StartFire(0);

            // Start Firing the Bot's Weapon
            FollowBot.Pawn.StartFire(0);

            // Code for Setting Bot WayPoint
            PickActor(TouchLocation, HitLocation, HitInfo);
            ExecuteBotMoveCommand(HitLocation);
    }
    else
    if(EventType == ZoneEvent_Update)
    {

    }
    else
    if (EventType == ZoneEvent_UnTouch)
    {
            // Stop Firing Pawn's weapon
            StopFire(0);

            // Stop Firing the Bot's weapon
            FollowBot.Pawn.StopFire(0);
    }
    return retval;
}
```

In the SpawnBot() function we added the line of code to add in the bot pawn's default inventory which includes a weapon when the bot is created. Also in the SwipeZoneCallback() function we added code to start and stop the firing of the bot's weapon for testing purposes. When the player fires his weapon the bot will fire its weapon.

Modifying the Player's Pawn to take Damage.

Next, we need to add in some more code to the player pawn JazzPawnDamage (see Listing 5–18). The code in bold is the new code that must be added. For a full listing of this class with both the new and old code in it please download the full source code.

Listing 5–18. *Modifying JazzPawnDamage to take Damage*

```
var SoundCue PawnHitSound;

event TakeDamage(int Damage, Controller InstigatedBy, vector HitLocation, vector
Momentum, class<DamageType> DamageType, optional TraceHitInfo HitInfo, optional Actor
DamageCauser)
{
    PlaySound(PawnHitSound);
    Health = Health - Damage;
    WorldInfo.Game.Broadcast(self,self @ " Has Taken Damage IN TAKEDAMAGE, HEALTH = " @
Health);

    if (Health <= 0)
```

```
    {
        SetLocation(InitialLocation);
        SetPhysics(PHYS_Falling);
        Health = 100;
    }
}
defaultproperties
{
    Begin Object Class=SkeletalMeshComponent Name=JazzMesh
        SkeletalMesh=SkeletalMesh'KismetGame_Assets.Anims.SK_Jazz'
        AnimSets(0)=AnimSet'KismetGame_Assets.Anims.SK_Jazz_Anims'
        AnimTreeTemplate=AnimTree'KismetGame_Assets.Anims.Jazz_AnimTree'
        BlockRigidBody=true
        CollideActors=true
    End Object
    Mesh = JazzMesh; // Set The mesh for this object
    Components.Add(JazzMesh); // Attach this mesh to this Actor

    CamAngle=3000;
    CamOffsetDistance= 484.0

    InventoryManagerClass=class'ExampleCh5.WeaponsCh5IM1'

    PawnHitSound =
SoundCue'A_Character_CorruptEnigma_Cue.Mean_Efforts.A_Effort_EnigmaMean_Death_Cue'
}
```

The new function TakeDamage() processes damage from projectiles. Also, it resets the player's position to the player's start position if the player's health becomes less than or equal 0. Health is then reset to 100.

Also, a sound effect is played whenever the pawn is hit.

Modifying the Player's Weapon to Give Damage

Next, we need to add code to the projectiles coming out of the player's weapon in JazzBulletDamage (see Listing 5–19). The additional code is in bold print. You can see the full updated JazzBulletDamage class in the source code.

Listing 5–19. *Making additions to JazzBulletDamage*

```
simulated singular event Touch(Actor Other, PrimitiveComponent OtherComp, vector
HitLocation, vector HitNormal)
{
    Other.TakeDamage(33, InstigatorController, HitLocation, -HitNormal, None);
}
```

The Touch() function damages the object it has hit by calling that object's TakeDamage() function. The value 33 is the amount of damage to cause to the object that touches this projectile.

Running the Game

Bring up the Unreal Frontend and compile your scripts. Bring up the Unreal Editor and run the game on the Mobile Previewer. See Figures 5–9 and 5–10.

Figure 5–9. *Your bot firing its weapon*

Figure 5–10. *Your bot falling just after dying and then being reset to its start position*

Summary

In this chapter we discussed bots. We started off with a basic overview of bots. Then we discussed Artificial Intelligence path finding using bots. We covered and demonstrated how to set up a bot to follow the player using both path nodes and the navigation mesh methods of path finding. Next, we showed you how to have the player direct a bot to a specific location in the world. Finally, we demonstrated how you could add a weapon to your bot and have the player and the bot take damage from each other's weapons. In the following Chapter 6, we will cover sound effects, create moving gates and platforms using Kismet, and create a Heads Up Display. Then in Chapter 7, we pull everything together to create a basic game framework using enemy computer controlled bots and focus on key elements in developing exceptional gameplay.

Environment: Sounds, Kismet, and HUD

In this chapter, we will cover several key topics for your gaming environment. These include sound, moving elements like platforms and gates, and information displays. These constitute the last pieces before we move to an actual gameplay example in the next chapter.

Sounds in the UDK are generated through Sound Cues that can combine sound data with functions that alter or process sound effects like looping and attenuation. In a hands-on example we show you how to add sounds to a weapon through the weapon's projectile class. This is followed by a brief discussion of Kismet and Matinee with respect to moving objects including platforms and locked gates. Finally, the Unreal Heads Up Display, or HUD, is covered and a hands-on example is given that displays important items like the player's score, lives left, and current health.

UDK Sound Cues

In this section we will cover Sound Cues. First we will give you an overview of the Sound Cue Editor and its major features such as attenuation and sound looping. Next, we will show you how to place Sound Cues in a level using the Unreal Editor. We then show you how to use UnrealScript to play a Sound Cue dynamically from within a program. In the next chapter, we present a hands-on example that uses the information and code presented here.

Overview of the UDK Sound Cue Editor

The Sound Cue Editor is where you can create new Sound Cues as well as modify existing Sound Cues. Sound Cues consist of one or more SoundNodeWave items (which hold the actual sound data) and sound operators which alter the final sound that is output. We won't describe every aspect of the Sound Cue Editor but touch on the key points that are needed to give you a basic working knowledge of Sound Cues.

> **NOTE:** Since Sound Cues are based on sound files of .wav format, any program that can capture and save or convert sounds to .wav format can be used to create audio data for Sound Cues. You can import .wav files by pressing the Import button located in the Content Browser. One program to record and save sound files in .wav format is Audacity which is a free, public-domain program.

Attenuation

Search for the Sound Cue called **A_Powerup_UDamage_SpawnCue** in the Content Browser by typing its name into the asset search box. Also check the Sound Cues checkbox under **Object Types ➤ Favorites** to make sure only Sound Cues are shown in the Preview Pane. Right-click on the item and select Edit Using Sound Cue Editor. This should bring up the Sound Cue Editor. See Figure 6–1.

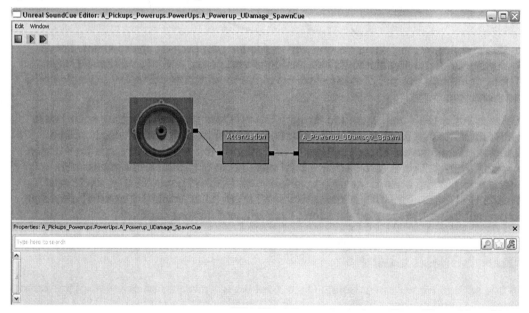

Figure 6–1. *Sound Cue for A_Powerup_UDamage_SpawnCue*

This Sound Cue uses attenuation. Attenuation allows your sound to fade away according to the distance from the sound's source in the game world. For example, when a car is on fire, the sound of the fire naturally fades away with a greater distance from the fire. In the UDK the sound cue Vehicle_Damage_FireLoop_Cue uses attenuation to simulate this real-world situation.

Click the Attenuation node to bring up the attenuation properties. See Figure 6–2.

▼ Attenuation	
Attenuate	☑
Spatialize	☑
d BAttenuation At Max	-60.000000
Distance Algorithm	ATTENUATION_Logarithmic
Distance Type	SOUNDDISTANCE_Normal
Radius Min	40.000000
Radius Max	2700.000000

Figure 6–2. *Attenuation properties*

The most important properties are the Distance Algorithm, Radius Min, and Radius Max.

- Distance Algorithm—Determines exactly how the sound decreases with distance from the source. You probably should experiment with this to determine your personal preference. Options include ATTENUATION_Linear, ATTENUATION_Logarithmic, ATTENUATION_Inverse, ATTENUATION_LogReverse, and ATTENUATION_NaturalSound

- Radius Min—Sound will start to attenuate or decrease starting at this distance from the sound source. Up to this radius the sound volume will be normal.

- Radius Max—Sound will attenuate between Radius Min and this value. At Radius Max the sound volume is zero.

Looping

Looping is the repetition of the same sound. This is appropriate for sounds that must be played continuously forever or for a short period of time. For example, the sound of the ocean hitting the shore can be played continuously if you are near a beach. Another example would be to play the sound of an alarm four times to indicate that an intruder has breached an area in your game world.

Now, search for **Vehicle_Damage_FireLoop_Cue** by typing that asset name into the search box. Right-click on the item in the preview pane and select Edit Using Sound Cue Editor to bring up the Sound Cue Editor. The set up of the Sound Cue is shown in Figure 6–3.

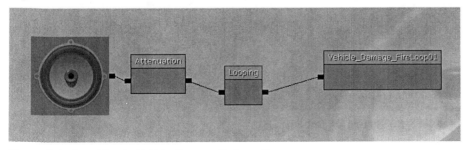

Figure 6–3. *Sound Cue for Vehicle_Damage_FireLoop_Cue*

This Sound Cue uses both attenuation and looping to modify the behavior of the output sound. Click on the Looping node. The looping properties should be displayed as in Figure 6–4.

▼ Looping	
Loop Indefinitely	☑
Loop Count Min	1000000.000000
Loop Count Max	1000000.000000

Figure 6–4. *Looping properties*

There are three values in the Looping node:

- Loop Indefinitely—If this is checked then the sound loops forever regardless of the values of Loop Count Min or Loop Count Max

- Loop Count Min—The minimum number of times to play this sound in a loop.

- Loop Count Max—The maximum number of times to play this sound in a loop.

Random

The random node's purpose is to play different variations of the same general sound so that the listener does not find the sound repetitive. A good example is background noises like insects and other environmental noises.

An example of a Sound Cue that uses a Random Node to select random sounds to play back is the **S_BulletImpact_01_Cue**. Type this into the search box and right-click on the asset in the preview pane and bring it up into the Sound Cue Editor. The Sound Cue layout should look like Figure 6–5.

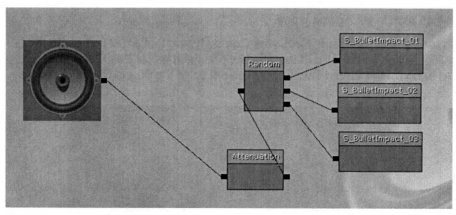

Figure 6–5. *Sound Cue S_BulletImpact_01_Cue*

This Sound Cue uses attenuation and randomness to produce the final sound from three possible sound effects. The final sound output will be affected by both attenuation and random selection. What this means is that final sound will be played from a random selection of sounds and will decrease in volume as the listener moves farther away from it.

The random properties are shown in Figure 6–6.

▼ Sound Node Random	
▼ Weights	... (3)
[0]	1.000000
[1]	1.000000
[2]	1.000000
Randomize Without Replacement	☑

Figure 6–6. *Random Property*

The Weights property allows you to set the probability that each sound would be selected. Here each is set to 1.0 which means that each sound effect has an equal chance of being selected for output.

Modulator

The purpose of the Modulator node is to change the volume and/or pitch of the sound data being played. This can be a quick and easy way to tweak a sound once it has been sampled.

Search for the Sound Cue **A_Effort_EnigmaMean_Death_Cue** by typing that term in the search box. Right-click the asset in the preview pane and bring it up in the Sound Cue Editor. The Sound Cue structure should look like Figure 6–7.

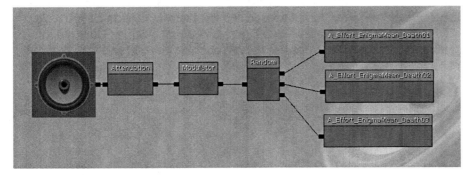

Figure 6–7. *Sound Cue A_Effort_EnigmaMean_Death_Cue*

This Sound Cue uses a combination of attenuation, modulation, and randomness in order to produce the final sound. The modulation properties are shown in Figure 6–8.

▼ Modulation	
Pitch Min	0.950000
Pitch Max	1.050000
Volume Min	0.950000
Volume Max	1.050000

Figure 6–8. *Modulation property*

The Modulation node is used to pick a random pitch and volume within a range. The range values are:

- Pitch Min—The minimum value for a random pitch.

- Pitch Max—The maximum value for a random pitch.

- Volume Min—The minimum value for a random volume.

- Volume Max—The maximum value for the random volume.

For example, you could set the Pitch Min and Pitch Max values to 5.0 and the Volume Min and Volume Max values to 2.0 to increase the pitch of the sound sample 5 times normal value and increase the volume of the sound sample to twice the normal value.

Adding Sound Cues Using the Unreal Editor

You can add Sound Cues directly to levels using the Unreal Editor. For example to put a fire sound that loops, select the **Vehicle_Damage_FireLoop_Cue** that was mentioned earlier. Right-click on an empty space just in front of the cube in the default level and select Add Ambient Sound to add this Sound Cue to the level. Run the level in the Mobile Previewer and walk toward and away from the cube to hear the sound increase in volume as you get closer to the sound source and decrease in volume as you walk away. To add this Sound Cue to the level see Figure 6–9. Adding Sound Cues via this method is good for stationary environmental sounds such as insects, and the sound of an ocean near the beach.

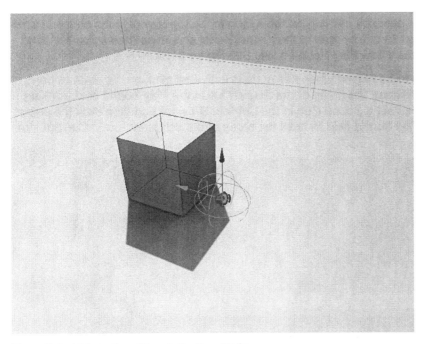

Figure 6–9. *Adding a Sound Cue via the Unreal Editor*

Adding Sound Cues Dynamically using UnrealScript

If a sound is not stationary and/or needs to be generated when an action in the game occurs then it should be created dynamically using UnrealScript.

In order for an UnrealScript class to play a Sound Cue it must be derived from the `Actor` class which contains the `PlaySound()` function. The `PlaySound()` function is defined in the `Actor` class as follows:

```
PlaySound(SoundCue InSoundCue,
 optional bool bNotReplicated,
 optional bool bNoRepToOwner,
 optional bool bStopWhenOwnerDestroyed,
 optional vector SoundLocation,
 optional bool bNoRepToRelevant);
```

The important parameters that are relevant to our needs are the parameters `InSoundCue` and `bStopWhenOwnerDestroyed`.

`InSoundCue` is the reference to the Sound Cue to play and `bStopWhenOwnerDestroyed` allows you to stop playing the Sound Cue when the owner playing it is destroyed.

Adding Sound Cues Using Kismet

If the sound needs to be attached to a Kismet related action such as the opening of a door or a gate then an easy way to provide sound effects is through Kismet.

Bring up the Kismet panel by clicking on the K icon in the top row of icons on the Unreal Editor. Right-click on an empty area of the Kismet panel and select **New Action** ➤ Sound ➤ **Play Sound** to create a new Play Sound node. See Figure 6–10.

To set a sound cue to be played when this node is activated click on the node to bring up its properties and enter the name of the Sound Cue in the Play Sound field. An easy way to do this is to select a Sound Cue in the Content Browser and then click the arrow to the right of the Play Sound field to have the name of the selected Sound Cue put into the field.

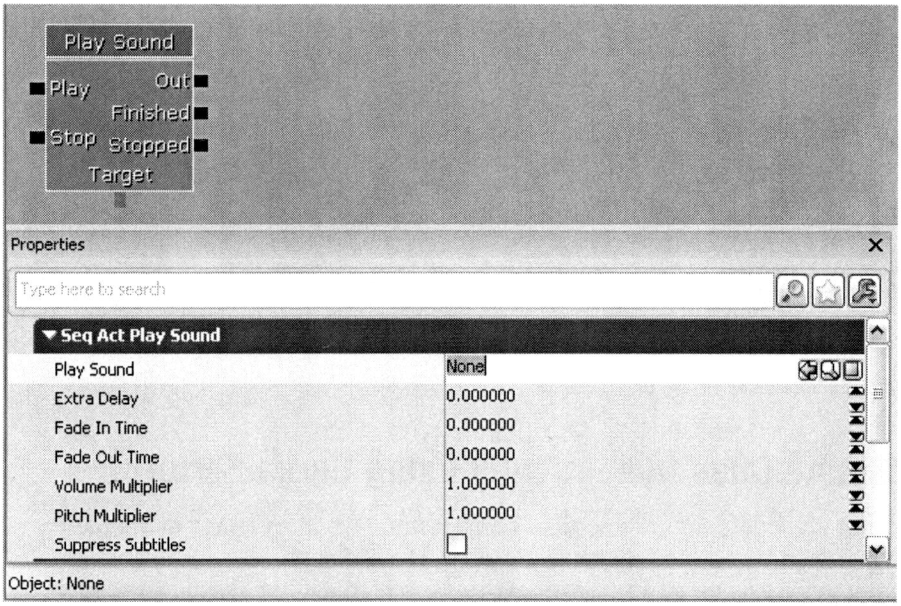

Figure 6–10. *The Play Sound node and properties in Kismet*

Hands-On Example: Adding Sound Cues to a Weapon

In this example, we will begin a larger project for the next chapter. We will create a new weapon class and projectile class that incorporate Sound Cues. Remember all classes that are derived from the Actor class, which is most classes, are able to produce sounds via the PlaySound() function defined in the Actor class and is accessible to derived or extended classes. Both the Weapon and Projectile classes are derived from the Actor class. We choose the Projectile class to add the sounds into because this is where the projectiles are actually initialized and explosions of the projectiles are handled. This is designed to illustrate how to incorporate Sound Cues into a real world UnrealScript example and demonstrate how to use Sound Cues dynamically.

Creating the Weapon

First you need to create a new directory for this project. Create a new directory called **ExampleCh6** under your default UDK installation directory at C:\UDK\UDK-2011-06\Development\Src. The exact base directory will depend on which version of the UDK you are using. The above base directory is set for the June 2011 UDK version.

Create another directory called **Classes** under the directory you just created. You should store all the UnrealScript files for this project under the Classes directory.

Next, you need to create a new class called JazzWeaponSound and save it to the Classes directory under the filename JazzWeaponSound.uc. See Listing 6–1.

> **NOTE:** Remember that all UnrealScript files must be named after the class in them with a .uc extension and placed in a Classes directory under a main project directory.

Listing 6–1. *JazzWeaponSound Class*

```
class JazzWeaponSound extends Weapon;

defaultproperties
{
 Begin Object Class=SkeletalMeshComponent Name=FirstPersonMesh
 SkeletalMesh=SkeletalMesh'KismetGame_Assets.Anims.SK_JazzGun'
 End Object
 Mesh=FirstPersonMesh
 Components.Add(FirstPersonMesh);

 Begin Object Class=SkeletalMeshComponent Name=PickupMesh
 SkeletalMesh=SkeletalMesh'KismetGame_Assets.Anims.SK_JazzGun'
 End Object
 DroppedPickupMesh=PickupMesh
 PickupFactoryMesh=PickupMesh

 WeaponFireTypes(0)=EWFT_Projectile
 WeaponFireTypes(1)=EWFT_NONE

 WeaponProjectiles(0)=class'JazzBulletSound'
 WeaponProjectiles(1)=class'JazzBulletSound'

 FiringStatesArray(0)=WeaponFiring
 FireInterval(0)=0.25
 Spread(0)=0
}
```

The important code is highlighted in bold print. The rest of code should look familiar from our coverage of weapons in Chapter 3.

We specify a new JazzBulletSound class for our projectile. It is in this class that we will add sounds associated with our bullets.

Creating the Projectile

Next, we need to create the JazzBulletSound class that is derived from the Projectile class. See Listing 6–2.

Listing 6–2. *JazzBulletSound class*

```
class JazzBulletSound extends Projectile;

var SoundCue FireSound;
var bool ImpactSoundPlayed;

simulated singular event Touch(Actor Other, PrimitiveComponent OtherComp, vector
HitLocation, vector HitNormal)
{
 Other.TakeDamage(33, InstigatorController, HitLocation, -HitNormal, None);
}

simulated function Explode(vector HitLocation, vector HitNormal)
{
 if (!ImpactSOundPlayed)
 {
 PlaySound(ImpactSound);
 ImpactSoundPlayed = true;
 }
}

function Init( Vector Direction )
{
 local vector NewDir;

 NewDir = Normal(Vector(InstigatorController.Pawn.Rotation));
 Velocity = Speed * NewDir;

 PlaySound(SpawnSound);
 PlaySound(FireSound, , , true,,);
}

defaultproperties
{
 Begin Object Class=StaticMeshComponent Name=Bullet
 StaticMesh=StaticMesh'EngineMeshes.Sphere'
 Scale3D=(X=0.050000,Y=0.050000,Z=0.05000)
 End Object
 Components.Add(Bullet)

 Begin Object Class=ParticleSystemComponent Name=BulletTrail
 Template=ParticleSystem'Castle_Assets.FX.P_FX_Fire_SubUV_01'
 End Object
 Components.Add(BulletTrail)

 MaxSpeed=+05000.000000
 Speed=+05000.000000

 FireSound = SoundCue'A_Vehicle_Generic.Vehicle.Vehicle_Damage_FireLoop_Cue'
```

```
ImpactSound = SoundCue'KismetGame_Assets.Sounds.S_BulletImpact_01_Cue'
SpawnSound = SoundCue'A_Pickups_Powerups.PowerUps.A_Powerup_UDamage_SpawnCue'

ImpactSoundPlayed = false
}
```

In this class we add sound effects for the impact of the projectile (ImpactSound), the firing of the weapon (SpawnSound) and the sound of the flames (FireSound) that are attached to the projectile via particle emitter.

The Sound Cues are set in the defaultproperties block and played back through the PlaySound() function.

This code will be incorporated in a hands-on example in the next chapter. In the mean time you can preview the sound effects by searching for these Sound Cues in the Content Browser in the Unreal Editor and double-clicking on them to play them.

Kismet, Matinee and Moving Objects

Kismet is the graphical version of UnrealScript. Kismet in combination with Unreal Matinee does an excellent job in controlling the movement of objects like platforms and the opening and closing of gates. Moving platforms that can move characters in the game world are created with InterpActors. Objects called triggers can be used to initiate the movement of closed gates or doors so that they become open.

Kismet is used to trigger the movement of platforms and gates and Unreal Matinee defines the exact movement that the platform, gate, or door should follow. Matinee uses a keyframe method of animation where you set certain frames that indicate the object's position in the world at certain times and then the Matinee will generate all the positions for the frames in between the keyframes. In this section we show you:

- How to use Kismet and Matinee to create a moving platform.
- How to create a moving gate that opens when your pawn touches a trigger.

> **NOTE:** There is also more information concerning Kismet and Matinee discussed back in Chapter 2.

Hands-On Example: Using Kismet to create a Moving Platform

In this hands-on example we will create a moving platform that can move the player's pawn from the ground level to the top of the cube of the default level.

1. Bring up the Unreal Editor.

2. Search for the static mesh **SM_Gate_02** in the search box in the Content Browser. Make sure to mark the Static Meshes checkbox.

3. Select this mesh in the Preview Pane, and double-click on it to load it into the UDK system and bring it up into the Mesh Viewer.

4. Put your cursor over an empty area in front of the cube in the default level.

5. Right-click and select Add InterpActor or simply drag and drop the gate into the level where you want it.

6. Rotate and move the gate mesh so that it is right in front of the cube and oriented as in Figure 6–11. Hit the spacebar while you have the gate selected to cycle between transformation, rotation, and scaling widgets.

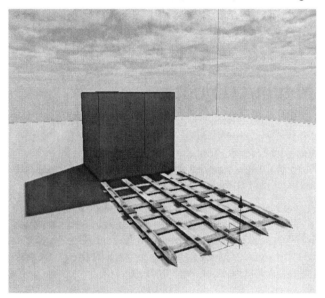

Figure 6–11. *Gate Mesh platform*

7. With the gate still selected open Kismet. Right-click and select **New Event Using InterpActor ➤ Mover**. This creates a new set of Kismet nodes as shown in Figure 6–12.

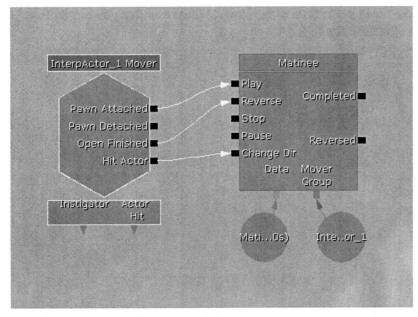

Figure 6–12. *Kismet nodes for moving a platform*

8. Double-click on the Matinee node to bring up Matinee. See Figure 6–13.

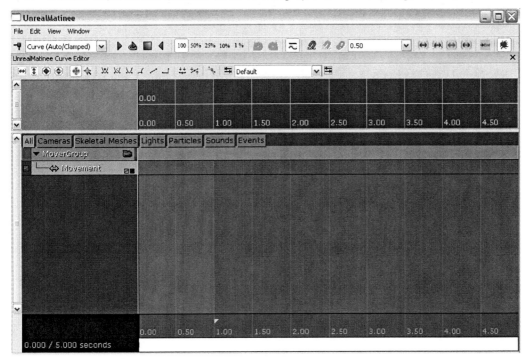

Figure 6–13. *Matinee node for our gate platform*

9. Scroll the white bar at the bottom of the Unreal Matinee so that you see the ending red marker. See Figure 6–14.

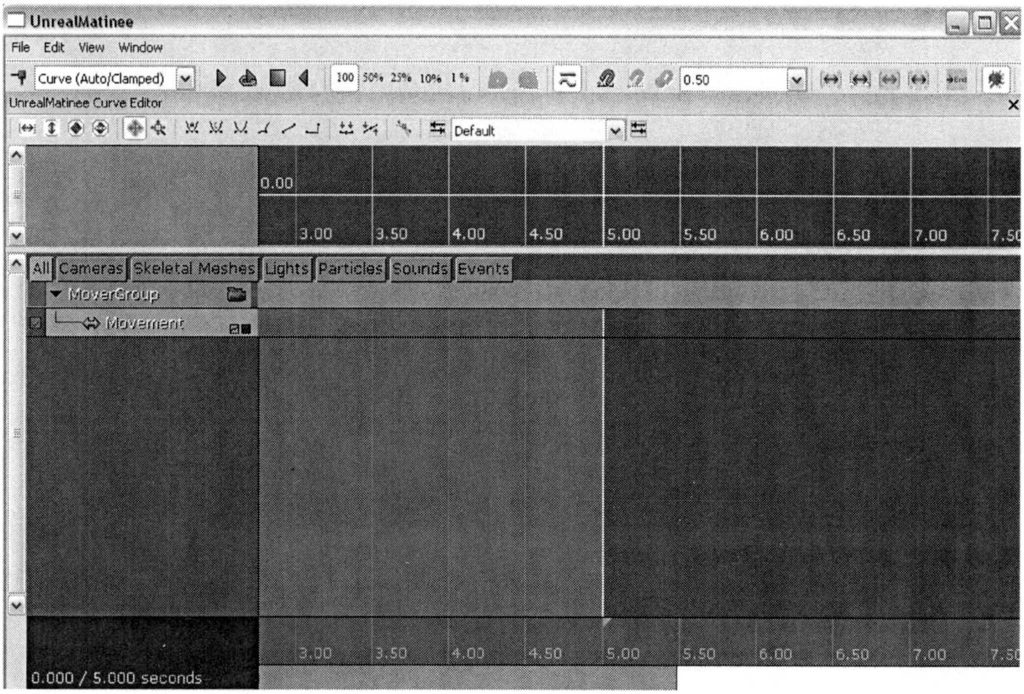

Figure 6–14. *Red marker that denotes the end of the Matinee sequence*

10. Move Red Marker which denotes the end of sequence from the 5.00 second mark to the 1 second mark. This shortens the time for the total animation to 1 second. See Figure 6–15.

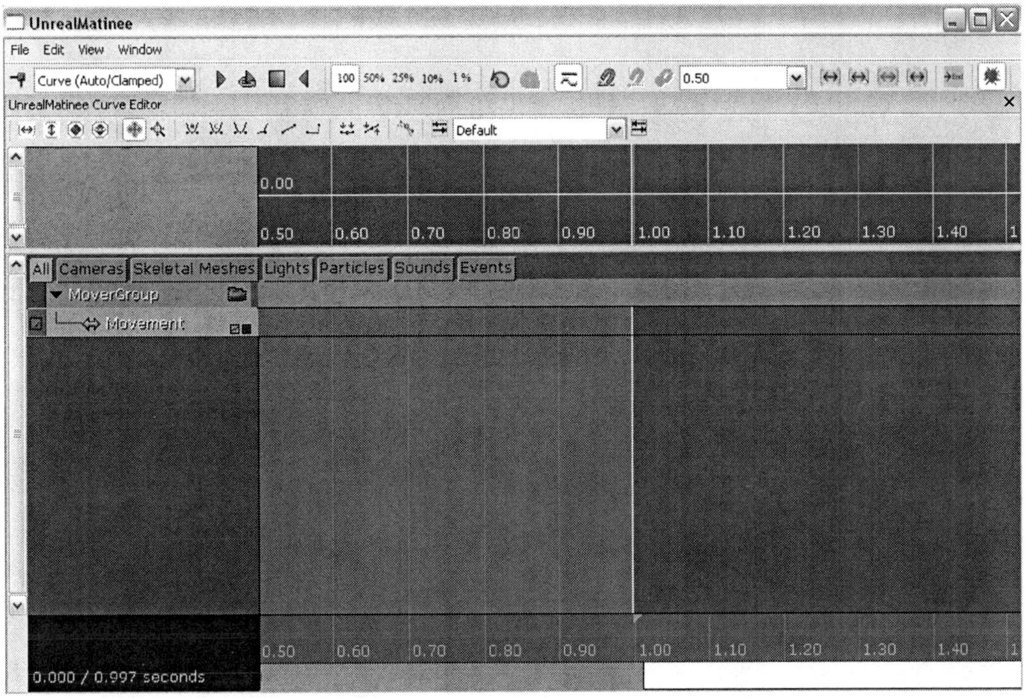

Figure 6–15. *Red Marker at new position at 1.00 second mark*

11. Slide the bar back to the front of the Matinee Sequence and make sure the black selection marker at the bottom area above the white bar is at the 0 seconds mark and hit the Enter key to mark the starting keyframe. A red outlined triangle should appear marking the new key frame. See Figure 6–16.

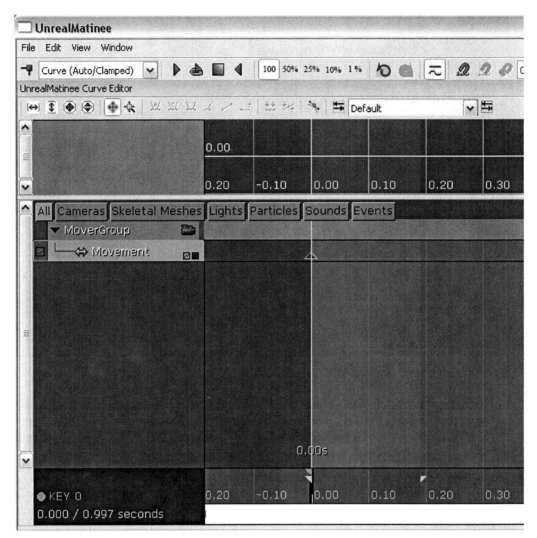

Figure 6–16. *Starting the first key frame with the gate at the default ground level.*

12. Slide the long black selection marker at the bottom of the keyframe panel to around the 1.0 second mark and hit the Enter key. A new keyframe is now being generated. See Figure 6–17.

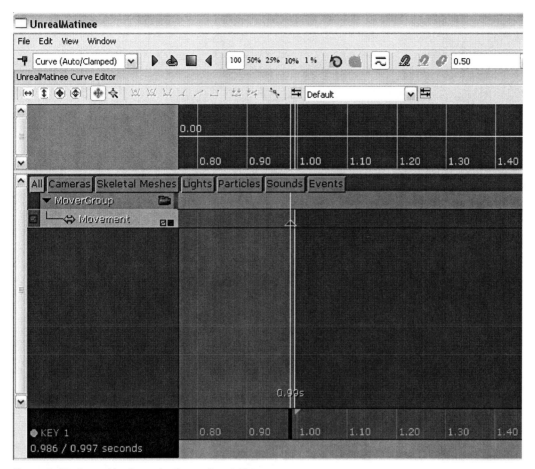

Figure 6–17. *Second keyframe for the moving platform*

13. Now, move the gate up using the transformation widget so that it is level with the top of the cube. Since we are recording this keyframe the gate should have lines to indicate the change in position from the last keyframe. See Figure 6–18.

Figure 6–18. *Changing the position of the gate for the final keyframe*

14. Close the Matinee Window.

15. Double-click on the gate to bring up its properties. Under the Collision category set the CollisionType to COLLIDE_Blockall. See Figure 6–19.

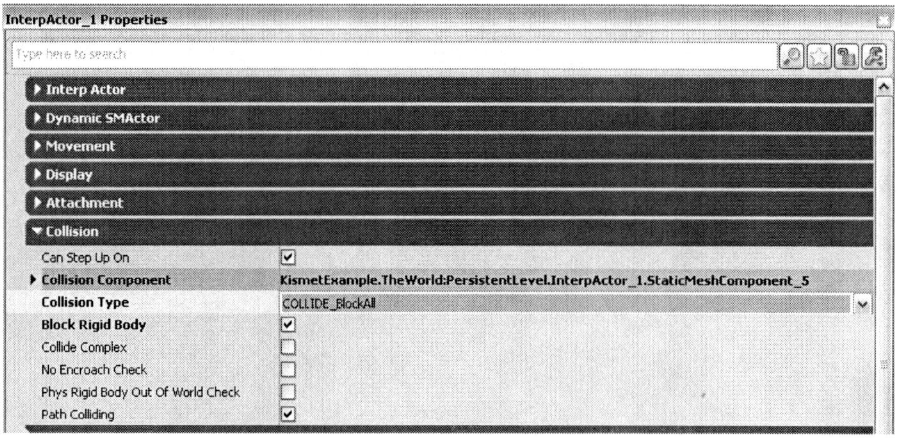

Figure 6–19. *Initializing the new moving gate platform*

Everything should now be set up so that you can have your pawn walk on the gate and have it move up. Select a game type from a previous chapter (such as Chapter 3) that allows you to see your pawn in the third person. A good choice would be the ExampleCh31Game game type.

Run the game on the mobile previewer. You should now be able to walk your pawn over the gate and the gate will automatically move up to the top of the cube. See Figure 6-20.

Figure 6-20. *A working platform from a gate static mesh*

Hands-on Example: Using Kismet to create Locked Gates

In this example we will create a gate that can be opened by the player touching a trigger.

1. Bring up the Unreal Editor.

2. Click on the cube in the default level, right-click and select Copy.

3. Put your cursor over an empty area in the level next to the cube, right-click and select Paste Here to paste a copy of this cube into the level.

4. In the Content Browser search for the same gate that you did for the last example. Select this mesh in the Preview Pane. Double-click on it to load it into the UDK and bring it up into the Mesh Viewer.

5. Right-click on the space between the blocks and select Add InterpActor to add the gate to the level as an InterpActor.

6. Position the gate between the blocks.

7. Right-click somewhere to the left or right of your gate and select **Add Actor ➤ Add Trigger**. This will create a new Trigger object to be used to open your gate. You can also put a static mesh at the trigger's location as a reminder of where the trigger is if you want to. A good mesh for this is a barrel mesh such as **Sm_Barrel_01** or **RemadePhysBarrel**. Type one of these names into the search box to bring it up in the preview panel. You can select one of these and drag and drop it into your level. See Figure 6–21.

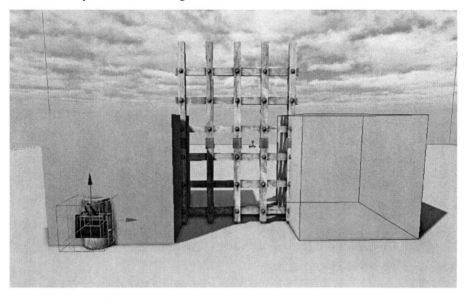

Figure 6–21. *Gate with trigger*

8. Select the trigger and open Kismet.

9. Right-click on an empty space in the Kismet panel and select **New Event Using Trigger ➤ Touch** to create a new Kismet Trigger Touch Node.

10. Right-click on an empty space in the Kismet panel and select New Matinee to create a new Matinee Node. Create a link between the Touched output on the trigger and the Play input on the Matinee by clicking on the Touched output and dragging your mouse to connect the wire to the Play input. See Figure 6–22.

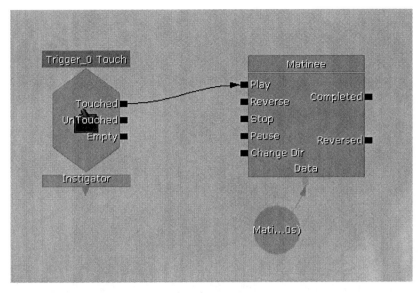

Figure 6–22. *Trigger controlling Matinee Sequence*

11. Make sure you have the gate selected. Double-click on the Matinee node to bring up Matinee.

12. Right-click on the main Matinee sequence panel and select Add New Empty Group. Add this new group by clicking the OK button on the dialog that pops up.

13. With your mouse on this new group right-click and select Add New Movement Track.

14. Click on the Movement track you just created. Make sure the long black sequence marker is at the 0.0 seconds mark and press the Enter key to start the keyframe for the starting position of the gate. See Figure 6–23.

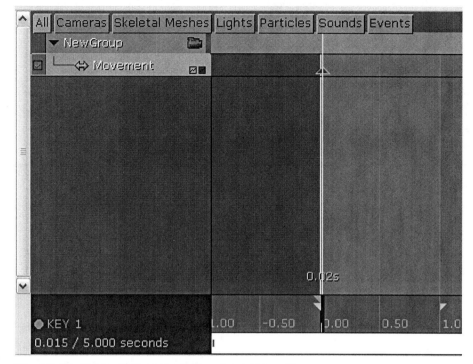

Figure 6–23. *Creating the keyframe for the gate's initial position.*

15. Next, we need to create a new keyframe for the gate's final position. Move the long black sequence marker to around the 5.0 marker. Hit the Enter key to create a new keyframe at this time. See Figure 6–24.

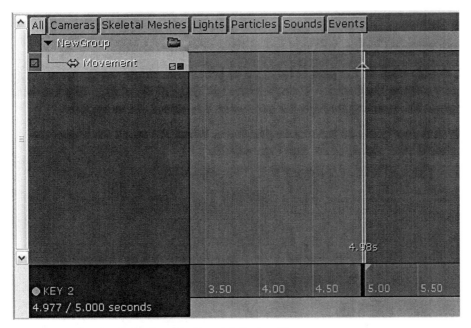

Figure 6–24. *Creating the keyframe for the gate's final position*

16. Next, move the gate using the transformation widget completely to one side as shown in Figure 6–25.

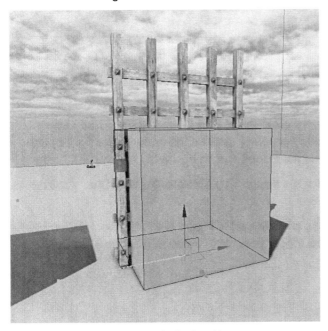

Figure 6–25. *Moving the gate to its final position*

17. Close Matinee.

18. Change the game type to one that has the player's pawn visible.

19. Next, double-click on the gate to bring up its properties. Under the Collision category change the Collision Type property to COLLIDE_BlockALL. This blocks your pawn from moving through the gate when it is closed. Save the level.

20. Finally, run your game on the mobile previewer. When you touch the trigger the gate should start sliding open. See Figure 6–26.

Figure 6–26. *Opening the gate by touching the trigger*

21. Bring up the Kismet panel. Right-click on an empty area and select **New Action ➤ Sound ➤ Play Sound** to create a Play Sound node.

22. In the Content Browser, search for **Elevator01_StartCue** and select the Sound Cue asset when it comes up.

23. Go back to the Kismet panel and click on the Play Sound Node to bring up its properties. Under the Play Sound property click on the arrow to the right of the field to place the currently selected Sound Cue in this field.

24. Repeat steps 21 through 23 for the Sound Cue **Elevator01_StopCue**. You should now have two Play Sound nodes.

25. Connect the Play Sound nodes as indicated in Figure 6–27. Connect the node with the StartCue sound to the trigger node and the node with the Stop Cue sound to the Matinee node.

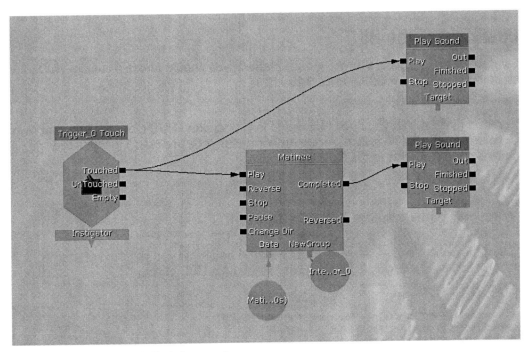

Figure 6–27. *Creating sound effects for our gate.*

26. Now try out the gate again using the Mobile Previewer. This time there should be a sound effect when the gate is first opened and another sound effect when the gate is fully opened.

UDK Heads Up Display

The last topic we cover in this chapter is the HUD in preparation for the topic that comes in the next chapter, which is gameplay. In term of the player's environment the HUD is probably the most apparent since it is right in the player's face literally. A HUD can be a basic one that displays the player's statistics or much more complex such as in a vehicle simulation that includes graphics that represent the vehicle's controls and the interior of the vehicle itself.

The Heads Up Display or HUD contains information that may be of interest to the player such as the number of lives left, current health, or score. The HUD can be drawn using Scaleform or the Canvas class. Scaleform refers to the Scaleform Gfx system that enables Adobe Flash based HUDs to run on the UDK.

Creating code that is compatible with Scaleform requires tools outside the UDK and requires the extra work of setting up scenes in Adobe Flash and graphics in programs like Adobe Photoshop. For these reasons only the Canvas method of HUD creation will be used in this book.

Overview of the HUD

For developing iOS games for the mobile platform you should create a custom HUD class that derives from UDKHud as follows:

```
class ExtendedHUD extends UDKHud;
```

The main function that you need to override in your custom HUD class to draw your own items is the DrawHUD() function. An example structure of a DrawHUD() function in a derived class that adds to the HUD is as follows:

```
function DrawHUD()
{
 super.DrawHUD();
 // Put your custom code here that draws to the HUD
}
```

In the class where you define the type of game to be played you need to set your HUDType in the defaultproperties to your new custom HUD class.

```
defaultproperties
{
 PlayerControllerClass=class'ExampleCh6.ExampleCh6PC'
 DefaultPawnClass=class'ExampleCh6.Jazz3Pawn'
 HUDType=class'ExampleCh6.ExtendedHUD'

 bRestartLevel=false
 bWaitingToStartMatch=true
 bDelayedStart=false
}
```

Displaying Text on the HUD

In order to draw text as well as do such things as set the color of the text, and the position of the cursor that draws the text on the HUD you use the Canvas object.

The Canvas object is created from the Canvas class which is a built-in class in the UDK that contains functions that allow the user to draw on the screen.

In the HUD class which is the base class for the HUD there is a variable called Canvas that can be used to draw text and graphics on our HUD.

```
Var Canvas Canvas;
```

The following is a list of key functions in the Canvas class. The examples show you how to use these functions from within the HUD class.

- DrawText() —To draw text on the screen use the DrawText() function.

    ```
    Canvas.DrawText("Hello World");
    ```

- SetDrawColor()—You can set the color of the text by calling the SetDrawColor() function. The input parameters R, G, B refer to the colors Red, Green, and Blue. These three values are used to define the color of the text that will be drawn. The values range from 0-255.

  ```
  Canvas.SetDrawColor(R, G, B);
  ```

- SetPos()—You can set the position of the cursor that draws the text on the HUD by calling the SetPos() function

  ```
  Canvas.SetPos(X, Y);
  ```

- TextSize()—Gets the horizontal and vertical size of the input text as it would appear on the screen in screen pixels and returns it in the last two parameters. The TextLabel variable holds the text in string format. The last two variables hold the numerical values of the size of the text in TextLabel in the X (horizontal) and Y (vertical) directions.

  ```
  Canvas.TextSize(TextLabel, TextSizeX, TextSizeY);
  ```

Displaying Textures on the HUD

You can draw textures to the HUD by using the DrawTextureBlended() function.

```
Canvas.DrawTextureBlended(DefaultTexture1, 1, BLEND_Masked);
```

The first parameter is a reference to the actual texture. The second parameter is the scale factor that will be applied to the horizontal and vertical lengths of the texture. The third parameter is the blend mode, with several options.

- Choose BLEND_Opaque to put the texture on the HUD without any alterations of the colors.

- Choose BLEND_Additive to add the colors of the texture and the background color already on the HUD to create a final color that will be placed on the HUD.

- Select BLEND_Masked to put the texture on the HUD without the black pixels.

Hands-on Example: Adding a Basic Heads Up Display

In this example we will create the basic custom HUD that we will use in the larger example that we will create later in the next chapter. Create a new file for this class in your Classes directory under the project directory called ExtendedHUD.uc and put in the following code. See Listing 6–3.

Listing 6–3. *Custom HUD class*

```
class ExtendedHUD extends UDKHud;

var Texture DefaultTexture1;
var Texture DefaultTexture2;
```

```
var Texture DefaultTexture3;
var Texture DefaultTexture4;
var Texture DefaultTexture5;

struct HUDInfo
{
 var string Label;
 var Vector2D TextLocation;
 var Color TextColor;
 var Vector2D Scale;
};

// HUD
var HUDInfo HUDHealth;
var HUDInfo HUDLives;
var HUDInfo HUDGameOver;
var HUDInfo HUDScore;

simulated function PostBeginPlay()
{
 Super.PostBeginPlay();

 HUDHealth.Label = "Health:";
 HUDHealth.TextLocation.x = 1100;
 HUDHealth.TextLocation.y = 50;
 HUDHealth.TextColor.R = 0;
 HUDHealth.TextColor.G = 0;
 HUDHealth.TextColor.B = 255;
 HUDHealth.Scale.X = 2;
 HUDHealth.Scale.Y = 4;

 HUDLives.Label = "Lives:";
 HUDLives.TextLocation.x = 600;
 HUDLives.TextLocation.y = 50;
 HUDLives.TextColor.R = 0;
 HUDLives.TextColor.G = 255;
 HUDLives.TextColor.B = 0;
 HUDLives.Scale.X = 2;
 HUDLives.Scale.Y = 4;

 HUDGameOver.Label = "GAME OVER";
 HUDGameOver.TextLocation.x = 400;
 HUDGameOver.TextLocation.y = 300;
 HUDGameOver.TextColor.R = 255;
 HUDGameOver.TextColor.G = 0;
 HUDGameOver.TextColor.B = 255;
 HUDGameOver.Scale.X = 7;
 HUDGameOver.Scale.Y = 7;

 HUDScore.Label = "Score:";
 HUDScore.TextLocation.x = 0;
 HUDScore.TextLocation.y = 50;
 HUDScore.TextColor.R = 255;
 HUDScore.TextColor.G = 0;
 HUDScore.TextColor.B = 0;
 HUDScore.Scale.X = 2;
 HUDScore.Scale.Y = 4;
```

```
}

function DrawHUDItem(HUDInfo Info, coerce string Value)
{
 local Vector2D TextSize;

 Canvas.SetDrawColor(Info.TextColor.R, Info.TextColor.G, Info.TextColor.B);
 Canvas.SetPos(Info.TextLocation.X, Info.TextLocation.Y);
 Canvas.DrawText(Info.Label, ,Info.Scale.X, Info.Scale.Y);
 Canvas.TextSize(Info.Label, TextSize.X, TextSize.Y);
 Canvas.SetPos(Info.TextLocation.X + (TextSize.X * Info.Scale.X), Info.TextLocation.Y);
 Canvas.DrawText(Value, , Info.Scale.X, Info.Scale.Y);
}

function DrawHUD()
{
 local int Lives;

 super.DrawHUD();

 /*
 // Blend Modes = BLEND_Opaque, BLEND_Additive, and BLEND_Modulate modes
 Canvas.SetPos(0,0);
 Canvas.DrawTextureBlended(DefaultTexture1, 1, BLEND_Opaque);

 Canvas.SetPos(150,0);
 Canvas.DrawTextureBlended(DefaultTexture2, 1, BLEND_Additive);

 Canvas.SetPos(300,0);
 Canvas.DrawTextureBlended(DefaultTexture3, 1, BLEND_Masked);

 Canvas.SetPos(450,0);
 Canvas.DrawTextureBlended(DefaultTexture4, 1, BLEND_Masked);

 Canvas.SetPos(600,0);
 Canvas.DrawTextureBlended(DefaultTexture5, 1, BLEND_Masked);
 */
 Canvas.Font = class'Engine'.static.GetLargeFont();

 // Score
 DrawHUDItem(HUDScore,ExampleCh6PC(PlayerOwner).Score);

 // Lives
 Lives = Jazz3Pawn(PlayerOwner.Pawn).Lives;
 DrawHUDItem(HUDLives, Lives);

 // Health
 DrawHUDItem(HUDHealth, PlayerOwner.Pawn.Health);

 // Game Over
 if (ExampleCh6PC(PlayerOwner).GameOVer)
 {
 DrawHUDItem(HUDGameOver, "");
 }
}
defaultProperties
{
```

```
DefaultTexture1= Texture2D'EditorResources.Ambientcreatures' // Yellow Chick 32 by 32
DefaultTexture2= Texture2D'EditorResources.Ammo' // Ammo Icon 32 by 32
DefaultTexture3= Texture2D'EditorResources.LookTarget' // Target 32 by 32
DefaultTexture4= Texture2D'EditorMaterials.Tick' // Green Check 32 by 32
DefaultTexture5= Texture2D'EditorMaterials.GreyCheck' // Grey Check 32 by 32
}
```

The key function in this class is the DrawHUDItem() function that draws the actual text on the HUD based on a HUDInfo entry along with the input value for that entry.

The HUD displays the player's score, lives left, and health. This custom HUD class also provides examples of how to draw various textures to the HUD in the commented out section. The preview of the HUD as part of the larger game play example that is created later in the next chapter is shown in Figure 6–28.

Figure 6–28. *Preview of the HUD for next chapter's gameplay example*

Summary

In this chapter we covered Sound Cues, the Sound Cue Editor that is used to create Sound Cues from sound data, how to use Sound Cues from within the Unreal Editor, from within UnrealScript in real-time during gameplay, and from within Kismet. Next, we discussed how to use Kismet and Matinee to control the movement of platforms and locked gates, as well as how to add sounds to the opening of a gate. We then covered the Unreal Heads Up Display and showed you how to create a custom HUD in UnrealScript.

Chapter 7

Sample Game and GamePlay

In this chapter we will discuss gameplay including the main categories that affect the quality of gameplay, which are game difficulty and game balance. Elements that make up game difficulty include such things as the characteristics of the enemies, the player, the weapons, and the projectiles used in the weapons. Game balance refers to finding the right combination of the above elements in order to create a fun game that the player will continue to come back to and play over and over again.

Finally, we cover an actual gameplay example where we create a small working game that involves an enemy Bot following the player around the level and firing a weapon at the player.

Gameplay Overview

In this section we will cover game difficulty and game balance, both of which are essential in producing gameplay that is both fun and challenging. We cover the different elements of gameplay that contribute to a game's difficulty level. We then discuss how balancing these different elements is also important to creating a fun game that the player will enjoy playing over and over again.

Game Difficulty

Game difficulty is an important part of creating good gameplay and making a game fun and entertaining. A game that is too difficult for the average user will frustrate him. A game that is too easy will lack any meaningful challenge and also make him lose interest in the game. The objective is to make a game easy enough for the average player but hard enough to keep him challenged.

Elements of gameplay that affect game difficulty are:

- Enemies: The number of enemies, the capabilities of the enemies (including their armor, weapons, health, and healing abilities), and other special abilities such as magic abilities are elements to consider concerning game difficulty.

- The Player: The fundamental characteristics of the player such as number of lives, health, healing ability, armor, weapons, and other special abilities are factors that are related to game difficulty.

- Power Ups: The nature, number, and location of power ups available inside the game world that would enhance the abilities of objects and characters, such as health bonus, weapon damage powerups, and extra lives, are also factors that would affect game difficulty.

- Level Design: The way the level is designed also affects the game difficulty level in terms of where the enemies are placed and the amount and types of cover available to the player and enemies. For example, do the player's enemies shoot at him from high ground in a fortified area? If so how much cover from hostile fire is there in the game arena?

- Game Play Rules: The rules of the game including how victory is achieved would also determine how difficult the game is. For example, if the objective of the game is to just survive for a certain amount of time, then hiding out in an easily defensible area with lots of cover from enemy fire would be desirable. However, once the player is able to find such an area in the game level, then the game would become very easy and perhaps not as fun and challenging.

Game Balance

Game Balance is also an important element in good gameplay and in creating a fun game. Game balance refers to finding the best combinations of the different levels of difficulty in each of the elements of gameplay listed in the Game Difficulty section previously.

For example, let's take the situation from the previous section where the goal of the game is to survive for a set time and the player has found a location in the game where he is well protected from enemy fire and can just sit and wait for the game to end. A way to change this game so that it is more balanced might be to:

- Change the Game Play Rules so that the objective would be to not only survive a set amount of time but to achieve other objectives such as destroying a certain target or killing a certain number of enemies.

- Change the Level Design so that any areas that are completely protected or mostly protected from enemy fire and attack are removed.

■ Increase the number of enemies around these heavily protected areas so that they are difficult to get to without the player taking heavy damage.

Basic GamePlay

In this section you will learn how to create a small working game with a working Heads Up Display, sound effects and the locked gate from the Kismet/Matinee section from the previous chapter. The knowledge used to create this game will be drawn from previous sections in this chapter and from previous chapters. A hands-on example will be presented to show you in detail how to create this basic game.

Hands-On Example: Creating a Basic Game Framework.

In this example we will create a small working game incorporating the code created in the Sound Cues, and HUD sections in this chapter. The final game will have a working HUD displaying the score, player's health, and number of lives left in the game. An enemy bot is created on a custom spawn pad and then follows the player and fires its weapon at the player. The objective of the game would be to kill the enemy bot and gain the highest score before all your lives have been used up.

Creating the Level

In this example we will extend the level that you created for the Kismet and Matinee controlled gate example in the previous chapter.

1. Bring up the Unreal Editor and load in the level you saved that contains the locked gate example using Kismet and Matinee.

2. Copy and paste the cube all across the level. Right-click on an empty area near the center of the level and select **Add Actor ➤ Add Pylon** to add a Pylon for the navigation mesh used to control the enemy Bot. Rebuild the navigation mesh by selecting **Build ➤ AI Paths** from the main Unreal Editor menu. The resulting level should look similar to Figure 7–1.

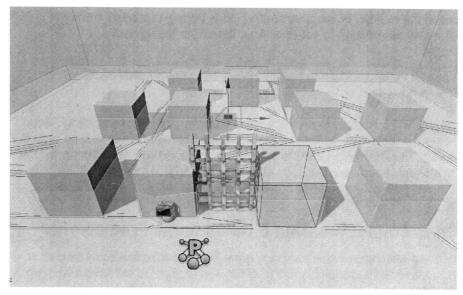

Figure 7–1. *Creating a simple game level*

The level is complete except for the Spawn Pad for the Bot which will be added later after code for the Spawn Pad has been created.

3.   Save the level.

Creating the Game Type

Next, we need to create a new game type class for this example (See Listing 7–1). Create this new class in the following directory:

`C:\UDK\UDK-2011-06\Development\Src\ExampleCh7\Classes`

You should have already created this directory to store code for the Sound Cue section and the HUD section that we created earlier in Chapter 6.

Listing 7–1. *Game Type*

```
class ExampleCh7Game extends FrameworkGame;

event OnEngineHasLoaded()
{
    WorldInfo.Game.Broadcast(self,"ExampleCh7Game Type Active - Engine Has Loaded
!!!!");
}
function bool PreventDeath(Pawn KilledPawn, Controller Killer, class<DamageType>
DamageType, vector HitLocation)
{
    return true;
}
static event class<GameInfo> SetGameType(string MapName, string Options, string Portal)
{
```

```
        return super.SetGameType(MapName, Options, Portal);
}
defaultproperties
{
        PlayerControllerClass=class'ExampleCh7.ExampleCh7PC'
        DefaultPawnClass=class'ExampleCh7.Jazz3Pawn'
        HUDType=class'ExampleCh7.ExtendedHUD'
        bRestartLevel=false
        bWaitingToStartMatch=true
        bDelayedStart=false
}
```

Note that we have specified a custom player controller, pawn class, and HUD for this game type. Remember that we have already created the custom HUD class in Chapter 6 so nothing more needs to be done with the HUD class.

Creating the Player's Code

Next, we need to create the UnrealScript code for the Player. This code consists of a custom pawn, controller, weapon, and weapon projectile

Pawn

The player's pawn is shown in Listing 7–2. The important modifications from previous code are shown in bold print.

The main addition here is the TakeDamage() function. This function processes damage to the player and if the player's health is equal to or less than zero and the player has more lives then reset the player's health and move the player to his starting location.

Listing 7–2. *Player's Pawn*

```
class Jazz3Pawn extends SimplePawn;

var float CamOffsetDistance;
var int CamAngle;

var Inventory MainGun;
var vector InitialLocation;

var SoundCue PawnHitSound;
var int Lives;

event TakeDamage(int Damage, Controller InstigatedBy, vector HitLocation, vector
Momentum, class<DamageType> DamageType, optional TraceHitInfo HitInfo, optional Actor
DamageCauser)
{
    PlaySound(PawnHitSound);
    Health = Health - Damage;
    WorldInfo.Game.Broadcast(self,self @ " Has Taken Damage IN TAKEDAMAGE, HEALTH = " @
Health);

    // If Died
    if (Health <= 0)
```

```
            {
                // Reduce number of lives left if above 0
                if (Lives > 0)
                {
                    Lives--;
                }

                // If player has more lives left then use them
                if (Lives > 0)
                {
                    SetLocation(InitialLocation);
                    SetPhysics(PHYS_Falling);
                    Health = 100;
                }
            }
        }
    }
    simulated singular event Rotator GetBaseAimRotation()
    {
        local rotator TempRot;
        TempRot = Rotation;
        TempRot.Pitch = 0;
        SetRotation(TempRot);
        return TempRot;
    }
    function AddGunToSocket(Name SocketName)
    {
        local Vector SocketLocation;
        local Rotator SocketRotation;

        if (Mesh != None)
        {
            if (Mesh.GetSocketByName(SocketName) != None)
            {
                Mesh.GetSocketWorldLocationAndRotation(SocketName, SocketLocation,
    SocketRotation);

                MainGun.SetRotation(SocketRotation);
                MainGun.SetBase(Self,, Mesh, SocketName);
            }
            else
            {
                WorldInfo.Game.Broadcast(self,"!!!!!!SOCKET NAME NOT FOUND!!!!!");
            }
        }
        else
        {
            WorldInfo.Game.Broadcast(self,"!!!!!!MESH NOT FOUND!!!!!");
        }
    }
    function AddDefaultInventory()
    {
        MainGun = InvManager.CreateInventory(class'JazzWeaponSound');
        MainGun.SetHidden(false);
        AddGunToSocket('Weapon_R');
        Weapon(MainGun).FireOffset = vect(0,0,-70);
    }
```

```
//////////////////////////////// Third Person View ////////////////////////////////
simulated function bool CalcCamera( float fDeltaTime, out vector out_CamLoc, out rotator
out_CamRot, out float out_FOV )
{
    local vector BackVector;
    local vector UpVector;
    local float  CamDistanceHorizontal;
    local float  CamDistanceVertical;

    // Set Camera Location
    CamDistanceHorizontal = CamOffsetDistance * cos(CamAngle * UnrRotToRad);
    CamDistanceVertical   = CamOffsetDistance * sin(CamAngle * UnrRotToRad);

    BackVector = -Normal(Vector(Rotation)) * CamDistanceHorizontal;
    UpVector   =  vect(0,0,1) * CamDistanceVertical;

    out_CamLoc = Location + BackVector + UpVector;

    // Set Camera Rotation
    out_CamRot.pitch = -CamAngle;
    out_CamRot.yaw   = Rotation.yaw;
    out_CamRot.roll  = Rotation.roll;

    return true;
}
defaultproperties
{
    Begin Object Class=SkeletalMeshComponent Name=JazzMesh
        SkeletalMesh=SkeletalMesh'KismetGame_Assets.Anims.SK_Jazz'
        AnimSets(0)=AnimSet'KismetGame_Assets.Anims.SK_Jazz_Anims'
        AnimTreeTemplate=AnimTree'KismetGame_Assets.Anims.Jazz_AnimTree'
        BlockRigidBody=true
        CollideActors=true
    End Object
    Mesh = JazzMesh; // Set The mesh for this object
    Components.Add(JazzMesh); // Attach this mesh to this Actor

    CamAngle=3000;
    CamOffsetDistance= 484.0

    InventoryManagerClass=class'WeaponsIM1'

    PawnHitSound =
SoundCue'A_Character_CorruptEnigma_Cue.Mean_Efforts.A_Effort_EnigmaMean_Death_Cue'
}
```

For this pawn we added a Lives variable to indicate the number of lives this pawn has
left. We also added code to the TakeDamage() function to only reset the player to the
starting level position if he has more lives left.

> **NOTE:** The number of player lives, and the player's health are key elements of gameplay that were discussed in the game overview section. In order to have a good game balance with a reasonable game difficulty level you can change the number of starting lives and the player's starting health accordingly to help get the desired game balance and difficulty you desire.

Controller

Next, we need to create our custom player controller. See Listing 7–3.

In this player controller we create the enemy bot on the bot spawn pad when the player is first created (PlayerTick() is first called). We also initialize the number of player's lives. In the main control loop for player which is the PlayerTick() function we continually check to see if the game is over, that is the number of player lives remaining is 0. The player's score is also kept in the variable Score. As in previous examples the function SwipeZoneCallback() handles touch input.

In this class we added the FindSpawnPadLocation() function to support spawning an enemy Bot on a pad that can be placed in the level using the Unreal Editor.

The ResetGame() function helps reset the player's score, lives, health, and so on after the player dies and the game is restarted.

Listing 7–3. *Player Controller*

```
class ExampleCh7PC extends SimplePC;

var Controller FollowBot;
Var Pawn FollowPawn;
var bool BotSpawned;

var bool GameOver;
var int Score;

function vector FindSpawnPadLocation()
{
    local SpawnPad TempSpawnPad;
    local vector TempLocation;
    foreach AllActors (class 'SpawnPad', TempSpawnPad )
    {
        TempLocation = TempSpawnPad.Location;
    }
    return TempLocation;
}
function SpawnBot(Vector SpawnLocation)
{
    SpawnLocation.z = SpawnLocation.z + 500;
    WorldInfo.Game.Broadcast(self,"SPAWNING A BOT AT LOCATION " @ Spawnlocation);
    FollowBot = Spawn(class'BotControllerAttack',,,SpawnLocation);
    FollowPawn = Spawn(class'BotPawn2',,,SpawnLocation);
    FollowBot.Possess(FollowPawn,false);
    BotControllerAttack(FollowBot).CurrentGoal = Pawn;
```

```
        Botpawn2(FollowPawn).AddDefaultInventory();
        BotPawn2(Followpawn).InitialLocation = SpawnLocation;
        FollowPawn.SetPhysics(PHYS_Falling);
        BotSpawned = true;
}
function ResetGame()
{
        GameoVer = false;
        Jazz3Pawn(Pawn).Lives = 3;
        Score = 0;
        Pawn.Health = 100;
        Pawn.SetHidden(false);
        Pawn.Weapon.SetHidden(false);
        Pawn.SetLocation(Jazz3Pawn(Pawn).InitialLocation);
}
function bool SwipeZoneCallback(MobileInputZone Zone,
                                float DeltaTime,
                                int Handle,
                                EZoneTouchEvent EventType,
                                Vector2D TouchLocation)
{
        local bool retval;
        retval = true;
        if (EventType == ZoneEvent_Touch)
        {
                WorldInfo.Game.Broadcast(self,"You touched the screen at = "
                                         @ TouchLocation.x @ " , "
                                         @ TouchLocation.y @ ", Zone Touched = "
                                         @ Zone);

                // Reset Game
                if (GameOver)
                {
                        ResetGame();
                }
                else
                {
                        // Start Firing pawn's weapon
                        StartFire(0);
                }
        }
        else
        if(EventType == ZoneEvent_Update)
        {
        }
        else
        if (EventType == ZoneEvent_UnTouch)
        {
                // Stop Firing Pawn's weapon
                StopFire(0);
        }
        return retval;
}
function SetupZones()
{
        Super.SetupZones();
```

```
          // If we have a game class, configure the zones
          if (MPI != None && WorldInfo.GRI.GameClass != none)
          {
              LocalPlayer(Player).ViewportClient.GetViewportSize(ViewportSize);

              if (FreeLookZone != none)
              {
                  FreeLookZone.OnProcessInputDelegate = SwipeZoneCallback;
              }
          }
    }
}
function PlayerTick(float DeltaTime)
{
    Super.PlayerTick(DeltaTime);
    if (!BotSpawned)
    {
        SpawnBot(FindSpawnPadLocation());
        BotSpawned = true;

        Jazz3Pawn(Pawn).InitialLocation = Pawn.Location;
        Jazz3Pawn(Pawn).Lives = 3;
    }
    If (Jazz3Pawn(Pawn).Lives <= 0)
    {
        GameoVer = true;
    }
    if (GameOver)
    {
        Pawn.SetHidden(true);
        Pawn.Weapon.SetHidden(true);
        Pawn.Velocity = vect(0,0,0);
    }
}
defaultproperties
{
    GameOver = false;
    BotSpawned = false;
}
```

> **NOTE:** The number of enemy bots in a level is one of the key gameplay elements. In this class you can modify the code so that additional enemy bots could be added to your level if needed to help you get the right game difficulty and game balance.

Weapon

The player's weapon has already been created in the Sound Cues section. See Listing 6-1 in the preceding chapter that covers the JazzWeaponSound class.

> **NOTE:** In terms of good gameplay the characteristics of the weapons used and projectiles used are extremely important. The most important property in the Weapon class in relation to game difficulty is the FireInterval variable that controls the delay between shots in seconds. Set this variable to make the player's weapon fire at a faster or slower rate.

Weapon Projectile

The player's weapon projectile class JazzBulletSound was created previously in the Sound Cues sections. See Listing 6-2.

> **NOTE:** In terms of the weapon's projectile the most important properties related to good gameplay are the projectile's speed and the amount of damage it does to the object it hits. Slower projectiles might be avoided especially if fired from a long distance. Projectiles that do small amounts of damage might not be effective against enemies that can heal themselves quickly for example.

Creating the Enemy Bot's Code

Next, we need to create the code for the enemy bot which involves the bot's pawn, controller, weapon, weapon projectile, and spawn pad.

Pawn

The code for the bot's pawn is in Listing 7–4. The pawn for the enemy bot is similar in structure to previous pawns.

The TakeDamage() function processes damage done to the enemy bot. The AddDefaultInventory() function creates the enemy bot's weapons, adds it into the bot's inventory and initialized it. The AddGunToSocket() function then physically attaches the bot's weapon's 3d mesh to the actual bot pawn so that it appears the enemy bot is holding the weapon.

Listing 7–4. *Enemy Bot's Pawn*

```
class BotPawn2 extends SimplePawn;

var Inventory MainGun;
var SoundCue JazzHitSound;
var vector InitialLocation;

var int KillValue;

event TakeDamage(int Damage, Controller InstigatedBy, vector HitLocation, vector
Momentum, class<DamageType> DamageType, optional TraceHitInfo HitInfo, optional Actor
DamageCauser)
```

```
    {
        PlaySound(JazzHitSound);
        Health = Health - Damage;
        WorldInfo.Game.Broadcast(self,self @ " Has Taken Damage IN TAKEDAMAGE, HEALTH = " @
Health);

        if (Health <= 0)
        {
            SetLocation(InitialLocation);
            SetPhysics(PHYS_Falling);
            Health = 100;

            // Process Kill
            if (PlayerController(InstigatedBy) != None)
            {
                // Add kill to Player's Score
                ExampleCh7PC(InstigatedBy).Score += KillValue;
            }
        }
    }
    function AddGunToSocket(Name SocketName)
    {
        local Vector SocketLocation;
        local Rotator SocketRotation;

        if (Mesh != None)
        {
            if (Mesh.GetSocketByName(SocketName) != None)
            {
                Mesh.GetSocketWorldLocationAndRotation(SocketName, SocketLocation,
SocketRotation);
                MainGun.SetRotation(SocketRotation);
                MainGun.SetBase(Self,, Mesh, SocketName);
            }
            else
            {
                WorldInfo.Game.Broadcast(self,"!!!!!!SOCKET NAME NOT FOUND!!!!!");
            }
        }
        else
        {
            WorldInfo.Game.Broadcast(self,"!!!!!!MESH NOT FOUND!!!!!");
        }
    }
    function AddDefaultInventory()
    {
        MainGun = InvManager.CreateInventory(class'JazzWeapon2Damage');
        MainGun.SetHidden(false);
        AddGunToSocket('Weapon_R');
        Weapon(MainGun).FireOffset = vect(0,13,-70);
    }

    defaultproperties
    {
        // Jazz Mesh Object
        Begin Object Class=SkeletalMeshComponent Name=JazzMesh
            SkeletalMesh=SkeletalMesh'KismetGame_Assets.Anims.SK_Jazz'
```

```
        AnimSets(0)=AnimSet'KismetGame_Assets.Anims.SK_Jazz_Anims'
        AnimTreeTemplate=AnimTree'KismetGame_Assets.Anims.Jazz_AnimTree'
        BlockRigidBody=true
        CollideActors=true
    End Object
    Mesh = JazzMesh;
    Components.Add(JazzMesh);

    // Collision Component for This actor
    Begin Object Class=CylinderComponent NAME=CollisionCylinder2
        CollideActors=true
        CollisionRadius=+25.000000
        CollisionHeight=+60.000000 //Nav Mesh
    End Object
    CollisionComponent=CollisionCylinder2
    CylinderComponent=CollisionCylinder2
    Components.Add(CollisionCylinder2)

    JazzHitSound = SoundCue'KismetGame_Assets.Sounds.Jazz_Death_Cue'
    InventoryManagerClass=class'WeaponsIM1'

    KillValue = 50;
}
```

The KillValue is the value that is added to the player's score when the pawn is killed. The TakeDamage() function adds the KillValue to the player's score if the pawn's health is zero or less.

> **NOTE:** The value of various enemies is another factor in creating good gameplay. Enemies that are harder to kill should be worth more points than enemies that are easier to kill. Enemies that are key to achieving some critical game objective should also be worth more points than enemies that are not related to any major objective.

Controller

Next, we need to create a new class for the bot's controller which is called BotControllerAttack. See Listing 7–5. The controller for our enemy bot is built upon the code for the bot that followed the player in Chapter 5.

The ExecuteWhatToDoNext() function is the main entry point for the enemy bot's AI decision making. The bot starts out in the Initial state and transitions to the FollowTarget state where the bot follows the player then to the Firing state where the enemy bot fires its weapon at the player. While in the FollowTarget state the bot uses the navigation mesh method of path finding to determine a path to the player. The GeneratePathTo() function generates the actual path using the navigation mesh and stores it in the NavigationHandle variable.

Listing 7–5. *Enemy Bot Controller*

```
class BotControllerAttack extends UDKBot;

var Actor CurrentGoal;
var Vector TempDest;
var float FollowDistance;
var Actor TempGoal;

event bool GeneratePathTo(Actor Goal, optional float WithinDistance, optional bool
bAllowPartialPath)
{
    if( NavigationHandle == None )
    return FALSE;

    // Clear cache and constraints (ignore recycling for the moment)
    NavigationHandle.PathConstraintList = none;
    NavigationHandle.PathGoalList = none;

    class'NavMeshPath_Toward'.static.TowardGoal( NavigationHandle, Goal );
    class'NavMeshGoal_At'.static.AtActor( NavigationHandle, Goal, WithinDistance,
bAllowPartialPath );

    return NavigationHandle.FindPath();
}
state FollowTarget
{
    Begin:
    WorldInfo.Game.Broadcast(self,"BotController-USING NAVMESH FOR FOLLOWTARGET STATE");
    // Move Bot to Target
    if (CurrentGoal != None)
    {
        if(GeneratePathTo(CurrentGoal))
        {
            NavigationHandle.SetFinalDestination(CurrentGoal.Location);

            if( NavigationHandle.ActorReachable(CurrentGoal) )
            {
                // then move directly to the actor
                MoveTo(CurrentGoal.Location, CurrentGoal,FollowDistance);
                GotoState('Firing', 'Begin');
            }
            else
            {
                // move to the first node on the path
                if( NavigationHandle.GetNextMoveLocation(TempDest,
Pawn.GetCollisionRadius()) )
                {
                    // suggest move preparation will return TRUE when the edge's
                    // logic is getting the bot to the edge point
                    // FALSE if we should run there ourselves
                    if (!NavigationHandle.SuggestMovePreparation(TempDest,self))
                    {
                        MoveTo(TempDest);
                    }
                }
            }
        }
    }
```

```
          else
          {
               //give up because the nav mesh failed to find a path
               `warn("FindNavMeshPath failed to find a path!");
               WorldInfo.Game.Broadcast(self,"FindNavMeshPath failed to find a path!,
CurrentGoal = " @ CurrentGoal);
               MoveTo(Pawn.Location);
          }
     }
     LatentWhatToDoNext();
}
state Firing
{
     Begin:
     WorldInfo.Game.Broadcast(self,"BotController-IN Firing State");
     Sleep(3);
     Pawn.StartFire(0);
     Sleep(0.5);
     LatentWhatToDoNext();
}
auto state Initial
{
     Begin:
     LatentWhatToDoNext();
}
event WhatToDoNext()
{
     DecisionComponent.bTriggered = true;
}
protected event ExecuteWhatToDoNext()
{
     if (IsInState('Initial'))
     {
          GotoState('FollowTarget', 'Begin');
     }
     else
     if (IsInState('Firing'))
     {
          Pawn.StopFire(0);
          GotoState('FollowTarget', 'Begin');
     }
     else
     {
          GotoState('FollowTarget', 'Begin');
     }
}
defaultproperties
{
     CurrentGoal = None;
     FollowDistance = 700;
}
```

The key difference between this class and the Bot controller class from the chapter on
UDK bots is the addition of the Firing state. The bot's pawn is given the command to
start firing its weapon in this state. In the previous chapter the bot just followed the
player around the level.

Now, the bot's behavior is to:

1. Move toward the player.

2. Stop and wait 3 seconds by suspending the state execution using the Sleep() function.

3. Fire the weapon at the player for a half a second

4. Go to step 1.

> **NOTE:** In terms of good gameplay the exact behavior of the bot concerning such things as how frequently it fires it weapon, does it seek cover from player fire, does it try to get a health powerup when its health is low, and other behaviors will affect the game difficulty and game balance. You can change these behaviors in this class by modifying the existing code framework.

Weapon

The weapon for the enemy bot is the JazzWeapon2Damage class which is already defined from Chapter 5. See Listing 5-13.

> **NOTE:** The issues regarding the bot's weapon characteristics and weapon projectile characteristics with respect to gameplay are similar to those of the player's weapon and weapon projectile discussed previously.

Weapon Projectile

The enemy bot's weapon's projectile is the JazzBullet2Damage class which we created previously in Chapter 5. See Listing 5-14.

SpawnPad

Next, we need to create the class that represents the enemy bot's spawn pad where new enemy bots are created and placed. See Listing 7–6.

> **NOTE:** The number and location of enemy bot spawn pads are also a factor in gameplay. You can expand on the existing game framework presented in this chapter by for example creating more spawn pads in different locations and modifying existing code to create many enemy bots attacking the player instead of just one enemy bot.

Listing 7–6. *Spawn Pad for the enemy Bot*

```
class SpawnPad extends Actor
placeable;

event Touch(Actor Other, PrimitiveComponent OtherComp, vector HitLocation, vector
HitNormal)
{
    WorldInfo.Game.Broadcast(self,"SpawnPad Has Been Touched");
}
defaultproperties
{
    Begin Object Class=StaticMeshComponent Name=StaticMeshComponent0
        StaticMesh=StaticMesh'HU_Deco.SM.Mesh.S_HU_Deco_SM_Metalbase01'
        Scale3D=(X=0.250000,Y=0.250000,Z=0.25000)
    End Object
    Components.Add(StaticMeshComponent0)

    Begin Object Class=CylinderComponent NAME=CollisionCylinder
        CollideActors=true
        CollisionRadius=+0040.000000
        CollisionHeight=+0040.000000
    End Object
    CollisionComponent=CollisionCylinder
    Components.Add(CollisionCylinder)

    bCollideActors=true
}
```

Creating the HUD Display

The custom HUD display was created in the HUD section in Chapter 6 as the ExtendedHUD class. You can use this same class for our example. See Listing 6-3.

Configuring the Game Type

Next, you need to configure your Unreal Script for compilation and the new game type to run on the mobile previewer. In your configuration files located at C:\UDK\UDK-2011-06\UDKGame\Config change the following configuration files.

For the UDKEngine.ini file make the following changes:

```
[UnrealEd.EditorEngine]
ModEditPackages=ExampleCh7
```

For the Mobile-UDKGame.ini file make the following changes:

```
[ExampleCh7.ExampleCh7Game]
RequiredMobileInputConfigs=(GroupName="UberGroup",RequireZoneNames=("UberStickMoveZone",
"UberStickLookZone","UberLookZone"))
```

Bring up the Unreal Frontend and compile your scripts.

NOTE: This sets up the dual virtual joysticks and the ability to process touch input for the rest of the screen. In terms of gameplay the final game should be play tested on an actual iOS device not just the mobile previewer. The reason is that the iOS device can handle multiple touches at one time where you can control both the movement and rotation of your pawn at the same time. In the mobile previewer you are limited to one touch at a time through the mouse. The differing user interfaces would affect the gameplay.

Setting up the Spawn Pad

Now, you need to place the spawn pad in your level.

1. Start up the Unreal Editor.

2. Load in the level you saved at the beginning of this exercise. A good place to put it would be behind the gates in an open area.

3. Go to the Actor Classes tab and search for **Spawnpad**. This should bring up that class in the viewing pane. Click on the class.

4. Right-click on the level where you wish to place the pad and select Add SpawnPad here. Save the level (see Figure 7–2).

Figure 7–2. *Creating the enemy bot's spawnpad*

Running the Game

Finally, it's time to run this new game on the Mobile Previewer.

1. Bring up the World Properties window by selecting **View ➤ World
    Properties** from the Unreal Editor menu.

2. Change the Default Game Type property under the Game Type category
    to ExampleCh7Game.

3. Run the game on the Mobile Previewer by selecting **Play ➤ On Mobile
    Previewer** from the main Unreal Editor menu. You should see something
    similar to Figures 7–3 and 7–4.

A quick rundown of some gameplay elements shown in this example are:

- Enemy bot behavior (Artificial Intelligence)

- Enemy bot weapon and projectiles

- Player weapon and projectiles

- Level design

As you test your game, you can adjust these elements until you get the right user
experience.

For example, note the behavior of the enemy bot. The general behavior of the enemy bot
is move toward the player so that the player is directly reachable to the enemy bot (no
obstructions), wait for a time period, and then fire at the player. This cycle then repeats.
Let's see how this appears in the game itself.

When the game first comes up in the mobile previewer, wait until the enemy bot comes
around the corner of the block and stops. See Figure 7–3.

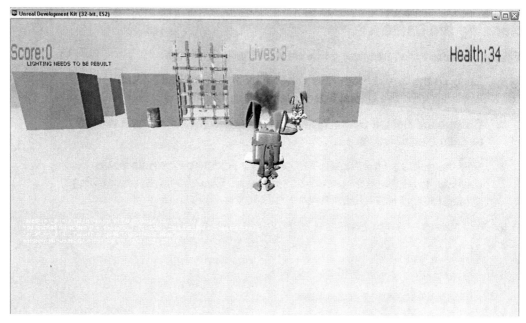

Figure 7–3. *At the Gates*

After three seconds, the enemy bot starts firing at the player. In terms of gameplay, here you can change the delay time between the enemy bot stopping and starting to fire to change the game difficulty as well as the game balance.

Next, try moving farther into the area with the large blocks. Move in between the blocks so that they obstruct the path directly to the enemy bot. The bot should follow you and move around these obstacles in order to get a clear shot at you. Once the enemy bot moves into a position where it gets a clear shot at you it stops again. (See Figure 7–4.) It then waits for three seconds and then fires its weapon at you. Here level design can affect gameplay by affecting game difficulty. Basically the player is exposed to enemy fire at the corners of each of the blocks where the enemy bot can get a clear shot at the player. If the blocks were longer or wider, for example, it would take more time for the bot to move into a good position to shoot at the player thus affecting game difficulty and gameplay generally since the enemy cannot jump over the blocks to get at the player.

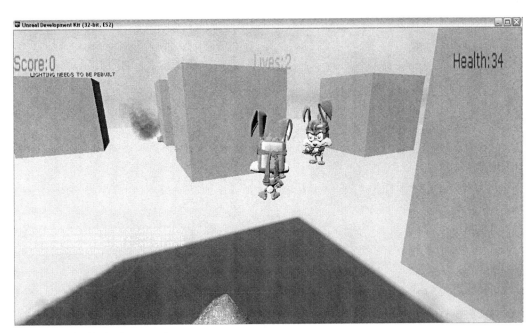

Figure 7-4. *Inside the Compound*

Summary

In this chapter we covered the elements of gameplay. First we gave background information on the elements that affect the quality of gameplay which are game difficulty and game balance. Then, we presented a hands-on example where we created a small game that incorporated Sound Cues, a custom HUD, a moving locked gate, and a custom enemy bot that follows and attacks the player. In the hands-on example important gameplay elements are highlighted and suggestions are given on how you could adjust the game difficulty and game balance of these elements in order to create superior gameplay.

Chapter 8

3D Math Review

In this chapter we will review some basic 3D math concepts needed to fully understand the hands-on examples presented in the other chapters, including the frameworks that follow.

Understanding 3D math is needed for such things as positioning objects such as a camera in a 3D world, applying forces to objects, finding distances in between two objects, and finding if a cover node protects an actor hiding behind it from enemy fire. In general anything that deals with positioning an object, motion (which is nothing more than positioning an object in different locations at certain time intervals), or with measuring angles in a 3D world will require some knowledge of 3D math.

In this chapter you will learn about:

- Vector addition
- Vector multiplication
- Dot products
- Cross products
- Cover nodes that protect an actor from the enemy.
- Third-person camera positioning
- Deriving the direction vector for kicking objects at an arbitrary angle

Vectors

Vectors are essential to understanding 3D math. Vectors are quantities that have a magnitude and a direction. Vectors can represent quantities like forces that are applied to objects or represent the location of objects in the game world. Vectors can also represent location, velocity, or acceleration of objects in the game world.

Scalars, by contrast, are quantities that just have magnitude, like a speed 55 miles per hour, for example. A velocity vector would have both magnitude and direction, such as 55 miles per hour in a northwest direction.

Direction with respect to vectors is indicated by an arrow. Magnitude can be shown graphically by the length of this arrow.

Some properties of vectors are that they:

■ Can be added together to produce a resultant vector that represents the net direction and magnitude of the vectors that are added.

■ Can be multiplied by a scalar to change the magnitude of a vector but not the direction.

■ Are used in dot products and cross products to find the angle between two vectors and to find a vector that is perpendicular to a pair of vectors.

You can visualize vectors as arrows that indicate direction and that have a length or magnitude like in Figure 8–1. This represents vectors on a 2D plane.

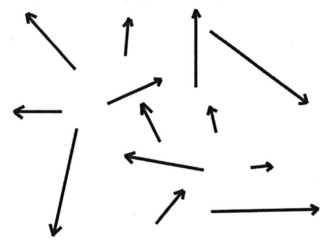

Figure 8–1. *Vectors represented as arrows with magnitude and direction on a 2D plane*

To visualize vectors within the Unreal 3D game world a better picture would be like in Figure 8–2.

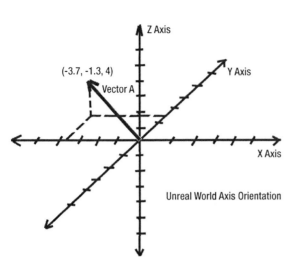

Figure 8–2. *A vector in the 3D Unreal world coordinate system*

In the Unreal world the X and Y axes represent the ground plane and the Z axis points upward toward the sky. As you can see from Figure 8–2 a vector is defined by two or three numbers in the form (X, Y, Z) depending if the vector is a 2D vector or a 3D vector.

The X, Y, and Z values represent the location of the head of the vector's arrow on the X, Y, and Z axes. For example, the Vector A in Figure 8–2 would be defined as –3.7 units on the X axis, -1.3 units on the Y axis, and 4 units on the Z axis. Based on these values we know the direction the vector is pointing. From these values we can also find the magnitude of this vector.

Vector Magnitude

The standard formula for finding the length or magnitude of a vector is as shown in Figure 8–3.

$$\|A\| = \sqrt{A_x^2 + A_y^2 + A_z^2}$$

Figure 8–3. *Finding the length of a vector*

The above formula states that the length of vector A is the square root of the sum of the squares of each component of vector A. The components of A being the X, Y, and Z values of the vector which are (Ax, Ay, Az). The ||A|| notation indicates the *absolute* value of A, which means the result is always a positive number.

Using Vector A in Figure 8–2 as an example, Ax would be –3.7, Ay would be -1.3, and Az would be 4. Each of these terms would be squared and then added together. Then the square root would be taken from the sum, and the result would be the magnitude of Vector A.

MagA = SquareRoot((-3.7 * -3.7) + (-1.3 * -1.3) + (4 * 4))

MagA = SquareRoot(13.69 + 1.69 + 16)

MagA = SquareRoot(31.38)

MagA = 5.60

You can do the above in an UnrealScript class function as:

```
local vector VectorA;
local float Length;
VectorA = vect(-3.7, -1.3, 4);
```

In UnrealScript there is a built in function to perform this operation which is the VSize() function. So in order to get the length of Vector A, you would just send Vector A as in input parameter like this:

```
Length = VSize(VectorA);
```

The Length variable would now contain the magnitude of Vector A.

Rotator to Vector Conversion

An Actor's rotation in the UDK game world is defined by a rotator which is a structure defined in the Object class.

```
struct immutable Rotator
{
    var() int Pitch, Yaw, Roll;
};
```

The pitch, yaw, and roll define an object's rotation around the X, Z, and Y axes.

You use the SetRotation() function to change the rotation of the Actor. The variable Rotation in the Actor class holds the object's rotation values in a Rotator structure.

For example to set an Actor to a state where it is not rotated you would use the following code in that Actor's class:

```
function ResetRotation()
{
    local Rotator TempRot;

    TempRot.pitch = 0;
    TempRot.yaw = 0;
    TempRot.Roll = 0;
    SetRotation(TempRot);
}
```

Since we are using the UDK, rotations are handled by the UDK graphics engine and we don't have to do any more work besides setting the rotation using SetRotation(). Without the UDK, we would need to rotate each object using matrix multiplication to get the desired rotation in the X, Y, and Z axes.

NOTE: If you are interested in the non UDK method of using matrices to transform and rotate objects then check out *3D Computer Graphics*, Third Edition, by Alan Watt.

In UnrealScript there is an easy way to convert the rotation of an object to a vector value that points in the direction the front of the object is facing. For example, to get a vector that points in the direction the player's pawn is facing you would do the following:

```
PawnFrontVector = Vector(Pawn.Rotation);
```

You would use this in your player controller class.

Normalizing Vectors

Normalized vectors are vectors of length 1 and are also called unit vectors. The importance of normalized vectors is that you can isolate the direction of the vector from the magnitude. That is, once you find the unit vector that indicates direction, then you can make this vector have any magnitude you want by multiplying the desired magnitude by the unit vector. Figure 8–4 shows the formula used for normalizing a vector.

Vector V = (Vx, Vy, Vz)

$$\text{Normalized V} = \left(\frac{Vx}{\|V\|}, \frac{Vy}{\|V\|}, \frac{Vz}{\|V\|} \right)$$

Figure 8–4. *Calculating Normal Vectors*

You normalize a vector by dividing each vector component by the magnitude of the original vector.

In UnrealScript there is a built in function called `Normal()` to perform this calculation. For example, the following would normalize vector V and return the new vector.

```
NormalizedV = Normal(V);
```

Vector Addition

Two vectors can be added by adding each of the components of the vectors. For example, two vectors A and B can be added together by adding the X, Y, and Z components of each vector.

```
ResultantVector = (Ax + Bx, Ay + By, Az + Bz);
```

For example, vector A is (1,0,0) which is a normal vector that points along the X axis, and vector B is (0,0,1) which is a normal vector that points upward along the Z axis. The resultant vector would be:

```
ResultantVector = (1 + 0, 0 + 0, 0 + 1)
```

```
ResultantVector = (1,0,1)
```

You can also add vectors graphically. However, this is not recommended as it gets complex quickly when dealing with many vectors.

Graphically, adding a group of vectors would look as in Figure 8–5.

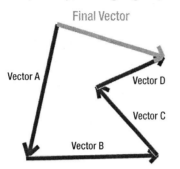

Figure 8–5. *Adding Vectors*

In order to add vectors together graphically you need to put them together head to tail. The resultant vector is the vector from the tail of the beginning vector to the head of the ending vector. Figure 8–5 illustrates how Vectors A, B, C, and D can be added together to get a final vector that is the net result of all the vectors combined.

It is much easier to add multiple vectors numerically. For example to add four vectors:

Vector A = (1,0,0)

Vector B = (0,0,1)

Vector C = (0,1,0)

Vector D = (1,1,1)

ResultantVector = (2,2,2)

In UnrealScript, you don't need to add the components but just add the vectors themselves as follows:

```
var vector VectorA,VectorB,VectorC,VectorD;
var vector ResultantVector;
VectorA = vect(1,0,0);
VectorB = vect(0,0,1);
VectorC = vect(0,1,0);
VectorD = vect(1,1,1);
ResultantVector = VectorA + VectorB + VectorC + VectorD;
```

Scalar Multiplication

A scalar value is a quantity that has only a magnitude and no direction, such as a number representing things like the speed of an object. A vector can be multiplied by a scalar value by multiplying each vector component by the scalar.

For example, assume we have a unit vector B that is pointing along the x axis:

Vector B = (1,0,0)

We want to multiply this vector by scalar S which is 10. The resulting vector would be:

Resultant Vector = (1 * 10, 0 * 10, 0 * 10)

Resultant Vector = (10,0,0)

A unit vector can be multiplied by a scalar so that the resulting vector is of length scalar. See Figure 8–6.

Unit Vector   Scalar Multiplier S

Figure 8–6. *Unit vector being scaled by a scalar*

The resulting vector is the same direction as the unit vector but the length has been changed to the value of S.

An example of where this would be useful is when you want to apply a certain amount of force to an object in a certain direction. You would make the direction vector into a unit vector of length 1, and then you would multiply the unit vector times the amount of force you want to apply to the object. The resulting vector is the force vector that includes the direction and amount of force to apply to the object. In the above example, Vector B would represent the unit direction vector and the scalar value S which is 10 would represent the force. The resultant vector represents a force of 10 along the x axis.

You can also change the direction of a vector to point in the opposite direction by multiplying it by a scalar value of –1. See Figure 8–7.

Figure 8–7. *Changing the direction of a vector*

For example, you want to find a vector that represents the back side of the player's pawn. In order to do this you would multiply the vector representing the front of the player's pawn by –1 to get a vector that points in the opposite direction.

Unit Circle

In order to understand fundamental trigonometry functions like sine and cosine you need to understand the unit circle. See Figure 8–8.

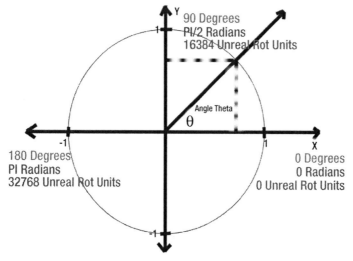

Figure 8–8. *The Unit Circle with an angle Theta shown*

A unit circle is a circle of radius of length 1 and is used to illustrate how cosine and sine values are derived. Understanding how cosine and sine values are derived from the unit circle is important since cosine and sine functions are involved in so many key things like vectors, dot products, and trigonometric identities that are needed to program games in a 3D world. The x axis of the unit circle defines cosine values which range from −1 to 1. The y axis defines sine values which also range from −1 to 1. An angle that is defined by Θ (theta) can range from 0 to 360 degrees.

> **NOTE:** Rotation angles in the UDK are measured in Unreal Rotation Units. For example, the value of PI is 32768 Unreal Rotation Units. The value UnrRotToRad is defined in the Object.uc file and is used to convert Unreal Rotation Units to Radians.

Sine and cosine values are determined by the angle's intersection with the unit circle. For example, at 0 degrees the cosine value is 1 and the sine value is 0. At 90 degrees the cosine value is 0 and the sine value is 1. At 180 degrees the cosine value is −1 and the sine value is 0.

Right Triangle

The right triangle is important because it is used in several important trigonometric identities. See Figure 8–9.

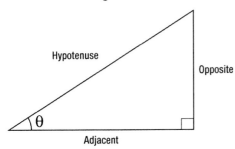

Figure 8–9. *The right triangle*

Key trigonometric identities are:

- Sin(ϴ) = Opposite/Hypotenuse

- Cos(ϴ) = Adjacent/Hypotenuse

And

- Hypotenuse * Sin(ϴ) = Opposite

- Hypotenuse * Cos(ϴ) = Adjacent

The above identities are useful when trying to break a vector into its components. For example, imagine you kick an object that has a velocity vector that is 20 ft/s and makes an angle with the ground of 45 degrees. Let's assume you want to find the horizontal speed of the ball along the ground. The velocity vector can be considered the hypotenuse of a right triangle and the ground would be the adjacent side of the triangle:

Adjacent = Hypotenuse * cos(45)

VelocityGround = VelocityTotal * cos(45)

VelocityGround = 20 * cos(45) = 14.14

Dot Product

Imagine two vectors with an angle theta between them as in Figure 8–10.

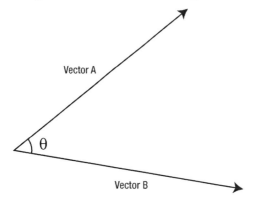

Figure 8–10. *Two vectors with an angle theta*

The definition of the dot product is given in Figure 8–11.

A dot B = ‖A‖ ‖B‖cos(θ)

Figure 8–11. *Dot Product definition*

The dot product of two vectors is equal to the magnitude of vector A multiplied by the magnitude of vector B multiplied by the cosine of the angle between the two vectors.

To find the angle between the two vectors from the dot product you would use the formula in Figure 8–12.

$$\theta = \arccos\left(\frac{A \text{ dot } B}{\|A\| \ \|B\|}\right)$$

Figure 8–12. *Finding an angle from the dot product of two vectors*

The angle between objects in the 3D game world can be an important factor. One example is displaying information about important game objects only when they are in the view of the player. To do this you would only display information onscreen when these objects are within a certain angle with respect to the front of the player's pawn. One vector would be the one from the player to the object you are testing. The other vector would be the one pointing outward from the front of the player's pawn. You can then find the angle between these vectors using the equation in Figure 8–12. If the angle is within a certain range then you can display information about this object on screen.

In UnrealScript there is a built in dot function to perform the dot product between two vectors. For example, the following code finds the angle in degrees between two vectors assuming the two vectors have already been normalized.

```
AngleDegrees = acos(SlotNormal Dot DirectionToThreat) * RadToDeg;
```

A dot product can also be used to project a vector onto a unit vector as shown in Figure 8–13.

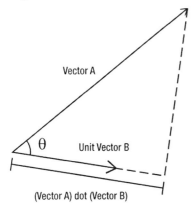

Figure 8–13. *Dot product projection onto a unit vector*

Note in the figure that using the dot product to project an arbitrary vector on a unit vector is basically another way of finding out the value of the Adjacent side of a right triangle. The Adjacent side of the triangle would be the one with the unit vector.

Cross Product

The cross product between two vectors generates a vector that is perpendicular to both vectors. See Figure 8–14.

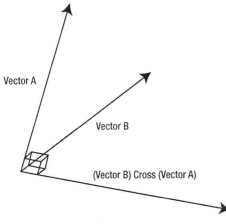

Figure 8–14. *Cross Product*

The cross product comes in handy when trying to find a vector to the left and right side of an Actor. For example, an enemy bot is hiding in cover and you want it to move sideways out of cover and fire at the player and then move back into cover. In order to do this you will need to find a vector that is perpendicular to both the bot's pawn front vector and the game world's up vector which would be the same as the positive Z axis. To do this you would take the cross product of these two vectors.

In UnrealScript there is a built in cross operator that calculates the cross product of two vectors. For example, the code below generates a perpendicular vector to the two input vectors using the cross operator.

```
RightVec = FrontVec cross vect(0,0,1);
```

Cover Nodes

A good applied example that uses vectors, angles, dot products, and trigonometric functions like sine and cosine is an example that involves creating cover nodes. In this section we will give an overview of cover nodes and a hands-on example that demonstrates their use in the Unreal world.

Cover Node Overview

A cover node is an area designated by the user that can provide protection or cover to a player or a computer-controlled bot from enemy fire. The cover node is implemented in the UDK in the class CoverLink. See Figure 8–15.

Figure 8–15. *The UDK Cover Link (green and black image on the right) and Cover Slot (red block)*

The cover node in the UDK consists of the actual node which is represented by a circular image with a picture of a man in the center and one or more cover slots. The cover slots are represented by a red block with an arrow pointing outward representing the cover slot's normal or perpendicular vector. For the examples in this book we assume a cover node has only 1 cover slot. Multiple cover slots per cover node are supported by the UDK; however, for simplicity we assume only 1 cover slot per cover node.

The general idea is that the cover slot be placed against an object that will serve as the cover with the cover slot's normal vector pointing toward the cover object. See Figure 8–16.

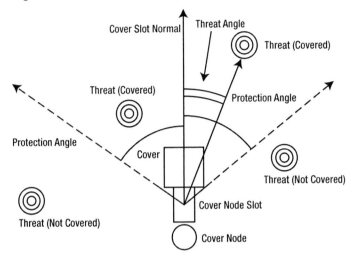

Figure 8–16. *New Custom Cover Node System*

In Figure 8–16 we have the cover node and a cover slot. The cover slot is placed against an object that will serve as cover from enemy fire. The cover slot's normal vector is oriented so that it faces the cover. The threat angle on the figure is the angle between the cover slot normal vector and the vector that goes from the cover node slot to the threat.

In addition, we have something new not in the default CoverLink class in the UDK base code. The cover protection angle is a new value that we have added to the new cover node class CoverLinkEx. This new class that is derived from the CoverLink class will be created in the hands-on example that follows this section. The cover protection angle is a value specified by the user which defaults to 45 degrees and measures from the cover slot normal to both the right and left sides of the normal.

A threat is covered if it is in the area between the two vectors that represent the cover protection angle. That is, the threat angle is less than the cover protection angle.

Hands-on Example: Cover Nodes

In this example we will be creating the new cover node class mentioned previously and showing it off in a demo where multiple bots take cover from the player who is considered by the bots to be the threat to take cover from. First we will create the new game type for this demo. Then, we will create the player controller, the bot's controller, the bot's pawn, and then the new cover node class. We will need to compile the code first so that the new cover node class is put into the UDK system before we start creating our new level that uses this new cover node class.

Creating the Game Type

We need to create a new directory under our source directory located at:

`C:\UDK\UDK-2011-06\Development\Src`

for the June 2011 version of the UDK. If you are using a different version of the UDK then the above default directory will be different. Under the above directory create the folder ExampleCh8. Under that directory create the Classes directory. You will be putting all your source code for this hands-on example in this Classes directory.

The new game type that you will need to create is in Listing 8–1.

Listing 8–1. *Game Type*

```
class ExampleCh8Game extends FrameworkGame;

event OnEngineHasLoaded()
{
    WorldInfo.Game.Broadcast(self,"ExampleCh8Game Type Active - Engine Has Loaded
!!!!");
}

function bool PreventDeath(Pawn KilledPawn, Controller Killer, class<DamageType>
DamageType, vector HitLocation)
{
    return true;
}
static event class<GameInfo> SetGameType(string MapName, string Options, string Portal)
{
    return super.SetGameType(MapName, Options, Portal);
}
defaultproperties
{
    PlayerControllerClass=class'ExampleCh8.ExampleCh8PC'
    DefaultPawnClass=class'JazzPawnDamage'
    HUDType=class'UDKBase.UDKHUD'

    bRestartLevel=false
    bWaitingToStartMatch=true
    bDelayedStart=false
}
```

The `PlayerControllerClass` variable points to our new custom player controller for this example.

Creating the Player Controller

Next, you will need to create the new player controller class shown in Listing 8–2. This code should be familiar from earlier chapters. The important changes are set in bold.

Listing 8–2. *Player Controller*

```
class ExampleCh8PC extends SimplePC;

var Controller FollowBot;
Var Pawn FollowPawn;
var bool BotSpawned;
var Actor BotTarget;
var float PickDistance;

function Actor PickActor(Vector2D PickLocation, out Vector HitLocation, out TraceHitInfo
HitInfo)
{
    local Vector TouchOrigin, TouchDir;
    local Vector HitNormal;
    local Actor  PickedActor;
    local vector Extent;

    //Transform absolute screen coordinates to relative coordinates
    PickLocation.X = PickLocation.X / ViewportSize.X;
    PickLocation.Y = PickLocation.Y / ViewportSize.Y;

    //Transform to world coordinates to get pick ray
    LocalPlayer(Player).Deproject(PickLocation, TouchOrigin, TouchDir);

    //Perform trace to find touched actor
    Extent = vect(0,0,0);
    PickedActor = Trace(HitLocation,
                        HitNormal,
                        TouchOrigin + (TouchDir * PickDistance),
                        TouchOrigin,
                        True,
                        Extent,
                        HitInfo);
    //Return the touched actor for good measure
    return PickedActor;
}
function SpawnBot(Vector SpawnLocation, optional Vector Offset)
{
    SpawnLocation = SpawnLocation + Offset;
    FollowBot = Spawn(class'BotCoverController',,,SpawnLocation);
    FollowPawn = Spawn(class'BotCoverPawn',,,SpawnLocation);
    FollowBot.Possess(FollowPawn,false);
    BotCoverController(FollowBot).BotThreat = Pawn;
    BotCoverpawn(FollowPawn).AddDefaultInventory();
    BotCoverPawn(Followpawn).InitialLocation = SpawnLocation;
    FollowPawn.SetPhysics(PHYS_Falling);
}
function bool SwipeZoneCallback(MobileInputZone Zone,
                                float DeltaTime,
                                int Handle,
                                EZoneTouchEvent EventType,
                                Vector2D TouchLocation)
{
    local bool retval;
    retval = true;
    if (EventType == ZoneEvent_Touch)
```

```
        {
            WorldInfo.Game.Broadcast(self,"You touched the screen at = " @
                                    TouchLocation.x @ " , " @ TouchLocation.y @
                                    ", Zone Touched = " @ Zone);
            // Start Firing pawn's weapon
            StartFire(0);
        }
        else
        if(EventType == ZoneEvent_Update)
        {
        }
        else
        if (EventType == ZoneEvent_UnTouch)
        {
            // Stop Firing Pawn's weapon
            StopFire(0);
        }
        return retval;
    }
    function SetupZones()
    {
        Super.SetupZones();
        // If we have a game class, configure the zones
        if (MPI != None && WorldInfo.GRI.GameClass != none)
        {
            LocalPlayer(Player).ViewportClient.GetViewportSize(ViewportSize);
            if (FreeLookZone != none)
            {
                FreeLookZone.OnProcessInputDelegate = SwipeZoneCallback;
            }
        }
    }
    function PlayerTick(float DeltaTime)
    {
        Super.PlayerTick(DeltaTime);
        if (!BotSpawned)
        {
            SpawnBot(Pawn.Location,vect(0,0,500));
            SpawnBot(Pawn.Location,vect(0,0,1000));
            SpawnBot(Pawn.Location,vect(0,0,1500));
            SpawnBot(Pawn.Location,vect(0,0,2000));
            SpawnBot(Pawn.Location,vect(0,0,2500));
            BotSpawned = true;
            JazzPawnDamage(Pawn).InitialLocation = Pawn.Location;
        }
    }
    defaultproperties
    {
        BotSpawned=false
        PickDistance = 10000
    }
```

Again, most of this code should look familiar to you from previous chapters. The key changes are in the SpawnBot() function where the bot's controller has been changed to the BotCoverController class and the bot's pawn has been changed to the BotCoverPawn class. The SpawnBot() function has also been modified to accept an offset vector that is added to `SpawnLocation`. The `PlayerTick()` function has been modified to create five bots that will be controlled by the new `BotCoverController` class using the new `SpawnBot()` function.

Creating the Bot's Pawn

Next, you need to create the pawn class for the bot. See Listing 8–3. You will recognize most of this code from previous examples. The line with the important change is set in bold.

Listing 8–3. *Bot Pawn*

```
class BotCoverPawn extends SimplePawn;

var Inventory MainGun;
var SoundCue JazzHitSound;
var vector InitialLocation;

event TakeDamage(int Damage, Controller InstigatedBy, vector HitLocation, vector
Momentum, class<DamageType> DamageType, optional TraceHitInfo HitInfo, optional Actor
DamageCauser)
{
    PlaySound(JazzHitSound);
    Health = Health - Damage;
    WorldInfo.Game.Broadcast(self,self @ " Has Taken Damage IN TAKEDAMAGE, HEALTH = " @
Health);

    if (Health <= 0)
    {
        SetLocation(InitialLocation);
        SetPhysics(PHYS_Falling);
        Health = 100;
    }
}
function AddGunToSocket(Name SocketName)
{
    local Vector SocketLocation;
    local Rotator SocketRotation;
    if (Mesh != None)
    {
        if (Mesh.GetSocketByName(SocketName) != None)
        {
            Mesh.GetSocketWorldLocationAndRotation(SocketName, SocketLocation,
SocketRotation);
            MainGun.SetRotation(SocketRotation);
            MainGun.SetBase(Self,, Mesh, SocketName);
        }
        else
        {
            WorldInfo.Game.Broadcast(self,"!!!!!!SOCKET NAME NOT FOUND!!!!!");
        }
    }
    else
    {
        WorldInfo.Game.Broadcast(self,"!!!!!!MESH NOT FOUND!!!!!");
    }
```

```
}
function AddDefaultInventory()
{
    MainGun = InvManager.CreateInventory(class'JazzWeapon2Damage');
    MainGun.SetHidden(false);
    AddGunToSocket('Weapon_R');
    Weapon(MainGun).FireOffset = vect(0,13,-70);
}
defaultproperties
{
    // Jazz Mesh Object
    Begin Object Class=SkeletalMeshComponent Name=JazzMesh
        SkeletalMesh=SkeletalMesh'KismetGame_Assets.Anims.SK_Jazz'
        AnimSets(0)=AnimSet'KismetGame_Assets.Anims.SK_Jazz_Anims'
        AnimTreeTemplate=AnimTree'KismetGame_Assets.Anims.Jazz_AnimTree'
        BlockRigidBody=true
        CollideActors=true
    End Object
    Mesh = JazzMesh;
    Components.Add(JazzMesh);

    // Collision Component for This actor
    Begin Object Class=CylinderComponent NAME=CollisionCylinder2
        CollideActors=true
        CollisionRadius=+15.000000
        CollisionHeight=+45.000000
    End Object
    CollisionComponent=CollisionCylinder2
    CylinderComponent=CollisionCylinder2
    Components.Add(CollisionCylinder2);

    JazzHitSound = SoundCue'KismetGame_Assets.Sounds.Jazz_Death_Cue'
    InventoryManagerClass=class'WeaponsIM1'
}
```

Most the code in the pawn was presented in previous chapters. The key change from previous versions is that the CollisionRadius is now set to 15 from 25. Refer to Chapter 5 (Figure 5-4) for a visual of a collision radius within a collision cylinder. The reason for this is that the collision radius was too large and was interfering with the movement of the bot around sharp corners of an object such as a box that had cover nodes on all four sides.

Creating the Bot's Controller

Next, we need to create the new controller for the bot. The first piece of code in Listing 8–4 deals with class variables and a function to free occupied slots in the UDK cover system.

The UnclaimAllSlots() function loops through the linked list of cover nodes pointed to by the WorldInfo.Coverlist variable and calls the Unclaim() function on the cover node to mark all the slots of that node as free that are occupied by the bot.

Listing 8–4. *Bot Controller*

```
class BotCoverController extends UDKBot;

// Navigation
var Actor CurrentGoal;
var Vector TempDest;
var Actor TempGoal;

// Cover Link
var CoverLink CurrentCover;
var bool BotInCover;

// Bot's Enemy
var Pawn BotThreat;

function UnclaimAllSlots()
{
    local CoverLink CoverNodePointer;
    local CoverLink TempNodePointer;
    local bool done;

    CoverNodePointer = WorldInfo.Coverlist;

    done = false;
    while (!done)
    {
        CoverNodePointer.Unclaim(Pawn, 0, true);
        if (CoverNodePointer.NextCoverLink != None)
        {
            TempNodePointer = CoverNodePointer.NextCoverLink;
            CoverNodePointer = TempNodePointer;
        }
        else
        {
            done = true;
        }
    }
    Pawn.ShouldCrouch(false);
    BotInCover = false;
}
```

The next piece of code, shown in Listing 8–5, deals with finding available cover nodes.

The FindClosestEmptyCoverNodeWithinRange() loops through all the available cover nodes and picks the cover node that is valid for the threat, available, and closest to the bot. The slot is tested for validity by calling the IsCoverSlotValid() function on the new cover node class object. The slot is tested for availability by calling the IsCoverSlotAvailable() function on the new cover node object.

Listing 8–5. *Finding the closest valid and empty cover node*

```
function CoverLink FindClosestEmptyCoverNodeWithinRange(Vector ThreatLocation, vector
Position, float Radius)
{
    local CoverLink CoverNodePointer;
    local CoverLink TempNodePointer;
    local bool done;
```

```
        local CoverLink ValidCoverNode;
        local bool SlotValid;
        local bool SlotAvailable;
        local bool NodeFound;
        local int DefaultSlot;

        local float Dist2Cover;
        local float ClosestCoverNode;

        CoverNodePointer = WorldInfo.Coverlist;
        DefaultSlot = 0;   // Assume only 1 slot per cover node.
        ClosestCoverNode = 999999999;

        ValidCoverNode = None;
        NodeFound = false;

        done = false;
        while (!done)
        {
            SlotValid = CoverLinkEx(CoverNodePointer).IsCoverSlotValid(0,ThreatLocation);
            SlotAvailable = CoverLinkEx(CoverNodePointer).IsCoverSlotAvailable(0);

            Dist2Cover =  VSize(CoverNodePointer.GetSlotLocation(DefaultSlot) - Position);
            if (SlotValid && SlotAvailable && (Dist2Cover < ClosestCoverNode))
            {
                ValidCoverNode = CoverNodePointer;
                ClosestCoverNode = Dist2Cover;
                NodeFound = true;
            }

            // Goto Next CoverNode
            if (CoverNodePointer.NextCoverLink != None)
            {
                TempNodePointer = CoverNodePointer.NextCoverLink;
                CoverNodePointer = TempNodePointer;
            }
            else
            {
                // No more Cover Nodes
                done = true;
            }
        }
        if (!NodeFound)
        {
            WorldInfo.Game.Broadcast(self,"!!! Can Not Find Valid CoverNode");
        }
        return ValidCoverNode;
}
```

The code in Listing 8–6 determines if the current cover is valid for the current threat. The FindEnemyLocation() returns the current location of the bot's enemy. The IsCurrentCoverValid() function returns true if the current cover node is valid and protects the bot from incoming fire from the enemy. Otherwise the function returns false.

Listing 8–6. *Determining if the current cover is valid*

```
function FindEnemyLocation(out vector EnemyLocation)
{
    EnemyLocation = BotThreat.Location;
}
function bool IsCurrentCoverValid()
{
    local bool RetVal;
    local vector ThreatLoc;

    RetVal = false;
    FindEnemyLocation(ThreatLoc);
    RetVal = CoverLinkEx(CurrentCover).IsCoverSlotValid(0, ThreatLoc);
    return Retval;
}
```

The next segment of code, shown in Listing 8–7, covers the function that is used to prepare the bot to move to another cover.

In the `PrepMoveToCover()` function:

1. The Threat's location is found (the Player's location)

2. The closest available cover node is found using the function `FindClosestEmptyCoverNodeWithinRange()` and returned in the variable `NextCover`.

3. If a cover has been found then the `CurrentCover` variable is set to the `NextCover`. The `CurrentGoal` of the bot is then set to this new cover node. All current cover nodes occupied by this bot are marked as empty. Next, the bot claims the cover node that it will move to which is held in `CurrentCover`.

Listing 8–7. *Preparing to move to a cover node*

```
function PrepMoveToCover()
{
    local vector ThreatLoc;
    local CoverLink NextCover;

    FindEnemyLocation(ThreatLoc);
    NextCover = FindClosestEmptyCoverNodeWithinRange(ThreatLoc, Pawn.Location, 9999999);
    if (NextCover != None)
    {
        WorldInfo.Game.Broadcast(self,"Moving to Next Cover " @ NextCover);
        CurrentCover = NextCover;
        CurrentGoal = CurrentCover;
        BotInCover = false;
        UnclaimAllSlots();
        CurrentCover.Claim(Pawn, 0);
    }
}
```

The code in Listing 8–8 generates the actual path to the goal using the navigation mesh. This function was originally presented in Chapter 5.

Listing 8–8. *GeneratePathTo*

```
event bool GeneratePathTo(Actor Goal, optional float WithinDistance, optional bool
bAllowPartialPath)
{
    if( NavigationHandle == None )
    return FALSE;

    // Clear cache and constraints (ignore recycling for the moment)
    NavigationHandle.PathConstraintList = none;
    NavigationHandle.PathGoalList = none;

    class'NavMeshPath_Toward'.static.TowardGoal( NavigationHandle, Goal );
    class'NavMeshGoal_At'.static.AtActor( NavigationHandle, Goal, WithinDistance,
bAllowPartialPath );

    return NavigationHandle.FindPath();
}
```

Listing 8–9 involves the TakeCover state. The TakeCover state moves the bot to the location of the current covernode as shown in Figure 8–16.

Listing 8–9. *TakeCover State*

```
state TakeCover
{
    Begin:

    //WorldInfo.Game.Broadcast(self,"NAVMESH, CurrentGoal = " @ CurrentGoal @ " ,
BotInCover = " @ BotInCover);

    if (CurrentGoal != None)
    {
        if(GeneratePathTo(CurrentGoal))
        {
            NavigationHandle.SetFinalDestination(CurrentGoal.Location);

            if( NavigationHandle.ActorReachable(CurrentGoal) )
            {
                // then move directly to the actor
                MoveTo(CurrentGoal.Location, BotThreat);
                BotInCover = true;
            }
            else
            {
                // move to the first node on the path
                if( NavigationHandle.GetNextMoveLocation(TempDest,
Pawn.GetCollisionRadius()) )
                {
                    // suggest move preparation will return TRUE when the edge's
                    // logic is getting the bot to the edge point
                    // FALSE if we should run there ourselves
                    if (!NavigationHandle.SuggestMovePreparation(TempDest,self))
                    {
                        MoveTo(TempDest, BotThreat);

                    }
                }
```

```
        }
    }
    else
    {
        //give up because the nav mesh failed to find a path
        WorldInfo.Game.Broadcast(self,"FindNavMeshPath failed to find a path!,
CurrentGoal = " @ CurrentGoal);
        MoveTo(Pawn.Location);
    }
}
LatentWhatToDoNext();
}
```

Figure 8–17. *Bots are Taking Cover from Player (shown on far left)*

The code for the bot's AI is shown in Listing 8–10.

Listing 8–10. *The main AI point*

```
auto state Initial
{
    Begin:
    LatentWhatToDoNext();
}
event WhatToDoNext()
{
    DecisionComponent.bTriggered = true;
}
protected event ExecuteWhatToDoNext()
{
    if (IsInState('Initial'))
    {
        PrepMoveToCover();
        GotoState('TakeCover', 'Begin');
    }
    else
```

```
        if (IsInState('TakeCover'))
        {
            if (BotInCover)
            {
                //Pawn.StopFire(0);
                if (IsCurrentCoverValid())
                {
                    GotoState('TakeCover', 'Begin');
                }
                else
                {
                    PrepMoveToCover();
                    GotoState('TakeCover', 'Begin');
                    //Pawn.StartFire(0);
                }
            }
            else
            {
                GotoState('TakeCover', 'Begin');
            }
        }
    }
}
defaultproperties
{
    CurrentGoal = None;
    BotInCover = false;
}
```

The main bot AI logic occurs in the ExecuteWhatToDoNext() function. After the bot is first created it is in the Initial state. From the Initial state the PrepMoveToCover() function is called to prepare the bot to move to a new cover. Next, the bot moves into the TakeCover state.

If the bot is already in the TakeCover state and if the bot has not reached the target cover node yet, then continue with the bot moving toward the cover node. The TakeCover state moves the bot toward the target cover node.

If the bot is already in cover then, check to see if the current cover node is valid. If the current cover node is valid then go back to the TakeCover state. If the current cover node is invalid then call the PrepMoveToCover() function and go to the TakeCover state.

Creating the New Cover Node Class

Next, we need to create the new cover node class called CoverLinkEx shown in Listing 8–11.

Listing 8–11. *CoverLinkEx Cover Node*

```
class CoverLinkEx extends CoverLink;

var() float CoverProtectionAngle;

function bool IsCoverSlotValid(int SlotIndex, vector ThreatLocation)
{
    local bool Valid;
```

```
    local vector SlotLocation;
    local Rotator SlotRotation;
    local vector SlotNormal;

    local vector DirectionToThreat;
    local float AngleDegrees;

    Valid = false;

    SlotLocation = GetSlotLocation(SlotIndex);
    SlotRotation = GetSlotRotation(SlotIndex);

    SlotNormal = Normal(Vector(SlotRotation));
    DirectionToThreat = Normal(ThreatLocation - SlotLocation);
    AngleDegrees = acos(SlotNormal Dot DirectionToThreat) * RadToDeg;

    if (AngleDegrees < CoverProtectionAngle)
    {
        Valid = true;
    }
    return Valid;
}
function bool IsCoverSlotAvailable(int SlotIndex)
{
    local bool SlotAvailable;

    SlotAvailable = false;
    if (Slots[SlotIndex].SlotOwner == None)
    {
        SlotAvailable = true;
    }
    return SlotAvailable;
}
defaultproperties
{
    CoverProtectionAngle = 45.0
}
```

The following are the key things to notice in the listing:

- This class is derived from the default cover node class CoverLink provided in the base UDK code. Here a key change is the addition of the CoverProtectionAngle variable that holds the angle measured from the cover slot normal in which the cover gives protection. The CoverProtectionAngle variable is shown in Figure 8–16 as the Protection Angle with one side of the angle denoted by dotted lines.

- The IsCoverSlotValid() function returns true if the cover slot is valid for the input slot number and threat location. The angle in degrees formed by the SlotNormal vector and the DirectionToThreat vector is calculated. This angle is called the Threat Angle in Figure 8–16. If this angle is less than the CoverProtectionAngle then this cover slot is valid for this threat.

- The `IsCoverSlotAvailable()` function returns true if the cover node slot indicated by the `SlotIndex` parameter is empty and has no owner. Otherwise a false value is returned.

- The `CoverProtectionAngle` is specified by default as 45 degrees but can be changed using the Editor since it is declared as a var(). The parentheses denote that this variable is editable in the Unreal Editor.

Setting Up the Game Configuration

Next, we need to set up this new example for compilation and for playing on the mobile previewer. In the configuration directory located at

`C:\UDK\UDK-2011-06\UDKGame\Config`

change the UDKEngine.ini and Mobile-UDKGame.ini configuration files to the following. (If you are using a different UDK version then the above directory will be different.)

```
UDKEngine.ini
[UnrealEd.EditorEngine]
ModEditPackages=ExampleCh8
Mobile-UDKGame.ini
[ExampleCh8.ExampleCh8Game]
RequiredMobileInputConfigs=(GroupName="UberGroup",RequireZoneNames=("UberStickMoveZone",
"UberStickLookZone","UberLookZone"))
```

Save the configuration files. You may need to write protect them to preserve the contents since the UDK sometimes overwrites them. Although this does not usually happen, it is advisable to take this precaution if you are working on a project over an extended period of time.

Bring up the Unreal Frontend and compile the scripts.

Setting Up the Level

Next, we need to actually the build the level that uses the new `CoverLinkEx` class that we created.

1. Bring up the Unreal Editor.

2. In the Content Browser search for **vendorcrate.**

3. This should bring up a static mesh of a crate. Select the crate and then copy and paste it, or drag and drop it into the empty default level in an open area.

4. In the Generic Browser, change to the Actor Classes tab.

5. Under the **Cover ➤ CoverLink** section select the `CoverLinkEx` class.

6. Right click on an empty area in the level and select the Add CoverLinkEx Here option to put the new modified coverlink in the level. See Figure 8–18.

Figure 8–18. *Creating the CoverLinkEx*

7. The arrow that points outward from the cover node slot is the cover node slot normal. This should be placed against the object that is going to serve as cover. Move and rotate the cover node until the slot normal faces one side of the crate and is located against it. See Figure 8–19.

Figure 8–19. *Rotating the Cover Node*

8. Repeat steps 6 and 7 to put cover nodes on all four sides of the vendor crate.

9. Select the vendor crate and all the cover nodes by holding down the Ctrl key and clicking on the crate and the cover nodes.

10. Copy the vendor crate and all the cover nodes by holding down the Alt key and moving these objects to another open area.

11. Create a total of five of these crates with cover nodes by repeating step 10 four more times.

12. Add a pylon to the level in an open area by right clicking and selecting **Add Actor ➤ Add Pylon**.

13. Build the AI paths by selecting **Build ➤ AI Paths** from the Unreal Editor menu.

14. Save this level by selecting **File ➤ Save Current Level** from the Unreal Editor menu. See Figure 8–20 to see what this level should roughly look like.

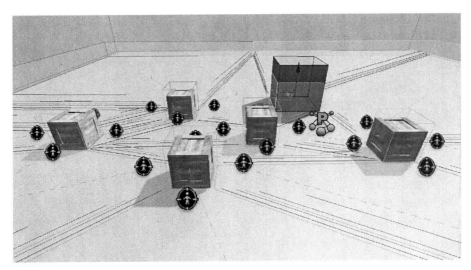

Figure 8–20. *Level with cover and cover nodes*

Running the Final Game

Next, while still in the Unreal Editor, change the default game type to ExampleCh8Game. Select the View ➤ World Properties menu item, and then set this value in the World Properties window.

Now run the game on the mobile previewer. Jazz bots should be dropping on your head and moving toward cover. Move your pawn around and you should see the bots trying to hide from you (see Figure 8–21 and 8–22). Ignore the message about the lighting needing to be rebuilt, as that does not have any effect on the actual gameplay.

Figure 8–21. *Bots taking cover from the player*

Figure 8–22. *Bots taking cover from player*

In-Depth Example Explanations

In this section we will provide more in depth explanations of key issues dealing with vectors, trigonometry, and 3D math.

Specifically we will cover

- How to position the camera in the world behind the player.
- How to apply a force to an object at a certain angle.

Third-Person Camera Positioning

In Chapter 3, we used third-person camera positioning to move the camera behind the player's pawn. The key issue is how to find the exact location to place the camera so that it is at a certain distance behind the player's pawn and makes a certain angle with the ground.

The key function in terms of moving the camera behind the player is the CalcCamera() function from the Jazz1Pawn class shown in Listing 8–12.

Listing 8–12. *CalcCamera function from the Jazz1Pawn class*

```
simulated function bool CalcCamera( float fDeltaTime, out vector out_CamLoc, out rotator
out_CamRot, out float out_FOV )
{
    local vector BackVector;
    local vector UpVector;

    local float  CamDistanceHorizontal;
    local float  CamDistanceVertical;

    // Set Camera Location
    CamDistanceHorizontal = CamOffsetDistance * cos(CamAngle * UnrRotToRad);
    CamDistanceVertical   = CamOffsetDistance * sin(CamAngle * UnrRotToRad);

    BackVector = -Normal(Vector(Rotation)) * CamDistanceHorizontal;
    UpVector   = vect(0,0,1) * CamDistanceVertical;

    out_CamLoc = Location + BackVector + UpVector;

    // Set Camera Rotation
    out_CamRot.pitch = -CamAngle;
    out_CamRot.yaw   = Rotation.yaw;
    out_CamRot.roll  = Rotation.roll;

    return true;
}
```

Here's what the code does:

- The camera's final position is the location of the player's pawn moved horizontally backward by the BackVector offset vector and upward by the UpVector offset vector.

- The BackVector points in the opposite direction from the player's front and has a magnitude of CamDistanceHorizontal units.

- The UpVector points upward and has a magnitude of CamDistanceVertical units.

- The CamDistanceHorizontal and CamDistanceVertical variables are calculated using the properties of a right triangle that were dicussed earlier in this chapter.

- The CamOffsetDistance is the distance between the player's pawn and the camera.

See Figure 8–23 for a diagram.

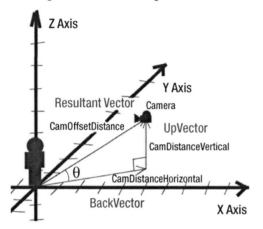

Figure 8–23. *Third-Person Camera Diagram*

The final position of the camera is calculated by adding the Resultant Vector to the player location. The Resultant vector is calculated by adding the BackVector to the UpVector. Graphically, to represent the addition of two vectors you put them head to tail with each other then draw the resultant vector from the tail of the first vector to the head of the last vector. CamDistanceVertical and CamDistanceHorizontal are scalar values derived from the CamOffsetDistance scalar value and the angle Theta which is the angle the camera makes with the ground. CamDistanceHorizontal is equal to CamOffsetDistance * cos(Theta). CamDistanceVertical is equal to CamOffsetDistance * sin(Theta).

Deriving a Direction Vector for Kicking an Object

In Chapter 4, we had to derive a direction vector for kicking an object in a 3D world. The issues involved finding the direction vector to kick the ball assuming a 2D world and then translating this vector into a full 3D world.

As part of determining the direction vector, we needed to first break it down into horizontal and vertical components. The key parts of the code in terms of setting the angle to kick an object are shown in Listing 8–13.

Listing 8–13. *Kicking an Object*

```
KickAngle = 15 * DegToRad;
ImpulseDir = (Normal(Vector(Pawn.Rotation)) * cos(KickAngle)) + (vect(0,0,1) *
sin(KickAngle));
ImpulseMag = 500;
```

The general idea is to first get the normalized vector that represents the direction that the object will be kicked. Then you can multiply this vector by the magnitude of the force you wish to apply to the object.

The first thing you will need to do is build the direction vector. The direction vector is composed of a horizontal component which is the FrontUnitVector and the vertical component which is vect(0,0,1). See Figure 8–24.

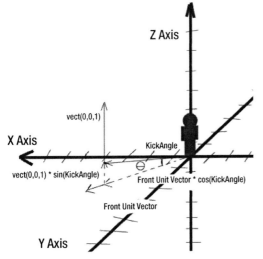

Figure 8–24. *Building the direction vector*

If we just added both vectors together then we would get a KickAngle of 45 degrees since the slope of the vector would be 1 since both vectors are unit vectors that have a length of 1.

To calculate the direction vector for an arbitrary angle is more complex. First let's find the direction vector for a KickAngle in 2 dimensions. See Figure 8–25.

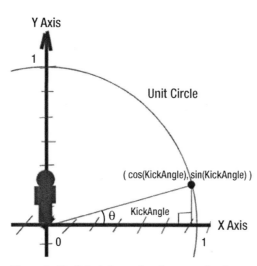

Figure 8–25. *Calculating a direction vector in 2D*

In Figure 8–25 you see the unit circle which has a radius of 1. According to the identities associated with a right triangle the horizontal value of the direction vector is cos(KickAngle) and the vertical value of the direction vector is sin(KickAngle).

Now we know how to get the direction vector from an arbitrary KickAngle on a 2D plane. However, our world is 3D so now we must somehow project this 2D direction vector into our 3D world.

We do this by multiplying the FrontUnitVector by cos(KickAngle) and the up unit vector which is vect(0,0,1) by sin(KickAngle) and adding them together to get the final direction vector in the 3D world.

Summary

In this chapter we covered vectors, vector addition, vector multiplication, dot and cross products using vectors. Next we went through a hands-on example that created a new cover node type where the user was able to set an angle of protection. If the threat was within this angle then the cover node provided protection to the occupant from this threat. Otherwise it does not. Finally we discussed in detail how certain things in previous chapters were accomplished such as the third-person camera and deriving the direction vector for kicking an object at a certain angle. The final few chapters are the framework chapters that will give you a good starting point for creating your own games.

Physics Game Framework

In this chapter we will build a basic game framework for a physics-based game. A physics game uses realistic models for such things as collisions, forces applied to game objects, behavior of game objects, and gravity. The goal is usually to destroy key objects and perhaps avoid destroying other key objects.

Probably the most famous physics game for the iOS platform, or any mobile platform for that matter, is Angry Birds. In Angry Birds the player throws birds at targets at a user defined angle. The level is complete when all the targets are destroyed. We develop a similar game in this chapter with the added benefit that the game is in 3D instead of 2D as in Angry Birds.

The basic physics game framework that will be presented in this chapter involves:

- Creating a collision object that is to be thrown
- Setting the angle that the object will be launched
- Launching the object and having it collide with other objects in a realistic manner
- Providing sound effects where appropriate
- Implementing a custom HUD (Heads Up Display) to keep track of vital game statistics
- Providing a mechanism to restart a new game or level

Physics Game Framework Overview

In this section we will give a general and specific overview of the physics game framework presented here in this chapter. The general overview explains in non-technical terms the framework and how you could extend the framework to meet your own needs. The specific overview outlines in detail the major elements of the framework and how to extend it.

General Overview

In a general sense this chapter provides you with a basic model and starting point for creating your own physics game.

This chapter provides the core information and techniques for creating a collision object. You are shown how to apply a force to this object at a user defined angle. You are also shown how to create other collision objects that will serve as the targets. These targets will be destroyed if enough force is applied to them.

This framework can be extended in many ways. For example, currently the force used to launch the object at the targets is fixed. The framework can be modified so that the user is able to set the force applied to the launch object. Also, the current game objective in the framework is to destroy all the target objects. This objective can be modified to include avoiding destroying other types of objects and deducting points or applying other penalties if these objects are destroyed.

Other kinds of physics-based games could be developed using this framework as a starting point. One way to do this is to change how the player launches the collision object. Instead of clicking on an object to launch it the player can throw it by touching it and moving the object with his finger and then releasing it. To implement this you would use the RB_Handle class which has built in functions to grab, release and move a KActor or KAsset type object. You can also change the player input so that the collision object is launched like an arrow. For example the player would pull the object back a certain distance then let go to launch it like an arrow.

Specific Overview

In a specific sense this chapter provides you with the detailed code you need to start implementing the ideas you have for your own physics game.

In the framework we create a custom class called GameBall which extends the KActorSpawnable class. This will be used as the player's launch object. This class can be created or spawned dynamically from within the game and can be used for realistic rigid body collisions with other objects. The key benefit here is that the Unreal physics engine takes care of all the difficult and time consuming calculations for you. You can extend this concept to the creation of dynamic collision objects that are skeletal meshes of the KAssetSpawnable class. Skeletal meshes are generally used for characters that have moveable parts. See Chapter 4 for more background information on KActors and KAssets.

The angle to launch the object can be set within a range of 0 to 90 degrees using the right controller. Move the right controller upward to increase the launch angle and downward to decrease the launch angle. You could extend this concept further by also allowing the user to set the amount of force applied to the launch object.

Currently the value is set to a constant in the variable ImpulseMag. ImpulseMag is set to 500 in the SwipeZoneCallback() function. The ApplyForceRigidBody() function is then called to actually apply the force.

The blocks that are destroyed by the player's ball are created from classes derived from the KActor class. Remember that the KActor and KAsset classes are the two types of collision objects that can be used in realistic rigid body collisions.

In terms of the target blocks you can extend the game's objectives to including penalties for destroying certain types of blocks. Currently the function AllBlocksDestroyed() checks to see if all of the target blocks of class RigidBodyCube have been destroyed using the built in AllActors() iterator and returns a true value when they have all been eliminated. A similar function based on this code could be used to determine if any blocks of another class were destroyed and impose penalties if they were.

A customized HUD has been created that displays the player's score, the time since the game has started and the launch angle of the player's ball. This HUD can be extended by adding other statistics that you find important. For example, you could add a variable that would track the total number of blocks destroyed and display that number on the HUD. A new variable of type HUDInfo called HUDTotalBlocksDestroyed could be created to hold the HUD related placement information. This variable would be initialized in the PostBeginPlay() function. The call to actually draw the new information onscreen will be called form the DrawHUD() function. For more background information on the HUD see Chapter 6.

Hands-on Example: A Basic Physics Game

In this hands-on example we will create a basic physics game that can serve as a basic framework for creating your own physics game. First we create code for a new game type, a new player controller, a game ball which the player kicks into a group of blocks, a new HUD, and a new class of block used to create the target blocks. We then set up the game to compile and run on the mobile previewer. After compiling the new code we build the level using the new RigidBodyCubeEx class that we created then run the game on the mobile previewer.

Creating the Game Type

The first thing we need to do is create a new directory for the code for this project. Create the ExampleCh9 directory under your default UDK installation directory at C:\UDK\UDK-2011-06\Development\Src.

> **NOTE:** As a reminder, we are using the June 2011 UDK. If you are using a different version of the UDK, then your default path will be different.

Create a directory called Classes under the new directory you just created and put all your source code files in this directory.

Create the following class and save it under the filename "ExampleCh9Game.uc". Again as with all previous examples in this book the filenames must match the classnames and the file extension must be ".uc". See Listing 9–1, and note that the PlayerControllerClass and HUDType variables are set to our new custom classes. Also note that the variable Score which keeps track of the player's score in this game type.

Listing 9–1. *Game Type*

```
class ExampleCh9Game extends FrameworkGame;

var int Score;

event OnEngineHasLoaded()
{
    WorldInfo.Game.Broadcast(self,"ExampleCh9Game Type Active - Engine Has Loaded
!!!!");
}

function bool PreventDeath(Pawn KilledPawn, Controller Killer, class<DamageType>
DamageType, vector HitLocation)
{
    return true;
}

static event class<GameInfo> SetGameType(string MapName, string Options, string Portal)
{
    return super.SetGameType(MapName, Options, Portal);
}

defaultproperties
{
    PlayerControllerClass=class'ExampleCh9.ExampleCh9PC'
    DefaultPawnClass=class'UDKBase.SimplePawn'
    HUDType=class'KickBallHUD'

    bRestartLevel=false
    bWaitingToStartMatch=true
    bDelayedStart=false
}
```

> **FRAMEWORK NOTE:** Here you can set your customized classes for the player controller, player's pawn, and player's HUD. You do this by setting the PlayerControllerClass, DefaultPawnClass, and HUDType variables to your new class.

Creating the Player Controller

Next, we need to create our player controller class. For a full version of the code in this section, without the explanations, please see the source code available for this book. Code that is new and not used in previous chapters is highlighted in bold print.

The first part of the controller code, shown in Listing 9–2, changes the behavior of the right virtual joystick controller so that pushing the virtual joystick up increases the kick angle and pushing it downward decreases the kick angle.

Key things to notice in the listing include:

- A function `InputDelayTimer()` is used to delay the update of the `KickAngle` variable. For example, originally the `KickAngle` variable would update too quickly and the rate of update needed to be slowed down.

- The `ProcessLookUpInput()` function updates the `KickAngle` based on the user's input. A call to the `SetTimer()` function initiates the call to `InputDelayTimer()` at a certain delay interval. During this delay interval the `KickAngle` is not updated. The `KickAngle` is also clamped to the range 0 to 90 degrees using the built in `Clamp()` function.

- The `UpdateRotation()` function is overridden by our custom function. The only difference here from the default function in the UDK base code is that the line

  ```
  DeltaRot.Pitch = PlayerInput.aLookUp;
  ```

  is commented out so that the player's up/down view is not changed and the function `ProcessLookUpInput()` is called to change the `KickAngle` instead of updating the player's up/down view.

Listing 9–2. *Customizing the Controls*

```
class ExampleCh9PC extends SimplePC;

var float PickDistance;
var int KickAngle;
var int BallCreationDist;
var float GameTime;
var bool bGameOver;
var Actor Ball;
var bool bInitDone;
var bool bInputDelayFinished;
var int GameTimeDelta;
var SoundCue BallHitSound;
var SoundCue BallSpawnSound;
function InputDelayTimer()
{
    bInputDelayFinished = true;
}
function ProcessLookUpInput()
```

```
{
    local float TimerDelta;

    if (!bInputDelayFinished)
    return;
    if (PlayerInput.aLookUp > 0)
    {
        KickAngle++;
    }
    else
    if (PlayerInput.aLookUp < 0)
    {
        KickAngle--;
    }
    KickAngle = Clamp(KickAngle,0,90);
    TimerDelta = 0.05;
    bInputDelayFinished = false;
    SetTimer(TimerDelta, false, 'InputDelayTimer');
}
function UpdateRotation( float DeltaTime )
{
    local Rotator DeltaRot, newRotation, ViewRotation;

    ViewRotation = Rotation;
    if (Pawn!=none)
    {
        Pawn.SetDesiredRotation(ViewRotation);
    }

    // Calculate Delta to be applied on ViewRotation
    DeltaRot.Yaw = PlayerInput.aTurn;

    //DeltaRot.Pitch = PlayerInput.aLookUp;
    ProcessLookUpInput();

    ProcessViewRotation( DeltaTime, ViewRotation, DeltaRot );
    SetRotation(ViewRotation);

    ViewShake( deltaTime );

    NewRotation = ViewRotation;
    NewRotation.Roll = Rotation.Roll;

    if ( Pawn != None )
        Pawn.FaceRotation(NewRotation, deltatime);
}
```

The next piece of the code, shown in Listing 9–3, creates and initializes the game timer. The GameTimer() function updates the amount of time that has passed since the level has started. The PostBeginPlay() function sets a looping timer which continuously calls the GameTimer() function to update the GameTime variable.

Listing 9–3. *The Game Timer*

```
function GameTimer()
{
    if (bGameOVer)
    {
        return;
    }
    GameTime = GameTime + GameTimeDelta;
}
simulated function PostBeginPlay()
{
    Super.PostBeginPlay();
    SetTimer(GameTimeDelta, true, 'GameTimer');
}
```

The next section of code, shown in Listing 9–4, should be familiar to you from Chapter 4, in which we covered UDK collisions. The `ApplyForceRigidBody()` function applies a force to a KActor or a KAsset object.

Listing 9–4. *Applying Force to a Rigid Body*

```
function ApplyForceRigidBody(Actor SelectedActor, Vector ImpulseDir,float ImpulseMag,
Vector HitLocation)
{
    if (SelectedActor.IsA('KActor'))
    {
        WorldInfo.Game.Broadcast(self,"*** Thrown object " @ SelectedActor @
                            ", ImpulseDir = " @ ImpulseDir @
                            ", ImpulseMag = " @ ImpulseMag @
                            ", HitLocation = " @ HitLocation);
        KActor(SelectedActor).ApplyImpulse(ImpulseDir,ImpulseMag, HitLocation);
    }
    else
    if (SelectedActor.IsA('KAsset'))
    {
        WorldInfo.Game.Broadcast(self,"*** Thrown object " @ SelectedActor @
                            ", ImpulseDir = " @ ImpulseDir @
                            ", ImpulseMag = " @ ImpulseMag @
                            ", HitLocation = " @ HitLocation);
        KAsset(SelectedActor).SkeletalMeshComponent.AddImpulse(ImpulseDir* ImpulseMag,
,'Bone06');
    }
    else
    {
        WorldInfo.Game.Broadcast(self,"!!!ERROR Selected Actor " @ SelectedActor @
                            "is not a KActor or KAsset, you can not apply
                            an impulse to this object!!!");
    }
}
```

The next section of code, shown in Listing 9–5, also should be familiar to you from Chapter 4. The `PickActor()` function determines if the user has touched an actor and returns a reference to this actor.

Listing 9–5. *Picking an Actor*

```
function Actor PickActor(Vector2D PickLocation, out Vector HitLocation, out TraceHitInfo
HitInfo)
{
    local Vector TouchOrigin, TouchDir;
    local Vector HitNormal;
    local Actor  PickedActor;
    local vector Extent;

    //Transform absolute screen coordinates to relative coordinates
    PickLocation.X = PickLocation.X / ViewportSize.X;
    PickLocation.Y = PickLocation.Y / ViewportSize.Y;

    //Transform to world coordinates to get pick ray
    LocalPlayer(Player).Deproject(PickLocation, TouchOrigin, TouchDir);

    //Perform trace to find touched actor
    Extent = vect(0,0,0);
    PickedActor = Trace(HitLocation,
                        HitNormal,
                        TouchOrigin + (TouchDir * PickDistance),
                        TouchOrigin,
                        True,
                        Extent,
                        HitInfo);
    //Return the touched actor for good measure
    return PickedActor;
}
```

The next piece of code, shown in Listing 9–6, is called to create the player's ball that will be used to destroy blocks in the level. Figure 9–1 shows the result of this code.

The `CreateNewGameBall()` function creates a new `GameBall` class object and applies a small force downward to activate the object's rigid body physics simulation. A sound is also played.

Listing 9–6. *Creating the Game Ball*

```
function CreateNewGameBall()
{
    local vector FrontVec;
    local vector BallLocation;

    local Vector HitLocation;
    local Vector ImpulseDir;
    local float ImpulseMag;

    FrontVec = Normal(Vector(Pawn.Rotation));
    BallLocation = Pawn.Location + (FrontVec * BallCreationDist);

    Ball = Spawn(class'GameBall',,,BallLocation);
    PlaySound(BallSpawnSound);

    ImpulseDir = Vect(0,0,1);
    ImpulseMag = 5;
    HitLocation = Vect(0,0,0);
```

```
    ApplyForceRigidBody(Ball, ImpulseDir, ImpulseMag, HitLocation);
}
```

Figure 9–1. *The Game Ball*

The next piece of code, shown in Listing 9–7, involves code related to player input through touching the screen. Key parts of the listing include:

- The `LoadLevel(string LevelName)` function loads in the level with the input `LevelName` string parameter.

- The `ResetGame()` function restarts the game by loading in the original level. In the UDK environment whenever a level is loaded, the game is restarted and all variables such as `Score` and `GameTime` are reset.

- In the `SwipeZoneCallback()` function, code has been added to create a new ball when the screen is touched and to reset the game if the current game is over. A sound is also played when the ball is kicked.

- The SetupZones() function initializes the input zones and this function should be familiar to you from the hands-on example in Chapter 2.

Listing 9–7. *Player Input*

```
function LoadLevel(string LevelName)
{
    local string Command;

    Command = "open " @ LevelName;
    ConsoleCommand(Command);
}

function ResetGame()
{
    LoadLevel("ExampleCh9Map");
}
function bool SwipeZoneCallback(MobileInputZone Zone,
                               float DeltaTime,
                               int Handle,
                               EZoneTouchEvent EventType,
                               Vector2D TouchLocation)
{
    local bool retval;
```

```
        local Actor PickedActor;
        local Vector HitLocation;
        local TraceHitInfo HitInfo;

        // Variables for physics
        local Vector ImpulseDir;
        local float ImpulseMag;
        local float RadKickAngle;

        retval = true;

        if (EventType == ZoneEvent_Touch)
        {
            // If screen touched then pick actor
            PickedActor = PickActor(TouchLocation,HitLocation,HitInfo);

            // Reset Game
            if (bGameOver)
            {
                ResetGame();
                return retval;
            }
            if (PickedActor.IsA('GameBall'))
            {
                RadKickAngle = KickAngle * DegToRad;

                ImpulseDir = (Normal(Vector(Pawn.Rotation)) * cos(RadKickAngle)) +
(vect(0,0,1) * sin(RadKickAngle));
                ImpulseMag = 500;

                ApplyForceRigidBody(PickedActor,ImpulseDir,ImpulseMag,HitLocation);
                PlaySound(BallHitSound);
            }
            else
            {
                CreateNewGameBall();
            }
        }
        else
        if(EventType == ZoneEvent_Update)
        {
        }
        else
        if (EventType == ZoneEvent_UnTouch)
        {
        }
        return retval;
    }
    function SetupZones()
    {
        Super.SetupZones();

        // If we have a game class, configure the zones
        if (MPI != None && WorldInfo.GRI.GameClass != none)
        {
            LocalPlayer(Player).ViewportClient.GetViewportSize(ViewportSize);
```

```
        if (FreeLookZone != none)
        {
            FreeLookZone.OnProcessInputDelegate = SwipeZoneCallback;
        }
    }
}
```

The next code section, shown in Listing 9–8, contains the main loop of code that is executed continuously in the function `PlayerTick()`. Notice the following things:

- The `AllBlocksDestroyed()` function returns true if all the target blocks have been destroyed by the player and false otherwise.

- The `InitKickBallGame()` function is called in the beginning to do any initialization after the player is first created and after `PlayerTick()` is first called.

- In the main `PlayerTick()` loop the function `AllBlocksDestroyed()` is continually called to check to see if all the target blocks in the level have been destroyed. If they have, then `bGameOver` is set to true.

Listing 9–8. *Main Loop*

```
function bool AllBlocksDestroyed()
{
    local RigidBodyCube TempBlock;
    local bool bAllBlocksDestroyed;

    bAllBlocksDestroyed = true;
    foreach AllActors(class'RigidBodyCube', TempBlock)
    {
        if (!TempBlock.bDestroyed)
        {
            bAllBlocksDestroyed = false;
        }
    }
    return bAllBlocksDestroyed;
}
function InitKickBallGame()
{
    bInitDone = true;
}
function PlayerTick(float DeltaTime)
{
    Super.PlayerTick(DeltaTime);

    if (!bInitDone)
    {
        InitKickBallGame();
    }
    if (AllBlocksDestroyed())
    {
        bGameOver = true;
    }
```

```
        if (bGameOver)
        {
            Pawn.SetHidden(true);
            Pawn.Velocity = vect(0,0,0);
        }
}
```

Listing 9–9 contains the final piece of the controller code, which defines the default values for some of the variables in this class.

Listing 9–9. *Default Properties*

```
defaultproperties
{
    PickDistance = 10000
    KickAngle = 45
    bInitDone = false;
    bInputDelayFinished = true
    BallCreationDist = 500
    GameTime=0
    GameTimeDelta = 1
    bGameOver = false;
    BallHitSound = SoundCue'A_Weapon_BioRifle.Weapon.A_BioRifle_FireImpactFizzle_Cue'
    BallSpawnSound = SoundCue'A_Pickups.Generic.Cue.A_Pickups_Generic_ItemRespawn_Cue'
}
```

> **FRAMEWORK NOTE:** Any changes on how the player interacts with the game should be implemented in this class.

Creating the Game Ball

Next, we need to create the GameBall class that will represent the player's ball that will be used to destroy the target blocks (see Listing 9–10). The important things to note in this code are

- The RigidBodyCollision() function plays a sound if the ball makes an impact with another object with a minimum force defined by the MinimumForceForSound variable.

- The Touch() function is called if another object touches this ball. Currently this function does nothing useful but is a placeholder in case you need this function in a future derived version of this class for your own game.

- The defaultproperties block defines the 3d mesh used for this ball as well as defining some default values such as the sound cue to use for the impact sound.

Listing 9-10. *The Player's Ball*

```
class GameBall extends KActorSpawnable;

var SoundCue BallImpact;
var float MinimumForceForSound;

event RigidBodyCollision(PrimitiveComponent HitComponent,
                         PrimitiveComponent OtherComponent,
                         const out CollisionImpactData RigidCollisionData,
                         int ContactIndex)
{
    local float CollisionForce;

    CollisionForce = VSize(RigidCollisionData.TotalNormalForceVector);
    if (CollisionForce >= MinimumForceForSound)
    {
        PlaySound(BallImpact);
    }
}

event Touch(Actor Other, PrimitiveComponent OtherComp, vector HitLocation, vector
HitNormal)
{
    WorldInfo.Game.Broadcast(self,"GameBall Has Been Touched");
}

defaultproperties
{
    Begin Object Class=StaticMeshComponent Name=GameBallMesh
        StaticMesh=StaticMesh'EngineMeshes.Sphere'
        Translation=(X=0.000000,Y=0.000000,Z=0.000000)
        Scale3D=(X=0.10000,Y=0.10000,Z=0.1000)

        CollideActors=true
        BlockActors=true
        BlockRigidBody=true
        bNotifyRigidBodyCollision=true
        ScriptRigidBodyCollisionThreshold=0.001
        RBChannel=RBCC_GameplayPhysics

RBCollideWithChannels=(Default=TRUE,BlockingVolume=TRUE,GameplayPhysics=TRUE,EffectPhysi
cs=TRUE)
    End Object
    Components.Add(GameBallMesh)
    CollisionComponent = GameBallMesh

    BallImpact =
SoundCue'A_Character_BodyImpacts.BodyImpacts.A_Character_RobotImpact_GibLarge_Cue'
    MinimumForceForSound = 50;
}
```

Creating the HUD

Next, we need to create the custom HUD class that will display the player's score, game time, and the KickAngle that defines the angle that a force will act on the ball (see Listing 9–11). The structure of this HUD class is similar to the one discussed previously in Chapter 6. The key differences are highlighted in bold print.

The following items are the key points to notice in the listing:

- The variables that hold the key information that is displayed on screen are HUDKickAngle, HUDGameTime, HUDScore.

- As before, the PostBeginPlay() function sets up the values of the HUD related variables.

- The DrawHUDItem() function draws the key statistics to the screen.

- The DrawHUD() function is overridden allowing us to add our own custom drawing routines to the HUD's normal drawing routines.

Listing 9–11. *Custom HUD*

```
class KickBallHUD extends UDKHud;

struct HUDInfo
{
    var string Label;
    var Vector2D TextLocation;
    var Color TextColor;
    var Vector2D Scale;
};
// HUD
var HUDInfo HUDKickAngle;
var HUDInfo HUDGameTime;
var HUDInfo HUDGameOver;
var HUDInfo HUDScore;
simulated function PostBeginPlay()
{
    Super.PostBeginPlay();

    HUDKickAngle.Label = "KickAngle:";
    HUDKickAngle.TextLocation.x = 1000;
    HUDKickAngle.TextLocation.y = 50;
    HUDKickAngle.TextColor.R = 0;
    HUDKickAngle.TextColor.G = 0;
    HUDKickAngle.TextColor.B = 255;
    HUDKickAngle.Scale.X = 2;
    HUDKickAngle.Scale.Y = 4;

    HUDGameTime.Label = "Time:";
    HUDGameTime.TextLocation.x = 600;
    HUDGameTime.TextLocation.y = 50;
    HUDGameTime.TextColor.R = 255;
    HUDGameTime.TextColor.G = 255;
```

```
    HUDGameTime.TextColor.B = 0;
    HUDGameTime.Scale.X = 2;
    HUDGameTime.Scale.Y = 4;

    HUDGameOver.Label = "Level Complete";
    HUDGameOver.TextLocation.x = 250;
    HUDGameOver.TextLocation.y = 300;
    HUDGameOver.TextColor.R = 255;
    HUDGameOver.TextColor.G = 0;
    HUDGameOver.TextColor.B = 255;
    HUDGameOver.Scale.X = 7;
    HUDGameOver.Scale.Y = 7;

    HUDScore.Label = "Score:";
    HUDScore.TextLocation.x = 0;
    HUDScore.TextLocation.y = 50;
    HUDScore.TextColor.R = 255;
    HUDScore.TextColor.G = 0;
    HUDScore.TextColor.B = 0;
    HUDScore.Scale.X = 2;
    HUDScore.Scale.Y = 4;
}
function DrawHUDItem(HUDInfo Info, coerce string Value)
{
    local Vector2D TextSize;

    Canvas.SetDrawColor(Info.TextColor.R, Info.TextColor.G, Info.TextColor.B);
    Canvas.SetPos(Info.TextLocation.X, Info.TextLocation.Y);
    Canvas.DrawText(Info.Label, ,Info.Scale.X,Info.Scale.Y);
    Canvas.TextSize(Info.Label, TextSize.X, TextSize.Y);
    Canvas.SetPos(Info.TextLocation.X + (TextSize.X * Info.Scale.X),
Info.TextLocation.Y);
    Canvas.DrawText(Value, , Info.Scale.X, Info.Scale.Y);
}
function DrawHUD()
{
    local int Time;

    super.DrawHUD();

    Canvas.Font = class'Engine'.static.GetLargeFont();
    // Score
    DrawHUDItem(HUDScore, ExampleCh9Game(WorldInfo.Game).Score);

    // Time
    Time = ExampleCh9PC(PlayerOwner).GameTime;
    DrawHUDItem(HUDGameTime, Time);

    // Kick Angle
    DrawHUDItem(HUDKickAngle,ExampleCh9PC(PlayerOwner).KickAngle);

    // Game Over
    if (ExampleCh9PC(PlayerOwner).bGameOVer)
    {
        DrawHUDItem(HUDGameOver, "");
    }
```

```
}
defaultProperties
{
}
```

> **FRAMEWORK NOTE:** Modify this class in order to add in more key statistics or change the key
> statistics that will be displayed in your game.

Creating the RigidBodyCubeEx Object

Next, we need to create the new RigidBodyCubeEx class that extends from our previously defined RigidBodyCube class from the Chapter 4.

Notice in Listing 9–12 that the RigidBodyCollision() function overrides the parent function in RigidBodyCube. It calls the parent function and also adds to the player's score the value of the cube and plays an explosion sound if the cube is destroyed.

Listing 9–12. *RigidBodyCubeEx class*

```
class RigidBodyCubeEx extends RigidBodyCube;

var SoundCue ExplosionSound;
var() float ItemValue;

event RigidBodyCollision(PrimitiveComponent HitComponent,
                         PrimitiveComponent OtherComponent,
                         const out CollisionImpactData RigidCollisionData,
                         int ContactIndex)
{
    super.RigidBodyCollision(HitComponent, OtherComponent, RigidCollisionData,
ContactIndex);

    if (bDestroyed)
    {
        PlaySound(ExplosionSound);
        ExampleCh9Game(WorldInfo.Game).Score += ItemValue;
    }
}

defaultproperties
{
    ExplosionSound = SoundCue'A_Weapon_ShockRifle.Cue.A_Weapon_SR_ComboExplosionCue'
    ItemValue = 10;
}
```

> **FRAMEWORK NOTE:** You can derive or extend a new class from this class to create a new type
> of target object for your own game.

Configuring the Game Type

Next, we need to set up this new example for compilation and for playing on the mobile previewer. In the configuration directory located at

```
C:\UDK\UDK-2011-06\UDKGame\Config
```

Change the UDKEngine.ini and Mobile-UDKGame.ini configuration files to the following.

```
UDKEngine.ini
[UnrealEd.EditorEngine]
ModEditPackages=ExampleCh9
Mobile-UDKGame.ini
[ExampleCh9.ExampleCh9Game]
RequiredMobileInputConfigs=(GroupName="UberGroup",RequireZoneNames=("UberStickMoveZone",
"UberStickLookZone","UberLookZone"))
```

Save the configuration files. You may need to write protect them to preserve the contents since the UDK sometimes overwrites them. Generally, this does not happen. However, if you are working on a project over a period of many months, then you probably should take this extra step. If you use this framework or the other frameworks in this book to build your own games, then I would advise you to write protect the configuration files.

Bring up the Unreal Frontend and compile the scripts.

Creating the Level

Next, we need to create the level. Follow these steps:

1. Bring up the Unreal Editor.

2. Type in **vendorcrate** into the search box in the Content Browser and the static mesh of a vendor crate should show up.

3. Click on the vendor crate static mesh and then drag and drop the crate into the default level (see Figure 9–2).

Figure 9–2. *Creating a vendor crate*

4. Create stacks of crates of various heights. An easy way to do this is to select multiple crates at once by holding down the Ctrl key and clicking on a stack of crates. After the crates are selected, release the Ctrl key, hold down the Alt key, and click on the transformation widget and move it to another location to create a copy of that stack of crates (see Figure 9–3).

Figure 9–3. *Duplicating Crates*

5. Click on the Actor Classes tab and search for **RigidbodyCubeEx**. Click on that class. Right-click on an empty area in the level and select the Add RigidBodyCubeEx Here option.

6. The Cube will be too big so double-click on it and set the Draw Scale under the Display category to 0.20 (see Figure 9–4).

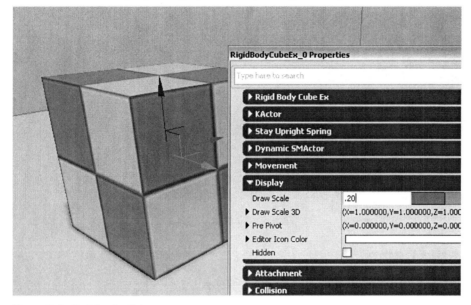

Figure 9–4. *Resizing the Cube*

7. Make copies of this cube and put them at the tops of the vendor crates you just created (see Figure 9–5).

Figure 9–5. *The Finished Level*

Running the Game

Now, we are ready to run our game. Follow these steps:

1. Select View ➤ World Properties from the Unreal Editor main menu. This would bring up the World Properties window.

2. In the World Properties window set the Default Game Type under the Game Type category to ExampleCh9Game.

3. Select the Play ➤ On Mobile Previewer option to run the game on the mobile previewer form the Editor.

Click somewhere on the screen to create a new ball. Click on this ball to kick it toward the checkered cubes. Use the left virtual joystick to move forward/backward and left/right. Use the right virtual joystick to turn left/right and raise and lower the KickAngle. You should see something like in Figure 9–6.

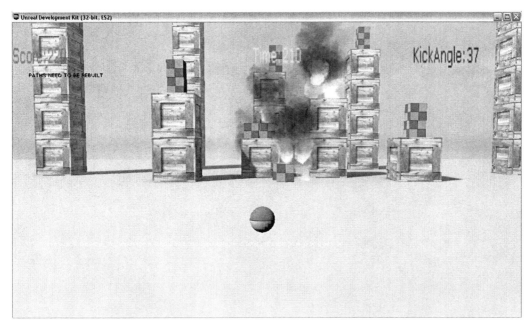

Figure 9–6. *Final Physics Game in Action*

Summary

In this chapter we created a basic framework for a physics game. Various custom collision objects were created such as the player's ball and the target cube that is to be destroyed. Sound effects were added in where appropriate. A level consisting of stacks of different heights of crates topped with target cubes was created. The final product was a basic playable physics game that the reader can use as a base to build his own physics games from. The last few chapters of this book will concentrate on creating basic game frameworks such as this one.

Chapter **10**

First-Person Shooter Game Framework

This chapter provides a framework for a first-person shooter based on a one-on-one deathmatch type combat game. The gameplay consists of a one player vs. one computer-controlled bot taking place in a level full of crates that serve as cover for the bot. Both the player and bot are respawned upon death.

This framework provides for a:

- First-person perspective weapon view and operation
- Custom bot controller that moves from cover to cover and attacks the player
- Spawning a bot on a spawnpad determined at random
- Custom HUD
- Health Power Up
- Mechanism to respawn dead bots and players

First the overall game framework will be discussed in both general and specific terms. This is followed by the actual hands-on example which will present the actual game framework.

Game Framework Overview

In this section we will cover a general overview and a specific overview for this chapter's game framework. The general overview will give you an idea of the key features of the game framework and the specific overview discusses features of the game framework in code-specific terms and tells you how you might be able to modify the framework for your own custom needs.

General Overview

This framework provides for a first-person player world viewpoint with a weapon that is visible within this view. The weapon is placed so that the player appears to be holding it. This framework can be modified to add in a different weapon and to place this new weapon in a different position within the player's view if needed.

A basic framework for a computer controlled bot that can use the cover nodes feature of the UDK is presented. The bot framework also features the ability to attack the player and to retrieve health powerups when its health is below a certain level. You can change the bot's behavior by adding in new states or modifying the states that already exist.

A method to randomly select a spawnpad from a set of spawnpads is presented. Code for respawning the enemy bot on one of these spawnpads is also given.

A custom Heads Up Display or HUD is presented. You can extend this HUD by adding or eliminating items to display using the existing HUD items in the framework as a guide.

A method to process health powerups is given in this game framework. This method could be expanded to include other types of powerups such as weapon powerups.

Specific Overview

In terms of generating a first-person perspective for weapons, the `PlaceWeapon()` function located in the player controller `ExampleCh10PC` actually does the work of placing the weapon 3d mesh in the 3d world in front of the player. In the `JazzCh10Pawn` class which is the player's pawn the function `AddDefaultInventory()` initialized the player's weapon which is the `JazzWeaponCh10` class and adds it into the player's inventory. The `WeaponsIM1` class is set as the inventory manager for the player's pawn.

You can expand on this basic framework through creating a new weapon and replacing it with the one now used by changing the `JazzWeaponCh10` weapon to your custom weapon in the `CreateInventory()` function in the `AddDefaultInventory()` function. For example, the code

```
InvManager.CreateInventory(class'YourCustomWeaponClass');
```

would place your new custom weapon in the player's inventory.

The bot controller is `BotAttackCoverController` and consists of three states:

- TakeCover—Bot moves to the cover node specified in the `CurrentGoal` variable. When the target cover node is reached, then `BotInCover` is set to true.

- GettingHealthPickup—Bot moves to the location of the Bonus specified in the `CurrentGoal` variable. When the Bonus has been reached then `bGotHealthPickup` is set to true.

- `AttackingEnemy`—Bot moves toward the enemy specified by the `BotThreat` variable and stops `AttackOffsetDist` distance from the threat if there is a clear path to the threat and then sets `bAttackDone` to true. Bot fires its weapon during this state.

When the bot is spawned it goes into the `TakeCover` state and the bot takes cover from the player. Once in cover, if the bot has health that is lower than the `HealthPickupTrigger` variable and a health powerup is available, it goes into the `GettingHealthPickup` state, picks up the bonus health, and then returns to the `TakeCover` state. If the bot is in cover and has been in the `TakeCover` state greater than the `AttackTimeInterval` time, then the bot goes into the `AttackEnemy` state and attacks the player. Once the attack is finished then the bot goes back into the `TakeCover` state and takes cover from the player.

You can extend this bot behavior by adding new states to the bot controller or changing the way the current states interact with one another.

In the `BotPawnCh10` class, which is the enemy bot's pawn class, the function `GetRandomSpawnPosition()` chooses a random pad from those in the game level and returns the position of that pad so that a new enemy bot can be respawned there.

You can expand this feature by increasing the number of pads available to the bot or how the bot selects a new pad to respawn on.

The game's custom HUD is defined in the class `FPSHUD`, and you can easily extend this class to provide for modifications of the key statistics displayed in the game.

The health powerup is implemented in the class `Bonus1` and can be used as a starting point template for other powerups you may have in mind.

Hands-On Example: First-Person Shooter Game Framework

In this hands-on example we build a first-person shooter deathmatch style game that involves one enemy computer controlled bot and one player. The bot will move from cover to cover and attack the player, retrieving health bonus powerups as needed. This section covers creating code for the game type, player related classes, enemy bot related classes, the HUD, and the health bonus powerup. Then a new game level is created and the game is configured to run on the mobile previewer.

Creating the Game Type

The first thing we need to do is create a new directory for the code for this project. Create the ExampleCh10 directory under your default UDK installation directory at `C:\UDK\UDK-2011-06\Development\Src`. (This is for the June 2011 UDK. If you are using a different version of the UDK then this directory will be different.) Create a directory called

Classes under the new directory you just created and put all your source code files in this directory.

Create the following class (see Listing 10–1) and save it under the filename "ExampleCh10Game.uc". Again as with all previous examples in this book the filenames must match the classnames and the file extension must be ".uc". The code in bold is specific to this example. (See the hands-on example in Chapter 2 for an example of the base game type class.)

In the listing, note the following variables:

- The variable Score holds the player's score.

- The variable MaxSpawnPads holds the maximum number of bot spawn pads in the level.

- The variable bGameOver indicates whether the current game is over.

Also, notice the following classes:

- The PlayerControllerClass is set to the custom player controller class for this framework.

- The DefaultPawnClass is set to the custom player pawn for this framework.

- The HUDType is set to the custom HUD class for this framework.

Listing 10–1. *Game Type*

```
class ExampleCh10Game extends FrameworkGame;
var int Score;
var int MaxSpawnPads;
var bool bGameOver;
event OnEngineHasLoaded()
{
    WorldInfo.Game.Broadcast(self,"ExampleCh10Game Type Active - Engine Has Loaded
!!!!");
}
function bool PreventDeath(Pawn KilledPawn, Controller Killer, class<DamageType>
DamageType, vector HitLocation)
{
    return true;
}
static event class<GameInfo> SetGameType(string MapName, string Options, string Portal)
{
    return super.SetGameType(MapName, Options, Portal);
}
defaultproperties
{
    PlayerControllerClass=class'ExampleCh10.ExampleCh10PC'
    DefaultPawnClass=class'JazzCh10Pawn'
    HUDType=class'FPSHUD'
    bRestartLevel=false
    bWaitingToStartMatch=true
    bDelayedStart=false
    Score = 0
```

```
    MaxSpawnPads = 4
    bGameOver = false;
}
```

> **FRAMEWORK NOTE:** You can expand the number of bot spawnpads in the level by increasing
> the MaxSpawnPads variable and placing additional number of spawnpads in your level using the
> Unreal Editor and setting the PadNumber in each additional pad.

Creating the Player-Related Classes

Next, we need to create the player related classes. These classes include the player
controller, the player's pawn, the player's weapon, and the player's projectile that is fired
from the weapon.

Creating the Player Controller

In this section we will discuss the player controller class. For a full version of this code
without the explanations, please download the source code for this book.

The first part of the code, shown in Listing 10–2, covers the class variables and the
function that resets the player:

- The variable EnemyBot holds a reference to the enemy bot's controller
  and the EnemyPawn variable holds a reference to the enemy bot's pawn.
  These variables are used in creating the enemy bot controller and
  enemy bot pawn when the player controller is first initialized.

- The SpawnPadLocations array holds the locations of the enemy bot's
  spawn pads for this level.

- The ResetGame() function resets key game variables such as player's
  score and player's health after the player dies and is respawned.

Listing 10–2. *Resetting the Game*

```
class ExampleCh10PC extends SimplePC;

var Controller EnemyBot;
Var Pawn EnemyPawn;
var bool BotSpawned;
var Actor BotTarget;
var bool bGameOver;
var array<vector> SpawnPadLocations;
function ResetGame()
{
    ExampleCh10Game(WorldInfo.Game).bGameOver = false;
    ExampleCh10Game(WorldInfo.Game).Score = 0;
    Pawn.Health = 100;

    Pawn.SetHidden(false);
```

```
        Pawn.Weapon.SetHidden(false);
        Pawn.SetLocation(JazzCh10Pawn(Pawn).InitialLocation);
}
```

The next piece of code, shown in Listing 10–3, covers the creation or spawning of the enemy bot. These are the important elements:

- The FindSpawnPad() function finds the spawnpad in the level that has a PadNumber equal to the input parameter and returns a reference to it or None if no pad is found.

- The SpawnBot() function spawns the enemy bot at a location in the 3d world with a bot controller BotAttackCoverController and bot pawn BotPawnCh10 and initializes it.

- The function SpawnBotOnRandomPad() randomly chooses a bot spawn pad in the level. It then finds a reference to the pad using the FindSpawnPad() function and creates this bot at that location using the SpawnBot() function.

Listing 10–3. *Spawning Bots*

```
function Actor FindSpawnPad(int PadNumber)
{
    local BotSpawnPad TempSpawnPad;
    local Actor ReturnSpawnPad;

    ReturnSpawnPad = None;
    foreach AllActors(class'BotSpawnPad', TempSpawnPad)
    {
        SpawnPadLocations.Additem(TempSpawnPad.Location);
        if(TempSpawnPad.PadNumber == PadNumber)
        {
            ReturnSpawnPad = TempSpawnPad;
        }
    }
    return ReturnSpawnPad;
}
function SpawnBot(Vector SpawnLocation, optional Vector Offset)
{
    SpawnLocation = SpawnLocation + Offset;
    EnemyBot = Spawn(class'BotAttackCoverController',,,SpawnLocation;
    EnemyPawn = Spawn(class'BotPawnCh10',,,SpawnLocation);
    EnemyBot.Possess(EnemyPawn,false);
    BotAttackCoverController(EnemyBot).BotThreat = Pawn;
    BotPawnCh10(EnemyPawn).AddDefaultInventory();
    BotPawnCh10(EnemyPawn).InitialLocation = SpawnLocation;
    BotPawnCh10(EnemyPawn).SpawnPadLocations = SpawnPadLocations;
    EnemyPawn.SetPhysics(PHYS_Falling);
}
function SpawnBotOnRandomPad(vector AlternateLocation, vector offset)
{
    local int RandomPadNumber;
    local Actor SpawnPad;
    local int MaxPads;
```

```
MaxPads = ExampleCh10Game(WorldInfo.Game).MaxSpawnPads;
RandomPadNumber = Rand(MaxPads);// Number from 0 to Max-1.
WorldInfo.Game.Broadcast(self,"RANDOMPADNUMBER = " @ RandomPadNumber);
SpawnPad = FindSpawnPad(RandomPadNumber);
if (SpawnPad != None)
{
    SpawnBot(SpawnPad.Location, offset);
}
else
{
    SpawnBot(AlternateLocation, Offset);
}
}
```

The next piece of code, which is in Listing 10–4, deals with player touch input. Again, the bold code is specific to this example, and the base code for the functions in this listing can be found in the hands-on example in Chapter 2.

In the SwipeZoneCallback() function code has been added to reset our game and to fire our weapon.

Listing 10–4. *Player Input*

```
function bool SwipeZoneCallback(MobileInputZone Zone,
                                float DeltaTime,
                                int Handle,
                                EZoneTouchEvent EventType,
                                Vector2D TouchLocation)
{
    local bool retval;
    retval = true;
    if (EventType == ZoneEvent_Touch)
    {
        // Reset Game
        if (ExampleCh10Game(WorldInfo.Game).bGameOver)
        {
            ResetGame();
        }
        else
        {
            // Start Firing pawn's weapon
        StartFire(0);
        }
    }
    else
    if(EventType == ZoneEvent_Update)
    {
    }
    else
    if (EventType == ZoneEvent_UnTouch)
    {
        // Stop Firing Pawn's weapon
        StopFire(0);
    }
    return retval;
```

```
}

function SetupZones()
{
    Super.SetupZones();
    // If we have a game class, configure the zones
    if (MPI != None && WorldInfo.GRI.GameClass != none)
    {
        LocalPlayer(Player).ViewportClient.GetViewportSize(ViewportSize);
        if (FreeLookZone != none)
        {
            FreeLookZone.OnProcessInputDelegate = SwipeZoneCallback;
        }
    }
}
```

The code segment in Listing 10–5 deals with placing the player's weapon in the first-person view. This PlaceWeapon() function is exactly the same as the one in Listing 3-18, which created the player controller class in Chapter 3.

Listing 10–5. *Placing the Weapon*

```
function PlaceWeapon()
{
    // First Person
    local vector WeaponLocation;
    local Rotator WeaponRotation,TempRot;
    local Weapon TestW;
    local vector WeaponAimVect;

    WeaponRotation.yaw = -16000; // 90 Degrees turn = OFFSET
    TempRot = Pawn.GetBaseAimRotation();
    WeaponRotation.pitch = TempRot.roll;
    WeaponRotation.yaw   += TempRot.yaw;
    WeaponRotation.roll  -= TempRot.pitch; // Switch due to weapon local axes
orientation
    WeaponAimVect = Normal(Vector(TempRot));
    WeaponLocation = Pawn.Location + (40 * WeaponAimVect) + vect(0,0,30);

    TestW = Pawn.Weapon; //Pawn.InvManager.GetBestWeapon();
    if (TestW != None)
    {
        TestW.SetLocation(WeaponLocation);
        TestW.SetRotation(WeaponRotation);
    }
    else
    {
        WorldInfo.Game.Broadcast(self,"Player has no weapon!!!!!");
    }
}
```

The code segment in Listing 10–6 is the PlayerTick() function, which is called continuously or "ticked". The PlayerTick() function adds in code for testing for the game over status and implementing code for a game over status. In terms of the game over status, if bGameOver is true, then the game is over because the player has died. If the player is still alive, bGameOver is false.

Listing 10–6. *PlayerTick Function*

```
function PlayerTick(float DeltaTime)
{
    Super.PlayerTick(DeltaTime);
    PlaceWeapon();
    if (!BotSpawned)
    {
        SpawnBotOnRandomPad(Pawn.Location, vect(0,0,500));
        BotSpawned = true;
        JazzCh10Pawn(Pawn).InitialLocation = Pawn.Location;
    }
    if (Pawn.Health <= 0)
    {
        ExampleCh10Game(WorldInfo.Game).bGameOver = true;
    }
    if (ExampleCh10Game(WorldInfo.Game).bGameOver)
    {
        Pawn.Health = 0;
        StopFire(0);
        Pawn.SetHidden(true);
        Pawn.Weapon.SetHidden(true);
        Pawn.Velocity = vect(0,0,0);
    }
}
defaultproperties
{
    BotSpawned = false;
}
```

FRAMEWORK NOTE: When adding a new weapon you may also have to modify the
PlaceWeapon() function which places the weapon mesh into the player's first-person view.

Creating the Player's Pawn

Next, the code for the player's pawn must be created (see Listing 10–7).

Several key elements from this listing:

- The key new function is the AddHealthBonus() function which
  processes the health powerup bonus. (Listing 3-17 in Chapter 3 is the
  base class for a player's pawn using the default first-person view.)

- The function TakeDamage() plays a sound when this pawn is hit and
  calculates damage to health.

- The AddDefaultInventory() function adds in our new custom weapon
  for this framework.

Listing 10–7. *Player's Pawn*

```
class JazzCh10Pawn extends SimplePawn;

var Inventory MainGun;
var vector InitialLocation;
var SoundCue PawnHitSound;

function AddHealthBonus(int Value)
{
    Health = Health + value;
}

event TakeDamage(int Damage, Controller InstigatedBy, vector HitLocation, vector
Momentum, class<DamageType> DamageType, optional TraceHitInfo HitInfo, optional Actor
DamageCauser)
{
    PlaySound(PawnHitSound);
    Health = Health - Damage;
}

function AddDefaultInventory()
{
    MainGun = InvManager.CreateInventory(class'JazzWeaponCh10');
    MainGun.SetHidden(false);
    Weapon(MainGun).FireOffset = vect(0,0,-70);
}

defaultproperties
{
    InventoryManagerClass=class'WeaponsIM1'
    PawnHitSound =
SoundCue'A_Character_CorruptEnigma_Cue.Mean_Efforts.A_Effort_EnigmaMean_Death_Cue'
}
```

Creating the Player's Weapon

Next, we need to create the player's weapon, as shown in Listing 10–8. The key new
code here is the setting of the WeaponProjectiles array to the new JazzBulletCh10
class.

Listing 10–8. *Player's Weapon*

```
class JazzWeaponCh10 extends Weapon;

defaultproperties
{
    Begin Object Class=SkeletalMeshComponent Name=FirstPersonMesh
        SkeletalMesh=SkeletalMesh'KismetGame_Assets.Anims.SK_JazzGun'
    End Object
    Mesh=FirstPersonMesh
    Components.Add(FirstPersonMesh);

    Begin Object Class=SkeletalMeshComponent Name=PickupMesh
        SkeletalMesh=SkeletalMesh'KismetGame_Assets.Anims.SK_JazzGun'
    End Object
```

```
    DroppedPickupMesh=PickupMesh
    PickupFactoryMesh=PickupMesh

    WeaponFireTypes(0)=EWFT_Projectile
    WeaponFireTypes(1)=EWFT_NONE

    WeaponProjectiles(0)=class'JazzBulletCh10'
    WeaponProjectiles(1)=class'JazzBulletCh10'

    FiringStatesArray(0)=WeaponFiring
    FireInterval(0)=0.25
    Spread(0)=0
}
```

The player's weapon in the first-person view should look like that shown in Figure 10–1.

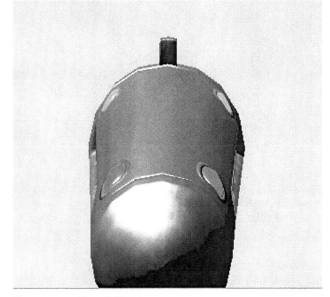

Figure 10–1. *Player's Weapon*

> **FRAMEWORK NOTE:** You can expand on this class by using a new custom class for the projectile or changing other weapon variables such as `FireInterval` which determines the time between shots.

Creating the Player's Projectile

Next, we need to create the projectile for the player's weapon (see Listing 10–9). The key changes from past versions of our custom projectile class here are new sound cues defined in variables `ImpactSound` and `SpawnSound`.

Listing 10–9. *Player weapon's bullet*

```
class JazzBulletCh10 extends Projectile;

var SoundCue FireSound;
var bool ImpactSoundPlayed;

simulated singular event Touch(Actor Other, PrimitiveComponent OtherComp, vector
HitLocation, vector HitNormal)
{
    Other.TakeDamage(33, InstigatorController, HitLocation, -HitNormal, None);
}
simulated function Explode(vector HitLocation, vector HitNormal)
{
    if (!ImpactSoundPlayed)
    {
        PlaySound(ImpactSound);
        ImpactSoundPlayed = true;
    }
    SetPhysics(Phys_Falling);
}
function Init( Vector Direction )
{
    super.Init(Direction);
    RandSpin(90000);
    PlaySound(SpawnSound);
    PlaySound(FireSound, , , true,,);
}
defaultproperties
{
    Begin Object Class=StaticMeshComponent Name=Bullet
        StaticMesh=StaticMesh'Castle_Assets.Meshes.SM_RiverRock_01'
        Scale3D=(X=0.300000,Y=0.30000,Z=0.3000)
    End Object
    Components.Add(Bullet)

    Begin Object Class=ParticleSystemComponent  Name=BulletTrail
        Template=ParticleSystem'Castle_Assets.FX.P_FX_Fire_SubUV_01'
    End Object
    Components.Add(BulletTrail)

    MaxSpeed=+05000.000000
    Speed=+05000.000000

    FireSound = SoundCue'A_Vehicle_Generic.Vehicle.Vehicle_Damage_FireLoop_Cue'
    ImpactSound =
SoundCue'A_Character_BodyImpacts.BodyImpacts.A_Character_RobotImpact_HeadshotRoll_Cue'
    SpawnSound = SoundCue'KismetGame_Assets.Sounds.S_WeaponRespawn_01_Cue'
    ImpactSoundPlayed = false
}
```

The player's projectile is shown in Figure 10–2.

Figure 10–2. *Player's Projectile*

Creating the Enemy Bot Related Classes

In this section we will create classes for our enemy bot. These classes will include those for the bot's pawn, controller, weapon, projectile, and spawnpad.

Creating the Bot Pawn

The first thing we need to do is create the enemy bot's pawn, as shown in Listing 10–10.

Key elements from the listing:

- New in this class are separate sounds that are played when an enemy bot dies which is DeathSound and when an enemy bot is injured which is HurtSound.

- The function GetRandomSpawnPosition() chooses a random pad from those stored in the array SpawnPadLocations and returns the location of that pad.

- The function AddHealthBonus() is used to process the bot's pickup of the bonus powerup and adds this bonus to the enemy bot's health.

Listing 10–10. *Enemy bot's pawn*

```
class BotPawnCh10 extends BotPawn2;

var array<vector> SpawnPadLocations;
var SoundCue DeathSound;
var SoundCue HurtSound;

function vector GetRandomSpawnPosition()
{
    local int RandPad;
    local int MaxPads;
    local vector returnvec;

    MaxPads = ExampleCh10Game(WorldInfo.Game).MaxSpawnPads;
    Randpad = Rand(MaxPads);
    WorldInfo.Game.Broadcast(self,"*************** " @ self @ " RESPAWNED at pad number
" @ RandPad);
    if (RandPad >= SpawnPadLocations.length)
    {
        // error
        return InitialLocation;
    }
    else
    {
        returnvec = SpawnPadLocations[RandPad];
    }
    return returnvec;
}
function AddHealthBonus(int Value)
{
    Health = Health + value;
}
event TakeDamage(int Damage, Controller InstigatedBy, vector HitLocation, vector
Momentum, class<DamageType> DamageType, optional TraceHitInfo HitInfo, optional Actor
DamageCauser)
{
    PlaySound(HurtSound);
    Health = Health - Damage;
    if (Health <= 0)
    {
        PlaySound(DeathSound);
        SetLocation(GetRandomSpawnPosition());
        SetPhysics(PHYS_Falling);
        Health = 100;
        BotAttackCoverController(Controller).ResetAfterSpawn();
        // Process Kill
        if (PlayerController(InstigatedBy) != None)
        {
            // Add kill to Player's Score
            ExampleCh10Game(WorldInfo.Game).Score += KillValue;
        }
    }
}
function AddDefaultInventory()
{
```

```
    MainGun = InvManager.CreateInventory(class'BotWeaponCh10');
    MainGun.SetHidden(false);
    AddGunToSocket('Weapon_R');
    Weapon(MainGun).FireOffset = vect(0,50,-70);
}
defaultproperties
{
    DeathSound = SoundCue'KismetGame_Assets.Sounds.Jazz_Death_Cue'
    HurtSound = SoundCue'KismetGame_Assets.Sounds.Jazz_SpinStop_Cue'
}
```

Creating the Bot Controller

Next, we need to create the bot's controller class. For a full version of this code without explanations, please download the source code for this book.

This new class builds upon the code presented in Chapter 8 where the bot moves from cover to cover and considers the player to be the threat. Important new code is highlighted in bold.

The first segment of code, shown in Listing 10–11, involves the variables that will be used in this class and cover node related functions:

- The bGotHealthPickup is true when the enemy bot has just taken the health bonus. If the enemy bot's health is less than the value of HealthPickupTrigger then the bot will retrieve a health powerup if one is available.

- The variable bJustRespawned is set to true just after the enemy bot is respawned and placed on a random spawn pad.

- When the bot is in the TakeCover state and an AttackTimeInterval has passed then bStartAttackEnemy is set to true and bot starts its attack on the player and bAttackDone is set to false. When the bot has a clear path to the player and is within AttackOffsetDist from the player then bAttackDone is set to true and the bot stops its attack.

Listing 10–11. *Class Variables and Cover Node Related Functions*

```
class BotAttackCoverController extends UDKBot;

// Navigation
var Actor CurrentGoal;
var Vector TempDest;
var Actor TempGoal;

// Cover Link
var CoverLink CurrentCover;
var bool BotInCover;

// Bot's Enemy
var Pawn BotThreat;
// Health Pickups
var bool bGotHealthPickup;
```

```
var int HealthPickupTrigger;
// Respawn
var bool bJustRespawned;
// Attack State
var int AttackOffsetDist;
var bool bAttackDone;
var int AttackTimeInterval;
var bool bStartAttackEnemy;

function UnclaimAllSlots()
{
    local CoverLink CoverNodePointer;
    local CoverLink TempNodePointer;
    local bool done;

    CoverNodePointer = WorldInfo.Coverlist;
    done = false;
    while (!done)
    {
        CoverNodePointer.Unclaim(Pawn, 0, true);
        if (CoverNodePointer.NextCoverLink != None)
        {
            TempNodePointer = CoverNodePointer.NextCoverLink;
            CoverNodePointer = TempNodePointer;
        }
        else
        {
            done = true;
        }
    }
    Pawn.ShouldCrouch(false);
    BotInCover = false;
}
function FindEnemyLocation(out vector EnemyLocation)
{
    EnemyLocation = BotThreat.Location;
}
function CoverLink FindClosestEmptyCoverNodeWithinRange(Vector ThreatLocation, vector
Position, float Radius)
{
    local CoverLink CoverNodePointer;
    local CoverLink TempNodePointer;
    local bool done;

    local CoverLink ValidCoverNode;
    local bool SlotValid;
    local bool SlotAvailable;
    local bool NodeFound;
    local int DefaultSlot;

    local float Dist2Cover;
    local float ClosestCoverNode;

    CoverNodePointer = WorldInfo.Coverlist;
    DefaultSlot = 0;   // Assume only 1 slot per cover node.
    ClosestCoverNode = 999999999;
```

```
        ValidCoverNode = None;
        NodeFound = false;

        done = false;
        while (!done)
        {
            SlotValid = CoverLinkEx(CoverNodePointer).IsCoverSlotValid(0,ThreatLocation);
            SlotAvailable = CoverLinkEx(CoverNodePointer).IsCoverSlotAvailable(0);
            Dist2Cover =  VSize(CoverNodePointer.GetSlotLocation(DefaultSlot) - Position);
            if (SlotValid && SlotAvailable && (Dist2Cover < ClosestCoverNode))
            {
                ValidCoverNode = CoverNodePointer;
                ClosestCoverNode = Dist2Cover;
                NodeFound = true;
            }

            // Goto Next CoverNode
            if (CoverNodePointer.NextCoverLink != None)
            {
                TempNodePointer = CoverNodePointer.NextCoverLink;
                CoverNodePointer = TempNodePointer;
            }
            else
            {
                // No more Cover Nodes
                done = true;
            }
        }
        if (!NodeFound)
        {
            WorldInfo.Game.Broadcast(self,"!!! Can Not Find Valid CoverNode");
        }
        return ValidCoverNode;
}
function bool IsCurrentCoverValid()
{
        local bool RetVal;
        local vector ThreatLoc;

        RetVal = false;
        if (CurrentCover != None)
        {
            FindEnemyLocation(ThreatLoc);
            RetVal = CoverLinkEx(CurrentCover).IsCoverSlotValid(0, ThreatLoc);
        }
        return Retval;
}
function PrepMoveToCover()
{
        local vector ThreatLoc;
        local CoverLink NextCover;

        FindEnemyLocation(ThreatLoc);
        NextCover = FindClosestEmptyCoverNodeWithinRange(ThreatLoc, Pawn.Location, 9999999);
        if (NextCover != None)
        {
            WorldInfo.Game.Broadcast(self, self @ " moving to Next Cover " @ NextCover);
```

```
            CurrentCover = NextCover;
            CurrentGoal = CurrentCover;
            BotInCover = false;
            UnclaimAllSlots();
            CurrentCover.Claim(Pawn, 0);
        }
    }
}
```

Listing 10–12 contains the next piece of code that contains the GeneratePathTo() function that actually generates the navigation path that the computer controlled bot will use. This is the exact same function that was used in Chapter 5 on bots.

Listing 10–12. *GeneratePathTo*

```
event bool GeneratePathTo(Actor Goal, optional float WithinDistance, optional bool
bAllowPartialPath)
{
    if( NavigationHandle == None )
    return FALSE;

    // Clear cache and constraints (ignore recycling for the moment)
    NavigationHandle.PathConstraintList = none;
    NavigationHandle.PathGoalList = none;
    class'NavMeshPath_Toward'.static.TowardGoal( NavigationHandle, Goal );
    class'NavMeshGoal_At'.static.AtActor( NavigationHandle, Goal, WithinDistance,
bAllowPartialPath );
    return NavigationHandle.FindPath();
}
```

The next code segment, in Listing 10–13, involves the TakeCover state in which the enemy bot uses the UDK cover node system to shield itself from incoming fire.

The AttackEnemyTimer() function is called after the AttackTimeInterval amount of time when the bot is in the TakeCover state to flag that the bot's attack on the player should start.

> **NOTE:** In the BeginState and EndState functions, the "Put Code Here" comments in the code refer to new code you can add to extend this framework for you own customized game.

Listing 10–13. *TakeCover State*

```
function AttackEnemyTimer()
{
    bStartAttackEnemy = true;
}
state TakeCover
{
    event BeginState( Name PreviousStateName )
    {
        // Put code here that is to only be executed when the state is first entered
        bStartAttackEnemy = false;
        SetTimer(AttackTimeInterval, false, 'AttackEnemyTimer');
    }
    event EndState( Name NextStateName )
    {
```

```
        // Put code here that is to be executed only when exiting this state
    }

    Begin:
    WorldInfo.Game.Broadcast(self,"********** In State TAKECOVER");
    if (CurrentGoal != None)
    {
        if(GeneratePathTo(CurrentGoal))
        {
            NavigationHandle.SetFinalDestination(CurrentGoal.Location);

            if( NavigationHandle.ActorReachable(CurrentGoal) )
            {
                // then move directly to the actor
                MoveTo(CurrentGoal.Location, BotThreat);
                BotInCover = true;
            }
            else
            {
                // move to the first node on the path
                if( NavigationHandle.GetNextMoveLocation(TempDest,
Pawn.GetCollisionRadius()) )
                {
                    if (!NavigationHandle.SuggestMovePreparation(TempDest,self))
                    {
                        MoveTo(TempDest, BotThreat);
                    }
                }
            }
        }
        else
        {
            WorldInfo.Game.Broadcast(self,"FindNavMeshPath failed to find a path!,
CurrentGoal = " @ CurrentGoal);
            MoveTo(Pawn.Location);
        }
    }
    LatentWhatToDoNext();
}
```

The next piece of code, shown in Listing 10–14, involves code related to the enemy bot retrieving the health powerup. These are the key components:

▩ The NeedHealthPickup() returns true if the enemy bot's health is less than the HealthPickupTrigger value. The HealthPickupAvailable() function returns a reference to the Health Bonus powerup closest to the enemy bot if one exists or None if no health powerups exist.

▩ The PrepGettingHealthPickup() function releases the ownership of any cover node that the bot may be occupying, sets the goal of the bot to point to the health bonus, and does other initializations in preparation for the bot transitioning to the GettingHealthPickup state.

▩ The GettingHealthPickup state moves the enemy bot toward the health powerup and sets bGotHealthPickup to true when the bot moves over it.

Listing 10–14. *Getting the Health Pickup*

```
function bool NeedHealthPickup()
{
    local bool bresult;
    if (Pawn.Health < HealthPickupTrigger)
    {
        bresult = true;
    }
    else
    {
        bresult = false;
    }
    return bresult;
}
function Actor HealthPickupAvailable()
{
    local Bonus1 TempBonus;
    local Actor ReturnActor;
    local float ClosestDist;
    local float TempDist;

    ReturnActor = None;
    ClosestDist = 999999;

    foreach AllActors(class'Bonus1', TempBonus)
    {
        TempDist = VSize(Pawn.Location - TempBonus.Location);
        If (TempDist < ClosestDist)
        {
            ReturnActor = TempBonus;
            ClosestDist = TempDist;
        }
    }
    return ReturnActor;
}
function PrepGettingHealthPickup(Actor Pickup)
{
    UnclaimAllSlots();
    CurrentGoal = Pickup;
    CurrentCover = None;
    bGotHealthPickup = false;
}
state GettingHealthPickup
{
    event BeginState( Name PreviousStateName )
    {
        // Put code here that is to only be executed when the state is first entered
    }
    event EndState( Name NextStateName )
    {
        // Put code here that is to be executed only when exiting this state
    }
    Begin:
```

```
    WorldInfo.Game.Broadcast(self,"-----------> In state GettingHealthPickup");
    if (CurrentGoal != None)
    {
        if(GeneratePathTo(CurrentGoal))
        {
            NavigationHandle.SetFinalDestination(CurrentGoal.Location);

            if( NavigationHandle.ActorReachable(CurrentGoal) )
            {
                // then move directly to the actor
                MoveTo(CurrentGoal.Location);
                bGotHealthPickup = true;
            }
            else
            {
                // move to the first node on the path
                if( NavigationHandle.GetNextMoveLocation(TempDest,
Pawn.GetCollisionRadius()) )
                {
                    if (!NavigationHandle.SuggestMovePreparation(TempDest,self))
                    {
                        MoveTo(TempDest, BotThreat);
                    }
                }
            }
        }
        else
        {
            MoveTo(Pawn.Location);
        }
    }
    LatentWhatToDoNext();
}
```

The code in Listing 10–15 deals with the enemy bot attacking the player:

- The PrepAttackingEnemy() function initializes the enemy bot for coming out of cover and entering the AttackingEnemy state by releasing any cover nodes that the bot currently occupies. The bot is ordered to start firing its weapon and other initializations take place.

- The AttackingEnemy state moves the enemy bot toward the player and when the player is directly reachable by the bot (has a clear line of sight without obstacles) within AttackOffsetDist distance bAttackDone is set to true and the attack is finished.

Listing 10–15. *Attacking the Player*

```
function PrepAttackingEnemy()
{
    bAttackDone = false;
    UnclaimAllSlots();
    CurrentGoal = BotThreat;
    CurrentCover = None;
```

```
    Pawn.StartFire(0);
}
state AttackingEnemy
{
    event BeginState( Name PreviousStateName )
    {
        // Put code here that is to only be executed when the state is first entered
        PrepAttackingEnemy();
    }
    event EndState( Name NextStateName )
    {
        // Put code here that is to be executed only when exiting this state
        Pawn.StopFire(0);
    }
    Begin:
    WorldInfo.Game.Broadcast(self,"############# In State AttackingEnemy");
    if (CurrentGoal != None)
    {
        if(GeneratePathTo(CurrentGoal))
        {
            NavigationHandle.SetFinalDestination(CurrentGoal.Location);

            if( NavigationHandle.ActorReachable(CurrentGoal) )
            {
                // then move directly to the actor
                MoveTo(CurrentGoal.Location, BotThreat, AttackOffsetDist);
                bAttackDone = true;
            }
            else
            {
                // move to the first node on the path
                if( NavigationHandle.GetNextMoveLocation(TempDest,
Pawn.GetCollisionRadius()) )
                {
                    if (!NavigationHandle.SuggestMovePreparation(TempDest,self))
                    {
                        MoveTo(TempDest, BotThreat);
                    }
                }
            }
        }
    }
    else
    {
        MoveTo(Pawn.Location);
    }
    }
    LatentWhatToDoNext();
}
```

The next code piece is shown in Listing 10–16. It involves resetting the enemy bot after it dies:

- The function ResetAfterSpawn() is called from the BotPawnCh10 class in the TakeDamage() function if the enemy bot dies.

- The function `ExecuteResetAfterSpawn()` actually executes the reset/respawn of the enemy bot when `bJustRespawned` is true. In addition this function unclaims any cover nodes owned by the enemy bot and sets up the move to the `TakeCover` state.

Listing 10–16. *Resetting the Bot*

```
function ResetAfterSpawn()
{
    bJustRespawned = true;
}
function ExecuteResetAfterSpawn()
{
    UnclaimAllSlots();
    CurrentCover = None;
    CurrentGoal = None;
    bGotHealthPickup = false;
    BotInCover = false;
    PrepMoveToCover();
}
```

Listing 10–17 shows the supporting code related to the enemy bot's Artificial Intelligence. This was originally presented in Chapter 5.

Listing 10–17. *AI-related code*

```
auto state Initial
{
    Begin:
    LatentWhatToDoNext();
}
event WhatToDoNext()
{
    DecisionComponent.bTriggered = true;
}
```

The piece of code in Listing 10–18 is related to the enemy bot's AI. A simplified state diagram of the enemy bot's AI is shown in Figure 10–3.

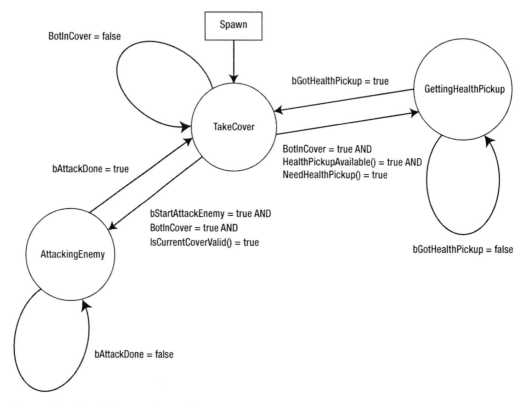

Figure 10–3. *Simplified state diagram for enemy bot*

In Listing 10-18, the ExecuteWhatToDoNext() function is the main decision-making function for the enemy bot. Here the bot makes the decision of which state to transition to based on certain conditions such as its health, whether it's time to attack the player or not.

Listing 10–18. *ExecuteWhatToDoNext*

```
protected event ExecuteWhatToDoNext()
{
    local Actor TempActor;

    if (bJustRespawned)
    {
        bJustRespawned = false;
        ExecuteResetAfterSpawn();
        GotoState('TakeCover', 'Begin');
    }
    else
    if (IsInState('Initial'))
    {
        PrepMoveToCover();
        GotoState('TakeCover', 'Begin');
    }
    else
```

```
if (IsInState('TakeCover'))
{
    if (BotInCover)
    {
        TempActor = HealthPickupAvailable();
        if (NeedHealthPickup() && (TempActor != None))
        {
            // Health Pickup available and needed
            PrepGettingHealthPickup(TempActor);
            GotoState('GettingHealthPickup','Begin');
        }
        else
        if (IsCurrentCoverValid())
        {
            if (bStartAttackEnemy)
            {
                GotoState('AttackingEnemy', 'Begin');
            }
            else
            {
                GotoState('TakeCover', 'Begin');
            }
        }
        else
        {
            PrepMoveToCover();
            GotoState('TakeCover', 'Begin');
        }
    }
    else
    {
        GotoState('TakeCover', 'Begin');
    }
}
else
if (IsInState('GettingHealthPickup'))
{
    if (!bGotHealthPickup)
    {
        GotoState('GettingHealthPickup','Begin');
    }
    else
    {
        // Got Pickup Now Take Cover
        PrepMoveToCover();
        GotoState('TakeCover', 'Begin');
    }
}
else
if (IsInState('AttackingEnemy'))
{
    if (!bAttackDone)
    {
        GotoState('AttackingEnemy', 'Begin');
```

```
        }
        else
        {
            PrepMoveToCover();
            GotoState('TakeCover', 'Begin');
        }
    }
}
```

Listing 10–19 contains the next piece of code for this class, which sets the default values for the variables in this class.

Here in the defaultproperties block, you can set key variables such as AttackTimeInterval which controls the time the bot waits in cover before attacking and AttackOffsetDist which controls how close the enemy bot will get to the player when attacking.

Listing 10–19. *Default Properties*

```
defaultproperties
{
    CurrentGoal = None
    CurrentCover = None
    BotInCover = false

    bGotHealthPickup = false
    HealthPickupTrigger = 49
    bJustRespawned = false

    AttackOffsetDist = 700
    bAttackDone = false
    AttackTimeInterval = 3
    bStartAttackEnemy = false
}
```

Creating the Bot Weapon

Next, we need to create the code for the enemy bot's weapon, shown in Listing 10–20. The key new code here is which class of projectiles the weapon will fire and is now set to the BotBulletCh10 class.

Listing 10–20. *Enemy bots's weapon*

```
class BotWeaponCh10 extends Weapon;
defaultproperties
{
    Begin Object Class=SkeletalMeshComponent Name=FirstPersonMesh
        SkeletalMesh=SkeletalMesh'KismetGame_Assets.Anims.SK_JazzGun'
    End Object
    Mesh=FirstPersonMesh
    Components.Add(FirstPersonMesh);

    Begin Object Class=SkeletalMeshComponent Name=PickupMesh
        SkeletalMesh=SkeletalMesh'KismetGame_Assets.Anims.SK_JazzGun'
    End Object
```

```
      DroppedPickupMesh=PickupMesh
      PickupFactoryMesh=PickupMesh

      WeaponFireTypes(0)=EWFT_Projectile
      WeaponFireTypes(1)=EWFT_NONE

      WeaponProjectiles(0)=class'BotBulletCh10'
      WeaponProjectiles(1)=class'BotBulletCh10'

      FiringStatesArray(0)=WeaponFiring
      FireInterval(0)=0.25
      Spread(0)=0
}
```

Creating the Bot Projectile

Next, we need to create the projectile class for the enemy bot's weapon. Listing 10–21 contains the code.

The key change here is the lowering of the amount of health damage this projectile does to the pawn that it hits from 33 in the JazzBulletSound class to 2 in this derived class. This makes it easier to play around with this framework and not get killed so often.

Listing 10–21. *Enemy bot's weapon's projectile*

```
class BotBulletCh10 extends JazzBulletSound;
simulated singular event Touch(Actor Other, PrimitiveComponent OtherComp, vector
HitLocation, vector HitNormal)
{
    Other.TakeDamage(2, InstigatorController, HitLocation, -HitNormal, None);
}
```

Creating the Bot Spawn Pad

Next, we need to create the enemy bot's spawn pad. The one created in Listing 10–22 is similar to the one we created for the sample game in Chapter 7. However, with this pad, we add a new 3d mesh graphic to represent our pad and we add a user editable variable called PadNumber. You can place an object of this class in a level using the Unreal Editor and edit its PadNumber in the properties window.

Listing 10–22. *Bot spawn pad*

```
class BotSpawnPad extends Actor
placeable;

var() int PadNumber;

defaultproperties
{
    Begin Object Class=StaticMeshComponent Name=StaticMeshComponent0
        StaticMesh=StaticMesh'Pickups.jump_pad.S_Pickups_Jump_Pad'
    End Object
    Components.Add(StaticMeshComponent0)
```

```
        Begin Object Class=CylinderComponent NAME=CollisionCylinder
            CollideActors=true
            CollisionRadius=+0040.000000
            CollisionHeight=+0040.000000
        End Object
        CollisionComponent=CollisionCylinder
        Components.Add(CollisionCylinder)

        bCollideActors=true
        PadNumber = 0
}
```

Creating the HUD

Next, we need to create a custom HUD class. Most of the code will be the same as other HUD code from Chapter 6. The custom HUD code is in Listing 10–23, and the difference are set in bold print. Notably in this listing,

- The variable HUDEnemyHealth displays the health of the enemy bot.

- The HUDEnemyHealth variable is initialized in the PostBeginPlay() function.

- Modifications have been made to the DrawHUD() function to draw the enemy bot's health on the HUD as well as changes needed due to the new game type which is ExampleCh10Game.

Listing 10–23. *The Custom HUD*

```
class FPSHUD extends UDKHud;

struct HUDInfo
{
    var string Label;
    var Vector2D TextLocation;
    var Color TextColor;
    var Vector2D Scale;
};

// HUD
var HUDInfo HUDHealth;

var HUDInfo HUDEnemyHealth;
var HUDInfo HUDGameOver;
var HUDInfo HUDScore;

simulated function PostBeginPlay()
{
    Super.PostBeginPlay();

    HUDHealth.Label = "Health:";
    HUDHealth.TextLocation.x = 1100;
    HUDHealth.TextLocation.y = 0;
    HUDHealth.TextColor.R = 255;
    HUDHealth.TextColor.G = 0;
    HUDHealth.TextColor.B = 0;
```

```
        HUDHealth.Scale.X = 2;
        HUDHealth.Scale.Y = 4;

        HUDEnemyHealth.Label = "Enemy Health:";
        HUDEnemyHealth.TextLocation.x = 500;
        HUDEnemyHealth.TextLocation.y = 0;
        HUDEnemyHealth.TextColor.R = 255;
        HUDEnemyHealth.TextColor.G = 0;
        HUDEnemyHealth.TextColor.B = 0;
        HUDEnemyHealth.Scale.X = 2;
        HUDEnemyHealth.Scale.Y = 4;

        HUDGameOver.Label = "GAME OVER";
        HUDGameOver.TextLocation.x = 400;
        HUDGameOver.TextLocation.y = 300;
        HUDGameOver.TextColor.R = 255;
        HUDGameOver.TextColor.G = 0;
        HUDGameOver.TextColor.B = 255;
        HUDGameOver.Scale.X = 7;
        HUDGameOver.Scale.Y = 7;

        HUDScore.Label = "Score:";
        HUDScore.TextLocation.x = 0;
        HUDScore.TextLocation.y = 0;
        HUDScore.TextColor.R = 255;
        HUDScore.TextColor.G = 0;
        HUDScore.TextColor.B = 0;
        HUDScore.Scale.X = 2;
        HUDScore.Scale.Y = 4;
}

function DrawHUDItem(HUDInfo Info, coerce string Value)
{
        local Vector2D TextSize;

        Canvas.SetDrawColor(Info.TextColor.R, Info.TextColor.G, Info.TextColor.B);
        Canvas.SetPos(Info.TextLocation.X, Info.TextLocation.Y);
        Canvas.DrawText(Info.Label, ,Info.Scale.X,Info.Scale.Y);
        Canvas.TextSize(Info.Label, TextSize.X, TextSize.Y);
        Canvas.SetPos(Info.TextLocation.X + (TextSize.X * Info.Scale.X),
Info.TextLocation.Y);
        Canvas.DrawText(Value, , Info.Scale.X, Info.Scale.Y);
}
function DrawHUD()
{
        super.DrawHUD();
        Canvas.Font = class'Engine'.static.GetLargeFont();
        // Score
        DrawHUDItem(HUDScore,ExampleCh10Game(WorldInfo.Game).Score);
        // Enemy Health
        DrawHUDItem(HUDEnemyHealth, ExampleCh10PC(PlayerOwner).EnemyPawn.Health);
        // Health
        DrawHUDItem(HUDHealth,PlayerOwner.Pawn.Health);
        // Game Over
        if (ExampleCh10Game(WorldInfo.Game).bGameOver)
        {
```

```
        DrawHUDItem(HUDGameOver, "");
    }
}
defaultProperties
{
}
```

Creating the Bonus

The next class we need to create is the class that represents the Health Bonus power-up class. This class is shown in Listing 10–24.

The key functions in this class are the Touch() and Tick() functions. The Touch() function is called when this object touches another object. If the object touched is a player then the player's health powerup function is called. If the object is an enemy bot then the enemy bot's health powerup function is called. The Tick() function is called continuously and is used to update the rotation of the health bonus 3d mesh in the game world.

The Value variable is the amount of health to add to the player or an enemy bot.

Listing 10–24. *Health Bonus power-up class*

```
class Bonus1 extends Actor
placeable;

var() float Value;
var SoundCue PickupSound;
var int SoundCueLength;

event Touch(Actor Other, PrimitiveComponent OtherComp, vector HitLocation, vector
HitNormal)
{
    WorldInfo.Game.Broadcast(self,"Health Bonus1 Has Been Touched by " @ Other @ ",
Bonus Value = " @ Value);
    if (Other.IsA('JazzCh10Pawn'))
    {
        JazzCh10Pawn(Other).AddHealthBonus(Value);
        PlaySound(PickUpSound);
        destroy();
    }
    else
    if (Other.IsA('BotPawnCh10'))
    {
        BotPawnCh10(Other).AddHealthBonus(Value);
        PlaySound(PickUpSound);
        destroy();
    }
}

function Tick(FLOAT DeltaTime)
{
    local Rotator TempRot;

    TempRot = Rotation;
```

```
        TempRot.yaw = Rotation.yaw + (15000 * DeltaTime);
        SetRotation(TempRot);
}

defaultproperties
{
        Begin Object Class=StaticMeshComponent Name=HealthMesh
            StaticMesh=StaticMesh'Pickups.Health_Large.Mesh.S_Pickups_Health_Large_Keg'
        End Object
        Components.Add(HealthMesh)

        Begin Object Class=CylinderComponent NAME=CollisionCylinder
            CollideActors=true
            CollisionRadius=+0040.000000
            CollisionHeight=+0040.000000
        End Object
        CollisionComponent=CollisionCylinder
        Components.Add(CollisionCylinder)

        bCollideActors=true
        bEdShouldSnap=True

        value = 25
        PickupSound = SoundCue'A_Pickups.Health.Cue.A_Pickups_Health_Super_Cue'
        SoundCueLength = 3
}
```

Configuring the Game Type

Next, we need to set up this new example for compilation and for playing on the mobile previewer. In the configuration directory located at

```
C:\UDK\UDK-2011-06\UDKGame\Config
```

change the UDKEngine.ini and Mobile-UDKGame.ini configuration files to the following. (This path is for the June 2011 version of the UDK. If you are using a different UDK version, then this default directory will be different.)

```
UDKEngine.ini
[UnrealEd.EditorEngine]
ModEditPackages=ExampleCh10
Mobile-UDKGame.ini
[ExampleCh10.ExampleCh10Game]
RequiredMobileInputConfigs=(GroupName="UberGroup",RequireZoneNames=("UberStickMoveZone",
"UberStickLookZone","UberLookZone"))
```

Save the configuration files. You may need to write protect them to preserve the contents since the UDK sometimes overwrites them (see the section "Configuring the Game Type" in Chapter 9).

Bring up the Unreal Frontend and compile the scripts.

Creating the Level

The next thing we need to do is create the level. Perform the following steps:

1. Bring up the Unreal Editor.
2. Load in the level that you created in Chapter 8 that involves the bot moving from cover to cover and hiding from the player. (You also can find the level— ExampleCh8Map.zip—with the source code for this book.)
3. Save the level as a new level by selecting **File ➤ Save As** from the main menu and entering a new filename for the map. Choose whatever filename you wish.
4. The level should consist of a group of crates with cover nodes placed on each side of the box with cover slots facing each side of the box. See Figure 10–4.

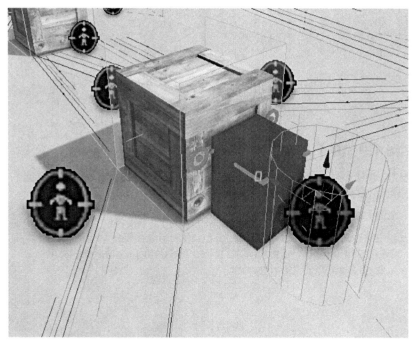

Figure 10–4. *Crate with cover nodes*

5. Select the crate and cover nodes by holding down the Ctrl key and clicking on the crate and all the cover nodes around it. Then make copies of these objects until they are spread across the level. Hold down the Alt key and move the transformation widget to create a new copy and move it to an open area. See Figure 10–5.

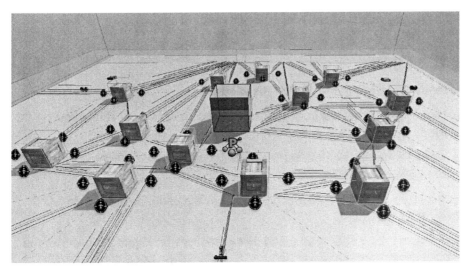

Figure 10–5. *Level with crates with cover nodes*

6. Now we need to create and place the enemy bot spawn pad. Go to the Actor Classes tab in the generic browser and type in BotSpawnPad into the search box to bring up the new BotSpawnPad class. Click on the class and drag and drop it into an empty corner of the level.

7. Type in Bonus1 into the search box in the Actor Classes tab to bring up the Bonus1 class. Click on this class and drag and drop it near the spawn pad you just placed in the level (see Figure 10–6).

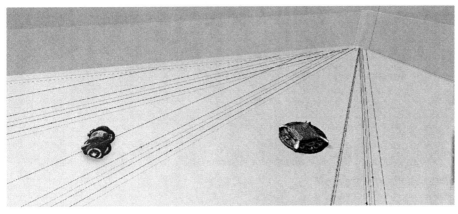

Figure 10–6. *Putting a bot spawn pad and bonus in a corner of the level*

8. Put spawn pads and Bonus power-ups in each of the four corners of the level. For the first bot spawn pad, set the number to 0 and number each one consecutively higher.

9. Rebuild the AI paths by selecting **Build ➤ AI Paths** from the Unreal Editor menu.

10. Save the level by selecting File ➤ Save Current Level.

Running the Game

Now, we are ready to run our game. Follow these steps:

1. Select View ➤ World Properties from the Unreal Editor main menu. This brings up the World Properties window.

2. In the World Properties window set the Default Game Type under the Game Type category to ExampleCh10Game.

3. Select the Play ➤ On Mobile Previewer option to run the game on the mobile previewer form the Editor.

Figure 10–7 shows the player being attacked by the enemy bot. Figure 10–8 shows the enemy bot taking cover from the player. Figure 10–9 shows the bot getting a health power-up.

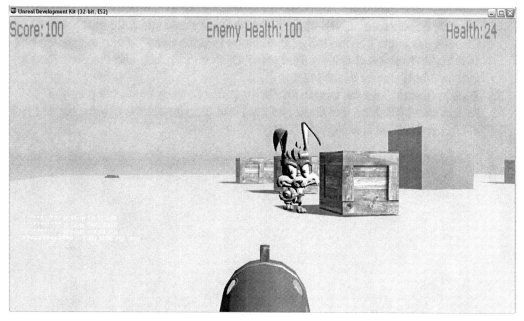

Figure 10–7. *Enemy bot attacking the player*

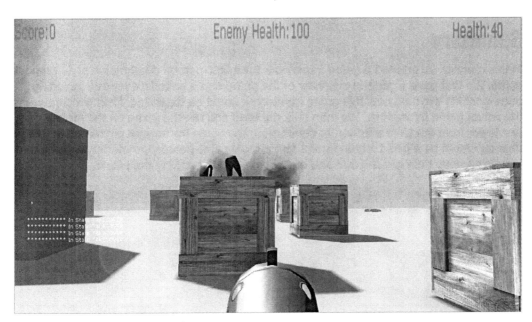

Figure 10–8. *Enemy bot taking cover from player*

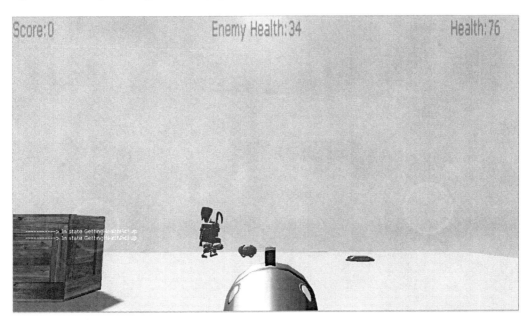

Figure 10–9. *Enemy bot retrieving a health power up*

Summary

In this chapter we created a game framework for a first-person deathmatch style combat game. We first gave a general overview of the game and a specific overview including code-specific ways on how this game framework could be extended. Next we created the actual game framework. We then built the level and ran the game on the mobile previewer from the Unreal Editor. In conclusion, the game framework presented in this chapter would be a good starting point for your own first-person shooter style game that involves enemy bots moving into and out of cover and attacking the player.

Chapter 11

Third-Person Shooter/Adventure Game Framework

In this chapter we will cover a third-person shooter / adventure game framework. A third-person shooter is distinct from a first-person shooter in that the player's pawn is visible. The great advantage of this is that it adds a movie like quality to the game. The player can see the in-game representation of himself perform various actions such as running, jumping, reloading, and firing weapons. An adventure game has the distinction of the player commanding other members of his party or squad to perform certain actions. This framework adds that feature whereby the player can command a computer-controlled character.

First a game framework overview is given. In this overview we give a general overview of the features of the framework, and then we give more code specific details on how these features are implemented. Next, we create the actual framework.

The general framework presented in this chapter consists of:

- A controllable player ally bot that can move to a location designated by the player, attack enemies selected by the player, and follows the player by default.

- An enemy bot that guards an asset and responds to attacks on that asset by attacking the player or bot responsible.

- An enemy asset that has a link to an enemy bot that guards it.

- A custom HUD that displays the player's health, the health of the player's bot ally, and the health of the objective (the enemy asset that is guarded) that the player must destroy.

- Framework code that tracks the health of the guarded enemy asset and displays a message when that enemy asset has been destroyed.

Game Framework Overview

In this section we give you an overview of the game framework from a general standpoint and a specific standpoint. The general overview will give you in general non-code specific terms the key features of this framework. The specific overview will give you a more detailed code specific overview of the game framework.

General Overview

This framework provides the basis for games you can define and create. It consists of various models, such as bots, meshes, and a HUD, that you can use or build on to produce the kind of game experience you want.

In this framework we build a player-controlled bot. This bot is issued commands by the player and then executes these commands. You can extend this framework by adding in new commands and the new states that will be needed to implement these commands. For a shooter type game a modification might be to modify the attack command so that your bot will attack certain target types with certain weapons that the player can specify. For an adventure style game a modification might be to add in a new set of commands specific to the needs of your adventure game. For example, you can expand the command set to include a command to have your bot negotiate with enemy forces.

In a general sense we have shown how to link the behaviors of objects of two different classes:

- We have created a computer-controlled bot that can respond to a threat to another Actor that it is guarding by attacking the threat and discontinuing that attack if certain conditions are true. Currently, that attack is broken off if the bot moves to a location that is too far away from the item it is guarding. You can expand on this framework by changing what specific type of Actor the bot is guarding, how the bot responds to a threat, and what conditions are needed for the bot to stop its attack on the threat.

- A new placeable class is created that includes a 3d mesh and is linked to another Actor that protects it. You can expand on this framework by changing the type of 3d mesh or the type of Actor that is associated with this class. For example, associate this object with the enemy that is assigned to destroy it.

This basic idea can be expanded to include any situation when you need to link events that occur to one type of object to behavior that needs to occur to another type of object.

A new HUD class that displays critical game statistics is presented. You can expand on this framework by adding or subtracting statistics that you want to add or delete from the HUD display using existing statistics as examples of how to do this.

Specific Overview

The artificial intelligence for the player's bot ally is implemented in the
BotAllyController class. The player issues commands to the bot through the player
controller class which is ExampleCh11PC. The ally bot is controlled by the player by
issuing the commands:

- Follow, to have the bot follow the player around the level

- Move, to have the bot move to a specific location in the game world, and

- Attack, to have the bot start its attack on the enemy bot that is guarding
  the objective.

The enemy bot's artificial intelligence is implemented in the BotControllerGuard class
and the bot's physical body is implemented in the GuardPawn class.

The player's objective which is the power generator is implemented in the Generator
class. This objective is guarded by an enemy bot that is referenced by the Guard variable
that is of the Pawn class.

The custom Heads Up Display is implemented in the Ch11HUD class and displays the
player's health, the player's bot's health, and the objective's health as well as displays
the mission accomplished message when the enemy asset is destroyed.

Hands-on Example: Third-Person Shooter/Adventure Game Framework

In this section we will build a framework suitable for a third-person shooter, third-person
adventure game or a perhaps a combination. You will be able to control an ally bot and
move it around the game world and order it to attack the enemy bot guarding the power
generator. Your objective would be to destroy this generator. We create new classes for
a game type, player controller, enemy guard controller, enemy guard pawn, player bot
ally controller, generator, HUD, and a custom bot marker that indicates toward what the
player's ally bot is to move.

Creating the Game Type

The first thing we need to do is create a new directory for the code for this project.
Create the ExampleCh11 directory under your default UDK installation directory at
C:\UDK\UDK-2011-06\Development\Src. If you are using a different version of the UDK
other than the June 2011 UDK then this default directory will be different. Create a
directory called Classes under the new directory you just created and put all your source
code files in this directory.

Create the following class, shown in Listing 11–1, and save it under the filename "ExampleCh11Game.uc". Again, as with all previous examples in this book, the filenames must match the classnames and the file extension must be ".uc".

The code in bold represents new or modified code from what was presented in previous chapters as well as important code that the reader should pay special attention to.

Listing 11–1. *Game type*

```
class ExampleCh11Game extends FrameworkGame;

event OnEngineHasLoaded()
{
    WorldInfo.Game.Broadcast(self,"ExampleCh11Game Type Active - Engine Has Loaded
!!!!");
}
function bool PreventDeath(Pawn KilledPawn, Controller Killer, class<DamageType>
DamageType, vector HitLocation)
{
    return true;
}
static event class<GameInfo> SetGameType(string MapName, string Options, string Portal)
{
    return super.SetGameType(MapName, Options, Portal);
}
defaultproperties
{
    PlayerControllerClass=class'ExampleCh11.ExampleCh11PC'
    DefaultPawnClass=class'JazzPawnDamage'
    HUDType=class'Ch11HUD'
    bRestartLevel=false
    bWaitingToStartMatch=true
    bDelayedStart=false
}
```

The PlayerControllerClass variable points to our custom player controller class ExampleCh11PC. The HUDType variable points to our custom HUD for this framework which is Ch11HUD.

Creating the Player Controller

Next, we need to create our custom player controller class. This class is similar to the player controller class in Chapter 5 covering bots in that the player can click on an area in the game world and have the bot move to that area. However, much has been changed and added. Now, the player must first select the ally bot and then direct the ally bot to an area to move to or an enemy bot to attack.

When the player is first initialized, the function SpawnAllyBot() is called to create the player's ally bot and the function CreateNewGuardBot() is called to create the enemy guard bot that guards the player's objective. In the PlayerTick() function that is continuously called, the FindObjectiveHealth() function is called to determine the damage done to the enemy structure and sets the bGameOver variable to true if this is true.

When the user touches the screen the function ProcessTouch() is called to process this user generated touch. It is this function that determines if the player is commanding the ally bot to move to a new location, to attack an enemy or is just firing the player's own weapon.

The listings in this section detail the controller class with explanations. You can find the complete source code listing without comments with the source code for the book.

The first section of code for this class is in Listing 11–2 and covers the class variables and the function that determines the objective's (which is the enemy power generator) health.

Listing 11–2. *Class Variables and FindObjectiveHealth*

```
class ExampleCh11PC extends SimplePC;
var Controller AllyBot;
Var Pawn AllyPawn;
var Controller GuardBot;
Var Pawn GuardPawn;
var bool BotSpawned;
var Actor BotTarget;
var float PickDistance;
var bool bBotCommandStateActive;
var int ObjectiveHealth;
var bool bGameOver;
function FindObjectiveHealth()
{
    local Generator TempGenerator;

    foreach AllActors(class'Generator', TempGenerator)
    {
        ObjectiveHealth = TempGenerator.Health;
    }
}
```

Key things to note in this listing are:

- The AllyBot and AllyPawn variables hold references to the controller for the player-controlled bot ally and the pawn for that ally.

- The GuardBot and GuardPawn variables are used to create the controller and pawn for the enemy guard that protects the enemy asset and is the player's goal to destroy.

- The bBotCommandStateActive variable is true if the player's bot ally is currently selected (last object touched). The next touch will be the enemy bot to attack or the place in the game world to move to.

- The ObjectiveHealth holds the health of enemy asset that the player needs to destroy in order to win the game.

- The bGameOver is true if the player has destroyed the generator, false otherwise.

■ The FindObjectiveHealth() function searches all the actors in the level and retrieves the health of the player's objective which is the power generator that needs to be destroyed.

The next piece of code is in Listing 11–3 and deals with picking an Actor. The PickActor() function determines if the user has touched and Actor on the screen and is the same function as in the hands-on example in Chapter 2.

Listing 11–3. *PickActor*

```
function Actor PickActor(Vector2D PickLocation, out Vector HitLocation, out TraceHitInfo
HitInfo)
{
    local Vector TouchOrigin, TouchDir;
    local Vector HitNormal;
    local Actor  PickedActor;
    local vector Extent;

    //Transform absolute screen coordinates to relative coordinates
    PickLocation.X = PickLocation.X / ViewportSize.X;
    PickLocation.Y = PickLocation.Y / ViewportSize.Y;

    //Transform to world coordinates to get pick ray
    LocalPlayer(Player).Deproject(PickLocation, TouchOrigin, TouchDir);

    //Perform trace to find touched actor
    Extent = vect(0,0,0);
    PickedActor = Trace(HitLocation,
                    HitNormal,
                    TouchOrigin + (TouchDir * PickDistance),
                    TouchOrigin,
                    True,
                    Extent,
                    HitInfo);

    //Return the touched actor for good measure
    return PickedActor;
}
```

The next code segment, shown in Listing 11–4, includes functions related to commanding the player's ally bot. The key ones to notice:

■ The SetBotMarkerGraphic() function creates a new botmarker if one does not currently exist and sets the position of it based on the Loc input parameter modified by the offset input vector.

■ The ExecuteBotMoveCommand() function sets the bot graphic marker to the input HitLocation position and sends a Move command to the player-controlled bot to move the bot to the location of the bot marker.

■ The ExecuteBotAttackCommand() function sets the bot marker graphic to a location above the attack target with the arrow pointing downward. The player-controlled bot is also given the Attack command directed against the Target.

■ The SelectBotAllyGraphic() function sets the location of the bot marker when selecting the player-controlled ally bot. The location of the bot marker is offset so that it is just above the ally bot.

Listing 11–4. *Bot Command Related Functions*

```
function SetBotMarkerGraphic(vector Loc, optional vector offset)
{
    Loc = Loc + offset;
    If (BotTarget == None)
    {
        WorldInfo.Game.Broadcast(None,"Creating New Move Marker!!!!!!!!!");
        BotTarget = Spawn(class'BotMarker2',,,Loc);
    }
    else
    {
        BotTarget.SetLocation(Loc);
    }
}
reliable server function ExecuteBotMoveCommand(Vector HitLocation)
{
    // 1. Set Marker
    Hitlocation.z += 50; // Add offset to help bot navigate to point
    SetBotMarkerGraphic(Hitlocation);
    // 2. Send Move Command to bot along with target location
    BotAllyController(AllyBot).SetCommand(Move, BotTarget);
}
function ExecuteBotAttackCommand(Actor Target)
{
    // 1. Set Marker
    SetBotMarkerGraphic(Target.Location, vect(0,0,200));
    // 2. Send Attack Command to bot along with target location
    BotAllyController(AllyBot).SetCommand(Attack, Target);
}
function SelectBotAllyGraphic(vector Loc)
{
    Loc.z += 200; // Add offset to help bot navigate to point
    SetBotMarkerGraphic(Loc);
}
```

The code segment in Listing 11–5 involves the creation of the enemy bot that guards the power generator. Note the following functions included in this listing:

■ The FindSpawnPad() function is the same as the one in the Chapter 10 framework.

■ The SpawnGuardBot() function creates a new enemy guard bot that will seek out a generator that is unguarded and will guard it. The bot uses the BotControllerGuard controller class and the GuardPawn pawn class and is created at SpawnLocation location offset by the Offset vector.

■ The CreateNewGuardBot() function finds the spawn pad in the level and creates the enemy guard bot on that spawn pad.

Listing 11–5. *Enemy Guard Bot Creation*

```
function Actor FindSpawnPad(int PadNumber)
{
    local BotSpawnPad TempSpawnPad;
    local Actor ReturnSpawnPad;
    ReturnSpawnPad = None;
    foreach AllActors(class'BotSpawnPad', TempSpawnPad)
    {
        if(TempSpawnPad.PadNumber == PadNumber)
        {
            ReturnSpawnPad = TempSpawnPad;
        }
    }
    return ReturnSpawnPad;
}

function SpawnGuardBot(Vector SpawnLocation,optional Vector Offset)
{
    SpawnLocation = SpawnLocation + Offset;
    GuardBot = Spawn(class'BotControllerGuard',,,SpawnLocation);
    GuardPawn = Spawn(class'GuardPawn',,,SpawnLocation);
    GuardBot.Possess(GuardPawn,false);
    GuardPawn(GuardPawn).AddDefaultInventory();
    GuardPawn(GuardPawn).InitialLocation = SpawnLocation;
    GuardPawn.SetPhysics(PHYS_Falling);
}
function CreateNewGuardBot()
{
    local Actor TempPad;
    TempPad = FindSpawnPad(0);
    if (TempPad != None)
    {
        SpawnGuardBot(TempPad.Location);
    }
}
```

In Listing 11–6, the Player's ally bot is created. The SpawnAllyBot() function creates a new player-controlled ally bot using the BotAllyController class for the controller and the BotPawn class for the pawn. The bot is created at SpawnLocation location offset by the Offset vector.

Listing 11–6. *Creating the Player's Ally Bot*

```
function SpawnAllyBot(Vector SpawnLocation, optional Vector Offset)
{
    SpawnLocation = SpawnLocation + Offset;
    AllyBot = Spawn(class'BotAllyController',,,SpawnLocation);
    AllyPawn = Spawn(class'BotPawn',,,SpawnLocation);
    AllyBot.Possess(AllyPawn,false);
    BotAllyController(AllyBot).SetCommand(Follow, Pawn);
    BotAllyController(AllyBot).BotOwner = Pawn;
    BotPawn(AllyPawn).AddDefaultInventory();
    BotPawn(AllyPawn).InitialLocation = SpawnLocation;
    AllyPawn.SetPhysics(PHYS_Falling);
}
```

The next piece of code involves functions that test whether the actor that is touched by the player is an ally bot or an enemy bot (see Listing 11–7):

- The IsActorAllyBot() function returns true if the touched Actor input in the TestBot parameter is of the type of pawn used by the bot ally.

- The IsActorGuardBot() function returns true if the tested Actor is of a pawn type used by the enemy guard bot.

Listing 11–7. *Ally or Enemy Bot Test Functions*

```
function bool IsActorAllyBot(Actor TestBot)
{
    local bool bretval;
    bretval = TestBot.IsA('BotPawn');
    return bretval;
}

function bool IsActorGuardBot(Actor TestBot)
{
    local bool bretval;
    bretval = TestBot.IsA('GuardPawn');
    return bretval;
}
```

The next code segment, shown in Listing 11–8, processes the player's touch input.

The ProcessTouch() function is the main processing function for user generated touches. If the bBotCommandStateActive is true that is the ally bot has been selected then if the touched actor is an enemy bot then execute the command to attack it. Otherwise if it is another location in the game world and not the ally bot's position then execute the command to move the ally bot to that location.

If the bBotCommandStateActive is false then if the touched actor is the ally bot then set the bBotCommandStateActive to true so that the next touch can execute a bot command either moving to a new location or attacking an enemy bot. Otherwise, start firing the player's weapon.

Listing 11–8. *Processing the Player's Touch Input*

```
function ProcessTouch(Actor TouchedActor, vector HitLocation)
{
    if (bBotCommandStateActive)
    {
        if (IsActorGuardBot(TouchedActor))
        {
            ExecuteBotAttackCommand(TouchedActor);
            bBotCommandStateActive = false;
        }
        else
        if (!IsActorAllyBot(TouchedActor))
        {
            ExecuteBotMoveCommand(HitLocation);
            bBotCommandStateActive = false;
        }
```

```
        }
        else
        {
            if (IsActorAllyBot(TouchedActor))
            {
                SelectBotAllyGraphic(TouchedActor.Location);
                bBotCommandStateActive = true;
            }
            else
            {
                // Start Firing pawn's weapon
                StartFire(0);
            }
        }
    }
}
```

The SwipeZoneCallback() function in Listing 11–9 is modified from previous versions
used in previous chapters, in that the ProcessTouch() function is now called to process
the user's touch input. The original function was defined in the hands-on example in
Chapter 2.

Listing 11–9. *SwipeZoneCallback*

```
function bool SwipeZoneCallback(MobileInputZone Zone,
                                float DeltaTime,
                                int Handle,
                                EZoneTouchEvent EventType,
                                Vector2D TouchLocation)
{
    local bool retval;
    local Actor TempActor;
    local Vector HitLocation;
    local TraceHitInfo HitInfo;

    retval = true;
    if (EventType == ZoneEvent_Touch)
    {
        // Code for Setting Bot WayPoint
        TempActor = PickActor(TouchLocation, HitLocation, HitInfo);
        ProcessTouch(TempActor, HitLocation);
    }
    else
    if(EventType == ZoneEvent_Update)
    {
    }
    else
    if (EventType == ZoneEvent_UnTouch)
    {
        // Stop Firing Pawn's weapon
        StopFire(0);
    }
    return retval;
}
function SetupZones()
{
    Super.SetupZones();
```

```
    // If we have a game class, configure the zones
    if (MPI != None && WorldInfo.GRI.GameClass != none)
    {
        LocalPlayer(Player).ViewportClient.GetViewportSize(ViewportSize);
        if (FreeLookZone != none)
        {
            FreeLookZone.OnProcessInputDelegate = SwipeZoneCallback;
        }
    }
}
```

The last chunk of code for this class is shown in Listing 11–10. It covers the
PlayerTick() function and default properties. The function has been modified to create
the enemy bot and player's ally bot when the controller is first ticked. Also, the health of
the player's objective is monitored and the game over status is set to true if the power
generator's health is equal to or less than 0.

Listing 11–10. *PlayerTick*

```
function PlayerTick(float DeltaTime)
{
    local vector AllyBotPos;
    Super.PlayerTick(DeltaTime);
    if (!BotSpawned)
    {
        AllyBotPos = Pawn.Location + Normal(Vector(Pawn.Rotation)) * 100;
        SpawnAllyBot(AllyBotPos,vect(0,0,500));
        BotSpawned = true;
        JazzPawnDamage(Pawn).InitialLocation = Pawn.Location;
        CreateNewGuardBot();
    }
    FindObjectiveHealth();
    if (ObjectiveHealth <= 0)
    {
        bGameOver = true;
    }
}
defaultproperties
{
    BotSpawned=false
    PickDistance = 10000
    bBotCommandStateActive = false
    bGameOver = false
}
```

> **FRAMEWORK NOTE:** This class can be modified in many ways such as to allow the player to
> control more bots or to change the way the player actually selects and gives the ally bot or bots
> their orders.

Creating the Bot Ally Controller

Next, we need to create the code for the controller for the player's ally bot.

The artificial intelligence for the player's bot ally is implemented in this class with the function ExecuteWhatToDoNext() being the main entry point for programmer defined custom behavior. The bot starts in the Initial state and goes to the FollowingTarget state. The bot is given the default command to follow the player when it is first created. Each of the available bot commands maps to a state within the BotAllyController class that implements that command.

The Follow command maps to the FollowingTarget state. The Move command maps to the MovingToMarker state. The Attack command maps to the AttackingEnemy state.

The first piece of code for this class, shown in Listing 11–11, involves bot commands. Key items in this listing are that:

- The FollowTarget holds a reference to the player's pawn that the ally bot will follow.

- The MoveToTarget holds a reference to the bot marker that the ally bot will move to.

- The AttackTarget holds a reference to the enemy bot's pawn that the ally bot will attack.

- The Command variable holds a player specified order for the ally bot. The orders are to Follow the player, Move to the location of the bot marker, or to Attack the enemy bot that is guarding the power generator.

- The SetCommand() function sets the command that the ally bot will follow as well as does some initializations that are command specific.

Listing 11–11. *Bot Commands*

```
class BotAllyController extends UDKBot;

var Vector TempDest;
var float FollowDistanceTarget;
var float FollowDistanceMarker;
var Actor TempGoal;
var float AttackOffsetDist;
var bool bAttackDone;
var int AttackDuration;
var Pawn BotOwner;
var Actor FollowTarget;
var Actor MoveToTarget;
var Actor AttackTarget;

enum BotCommand
{
    Follow,
    Move,
```

```
    Attack
};
var BotCommand Command;
function SetCommand(BotCommand Order, Actor Target)
{
    Command = Order;
    if (Command == Follow)
    {
        FollowTarget = Target;
    }
    else
    if (Command == Move)
    {
        MoveToTarget = Target;
    }
    else
    if (Command == Attack)
    {
        AttackTarget = Target;
        bAttackDone = false;
    }
}
```

The next piece of code is the GeneratePathTo() function from Chapter 5 that does the actual pathfinding using a navigation mesh (see Listing 11–12).

Listing 11–12. *GeneratePathTo*

```
event bool GeneratePathTo(Actor Goal, optional float WithinDistance, optional bool
bAllowPartialPath)
{
    if( NavigationHandle == None )
    return FALSE;
    // Clear cache and constraints (ignore recycling for the moment)
    NavigationHandle.PathConstraintList = none;
    NavigationHandle.PathGoalList = none;
    class'NavMeshPath_Toward'.static.TowardGoal( NavigationHandle, Goal );
    class'NavMeshGoal_At'.static.AtActor( NavigationHandle, Goal, WithinDistance,
bAllowPartialPath );
    return NavigationHandle.FindPath();
}
```

The FollowingTarget state, shown in Listing 11–13, makes this bot follow the player around the level. When the actor is directly reachable, the bot stops when it is within FollowDistanceTarget Unreal units of distance from the player.

> **NOTE:** In the BeginState and EndState functions, the "Put Code Here" comments in the code refer to new code you can add to extend this framework for you own customized game.

Listing 11–13. *FollowingTarget State*

```
state FollowingTarget
{
    event BeginState( Name PreviousStateName )
    {
        // Put code here that is to only be executed when the state is first entered
    }
    event EndState( Name NextStateName )
    {
        // Put code here that is to be executed only when exiting this state
    }
    Begin:
    WorldInfo.Game.Broadcast(self,"************* IN State FollowTarget ");
    // Move Bot to Target
    if (FollowTarget != None)
    {
        if(GeneratePathTo(FollowTarget))
        {
            NavigationHandle.SetFinalDestination(FollowTarget.Location);

            if( NavigationHandle.ActorReachable(FollowTarget) )
            {
                // then move directly to the actor
                MoveTo(FollowTarget.Location, ,FollowDistanceTarget);
            }
            else
            {
                // move to the first node on the path
                if( NavigationHandle.GetNextMoveLocation(TempDest,
Pawn.GetCollisionRadius()) )
                {
                    if (!NavigationHandle.SuggestMovePreparation(TempDest,self))
                    {
                        MoveTo(TempDest);
                    }
                }
            }
        }
        else
        {
            //give up because the nav mesh failed to find a path
            `warn("FindNavMeshPath failed to find a path!");
            WorldInfo.Game.Broadcast(self,"FindNavMeshPath failed to find a path!,
FollowTarget= " @ FollowTarget);
            MoveTo(Pawn.Location);
        }
    }
    LatentWhatToDoNext();
}
```

Listing 11–14 shows the MovingToMarker state. This state makes the bot move toward the bot marker, and when the bot marker is directly reachable, it stops the bot when it is within FollowDistanceMarker using Unreal units of distance of the marker.

Listing 11–14. *MovingToMarker State*

```
state MovingToMarker
{
    event BeginState( Name PreviousStateName )
    {
        // Put code here that is to only be executed when the state is first entered
    }
    event EndState( Name NextStateName )
    {
        // Put code here that is to be executed only when exiting this state

    }
    Begin:
    WorldInfo.Game.Broadcast(self,"************* IN State MoveToMarker ");
    // Move Bot to Target
    if (MoveToTarget != None)
    {
        if(GeneratePathTo(MoveToTarget))
        {
            NavigationHandle.SetFinalDestination(MoveToTarget.Location);

            if( NavigationHandle.ActorReachable(MoveToTarget) )
            {
                // then move directly to the actor
                MoveTo(MoveToTarget.Location, ,FollowDistanceMarker);
            }
            else
            {
                // move to the first node on the path
                if( NavigationHandle.GetNextMoveLocation(TempDest,
Pawn.GetCollisionRadius()) )
                {
                    if (!NavigationHandle.SuggestMovePreparation(TempDest,self))
                    {
                        MoveTo(TempDest);
                    }
                }
            }
        }
        else
        {
            //give up because the nav mesh failed to find a path
            `warn("FindNavMeshPath failed to find a path!");
            WorldInfo.Game.Broadcast(self,"FindNavMeshPath failed to find a path!,
MoveToTarget= " @ MoveToTarget);
            MoveTo(Pawn.Location);
        }
    }
    LatentWhatToDoNext();
}
```

The AttackingEnemy state shown in Listing 11–15 makes this bot move toward the enemy pawn and attack it. When the enemy bot is directly reachable, it stops the bot when it is within AttackOffsetDist Unreal units of distance of the enemy.

Listing 11–15. *AttackingEnemy State*

```
state AttackingEnemy
{
    event BeginState( Name PreviousStateName )
    {
        // Put code here that is to only be executed when the state is first entered
        Pawn.StartFire(0);
        bAttackDone = false;
    }
    event EndState( Name NextStateName )
    {
        // Put code here that is to be executed only when exiting this state
        Pawn.StopFire(0);
    }

    Begin:
    WorldInfo.Game.Broadcast(self,"############# In State AttackingEnemy");

    if (AttackTarget != None)
    {
        if(GeneratePathTo(AttackTarget))
        {
            NavigationHandle.SetFinalDestination(AttackTarget.Location);

            if( NavigationHandle.ActorReachable(AttackTarget) )
            {
                // then move directly to the actor
                MoveTo(AttackTarget.Location, AttackTarget, AttackOffsetDist);
                Sleep(AttackDuration);
                bAttackDone = true;
            }
            else
            {
                // move to the first node on the path
                if( NavigationHandle.GetNextMoveLocation(TempDest,
Pawn.GetCollisionRadius()) )
                {
                    if (!NavigationHandle.SuggestMovePreparation(TempDest,self))
                    {
                        MoveTo(TempDest, AttackTarget);
                    }
                }
            }
        }
        else
        {
            //give up because the nav mesh failed to find a path
            WorldInfo.Game.Broadcast(self,"FindNavMeshPath failed to find a
path!,AttackTarget = " @ AttackTarget);
```

```
            MoveTo(Pawn.Location);
        }
    }

    LatentWhatToDoNext();
}
```

Next is the code in Listing 11–16 that provides support to the bot's AI and originally appeared in Chapter 5.

Listing 11–16. *AI Support Code*

```
auto state Initial
{
    Begin:

    LatentWhatToDoNext();
}
event WhatToDoNext()
{
    DecisionComponent.bTriggered = true;
}
```

The final piece of code for this class is shown in Listing 11–17 and contains the ExecuteWhatToDoNext() function and default properties. The ExecuteWhatToDoNext() function processes the player's commands and executes them through state transitions.

Listing 11–17. *ExecuteWhatToDoNext*

```
protected event ExecuteWhatToDoNext()
{
    if (IsInState('Initial'))
    {
        GotoState('FollowingTarget', 'Begin');
    }
    else
    if (Command == Follow)
    {
        GotoState('FollowingTarget', 'Begin');
    }
    else
    if (Command == Move)
    {
        GotoState('MovingToMarker', 'Begin');
    }
    else
    if (Command == Attack)
    {
        if (!bAttackDone)
        {
            GotoState('AttackingEnemy', 'Begin');
        }
        else
        {
            Command = Follow;
            GotoState('FollowingTarget', 'Begin');
```

```
            }
        }
    }
defaultproperties
{
    FollowDistanceTarget = 250
    FollowDistanceMarker = 75
    AttackOffsetDist = 500
    bAttackDone = false
    AttackDuration = 2;
}
```

> **FRAMEWORK NOTE:** This bot controller class can be easily modified by adding in additional
> types of commands and processing them in the ExecuteWhatToDoNext() function. For
> example, you can add in the command Heal to the list of enumerations in BotCommand. You
> would add in a new state called HealingTarget that would move the bot to the target Actor you
> wanted to heal and then perform the healing. The new command would be tested for in the
> ExecuteWhatToDoNext() function and if true the bot's state would go to the HealingTarget state.

Creating the BotMarker

Next, we create the class for the bot marker that denotes the location the player wants
the bot to move to in the game world (see Listing 11–18). The Tick() function rotates the
marker continuously. The StaticMesh variable defines the actual 3d mesh graphic used
for the bot marker. The Scale3D variable resizes the marker to twice its normal size.

Listing 11–18. *BotMarker class*

```
class BotMarker2 extends Actor;

event Touch(Actor Other, PrimitiveComponent OtherComp, vector HitLocation, vector
HitNormal)
{
    //WorldInfo.Game.Broadcast(self,"BotMarker Has Been Touched");
}
function Tick(FLOAT DeltaTime)
{
    local Rotator TempRot;
    TempRot = Rotation;
    TempRot.yaw = Rotation.yaw + (15000 * DeltaTime);
    SetRotation(TempRot);
}
defaultproperties
{
    Begin Object Class=StaticMeshComponent Name=StaticMeshComponent0
        StaticMesh=StaticMesh'CastleEffects.TouchToMoveArrow'
        Scale3D=(X=2.0000,Y=2.0000,Z=2.000)
    End Object
    Components.Add(StaticMeshComponent0)
}
```

Creating the Enemy Guard Bot Controller

Next, we need to create the controller class for the enemy bot that guards the power generator.

After the guard bot is created it automatically tries to find an unguarded generator to guard. If an unguarded power generator is found then the bot goes into the Guarding state and guards the structure. While guarding the power generator if a threat occurs, the bot goes to the Attacking state and attacks the threat to the power generator. The bot will move toward the threat and attack it but if the bot is out of its patrol range then it will go back to the generator and go back into the Guarding state. The ExecuteWhatToDoNext() function is the key entry point to this AI behavior.

The first piece of code for this class is in Listing 11–19 and covers the class variables and navigation mesh pathfinding. Key things to notice:

- GuardedStructure references the asset that this enemy guard is protecting.

- Threat holds a reference to an Actor that has attacked the power generator this bot is guarding.

- The GeneratePathTo() function does the actual navigation mesh pathfinding and is the same function as in the hands-on examples presented in Chapter 5.

Listing 11–19. *Mesh Navigation*

```
class BotControllerGuard extends UDKBot;

var Actor CurrentGoal;
var Vector TempDest;
var Actor TempGoal;
var float GuardDistance;
var float AttackDistance;
var float GuardRadius;
var Actor GuardedStructure;
var Pawn Threat;

//////////////////// Navigation Mesh Related Functions  ////////////////////
event bool GeneratePathTo(Actor Goal, optional float WithinDistance, optional bool
bAllowPartialPath)
{
    if( NavigationHandle == None )
    return FALSE;

    // Clear cache and constraints (ignore recycling for the moment)
    NavigationHandle.PathConstraintList = none;
    NavigationHandle.PathGoalList = none;
    class'NavMeshPath_Toward'.static.TowardGoal( NavigationHandle, Goal );
    class'NavMeshGoal_At'.static.AtActor( NavigationHandle, Goal, WithinDistance,
bAllowPartialPath );
    return NavigationHandle.FindPath();
}
```

Next consider Listing 11–20, which involves functions related to guarding the power generator:

- The FindUnguardedGenerator() function finds a generator that has no enemy bot guarding it and returns a reference to it if one is found.

- The Guarding state moves the bot to the structure that it is going to guard against attack.

- The IsInPatrolRange() function returns true if the distance the bot is from the guarded structure is equal to or less than the GuardRadius. Otherwise a value of false is returned.

Listing 11–20. *Guarding Related Functions*

```
function Actor FindUnguardedGenerator()
{
    local Generator TempGenerator;
    local Actor ReturnGenerator;
    ReturnGenerator = None;
    foreach AllActors(class'Generator', TempGenerator)
    {
        if(TempGenerator.Guard == None)
        {
            ReturnGenerator = TempGenerator;
        }
    }
    return ReturnGenerator;
}
state Guarding
{
    event BeginState( Name PreviousStateName )
    {
        // Put code here that is to only be executed when the state is first entered
        CurrentGoal = GuardedStructure;
        Threat = None;
    }
    event EndState( Name NextStateName )
    {
        // Put code here that is to be executed only when exiting this state
    }

    Begin:
    // Move Bot to Target
    if (CurrentGoal != None)
    {
        if(GeneratePathTo(CurrentGoal))
        {
            NavigationHandle.SetFinalDestination(CurrentGoal.Location);

            if( NavigationHandle.ActorReachable(CurrentGoal) )
            {
                // then move directly to the actor
                MoveTo(CurrentGoal.Location,CurrentGoal,GuardDistance);
```

```
            }
            else
            {
                // move to the first node on the path
                if( NavigationHandle.GetNextMoveLocation(TempDest,
Pawn.GetCollisionRadius()) )
                {
                    if (!NavigationHandle.SuggestMovePreparation(TempDest,self))
                    {
                        MoveTo(TempDest);
                    }
                }
            }
        }
        else
        {
            //give up because the nav mesh failed to find a path
            `warn("FindNavMeshPath failed to find a path!");
            WorldInfo.Game.Broadcast(self,"GUARDING - FindNavMeshPath failed to find a
path!, CurrentGoal = " @ CurrentGoal);
            MoveTo(Pawn.Location);
        }
    }
    LatentWhatToDoNext();
}
function bool IsInPatrolRange()
{
    local bool retval;
    local float Distance;
    Distance = VSize(Pawn.Location - GuardedStructure.Location);
    if (Distance <= GuardRadius)
    {
        retval = true;
    }
    else
    {
        retval = false;
    }
    return retval;
}
```

Now, Listing 11–21 shows the Attacking state, in which the bot moves toward the
Threat and begins firing its weapon. If the bot is out of the patrol range, that is
IsInPatrolRange() returns false, then the attack is finished and the bot returns to the
Guarding state.

Listing 11–21. *Attacking State*

```
state Attacking
{
    event BeginState( Name PreviousStateName )
    {
        // Put code here that is to only be executed when the state is first entered
        CurrentGoal = Threat;
        Pawn.StartFire(0);
    }
    event EndState( Name NextStateName )
    {
        // Put code here that is to be executed only when exiting this state
        Pawn.StopFire(0);
    }
    Begin:
    // Move Bot to Target
    if (CurrentGoal != None)
    {
        if(GeneratePathTo(CurrentGoal))
        {
            NavigationHandle.SetFinalDestination(CurrentGoal.Location);

            if( NavigationHandle.ActorReachable(CurrentGoal) )
            {
                // then move directly to the actor
                MoveTo(CurrentGoal.Location,CurrentGoal,
                    AttackDistance);
            }
            else
            {
                // move to the first node on the path
                if( NavigationHandle.GetNextMoveLocation(TempDest,
Pawn.GetCollisionRadius()) )
                {
                    if (!NavigationHandle.SuggestMovePreparation(TempDest,self))
                    {
                        MoveTo(TempDest);
                    }
                }
            }
        }
        else
        {
            //give up because the nav mesh failed to find a path
            `warn("FindNavMeshPath failed to find a path!");
            WorldInfo.Game.Broadcast(self,"GUARDING - FindNavMeshPath failed to find a
path!, CurrentGoal = " @ CurrentGoal);
            MoveTo(Pawn.Location);
        }
    }
    if (!IsInPatrolRange())
    {
        GotoState('Guarding', 'Begin');
```

```
    }
    LatentWhatToDoNext();
}
```

Listing 11–22 involves functions that support the AI of the bot and were previously shown in Chapter 5.

Listing 11–22. *AI Support Functions*

```
auto state Initial
{
    Begin:
    LatentWhatToDoNext();
}
event WhatToDoNext()
{
    DecisionComponent.bTriggered = true;
}
```

Next is the ExecuteWhatToDoNext() function (see Listing 11–23), which is the main entry point for user defined AI and is a good place for testing to see if the bot needs to transition to a new state. The default properties for this class are also shown.

Listing 11–23. *The* ExecuteWhatToDoNext() *function*

```
protected event ExecuteWhatToDoNext()
{
    local Actor TempGenerator;
    if (IsInState('Initial'))
    {
        TempGenerator = FindUnguardedGenerator();
        if (TempGenerator != None)
        {
            Generator(TempGenerator).Guard = Pawn;
            GuardedStructure = TempGenerator;
            GotoState('Guarding', 'Begin');
        }
        else
        {
            GotoState('Inital', 'Begin');
        }
    }
    else
    if (IsInState('Guarding'))
    {
        if (Threat != None)
        {
            GotoState('Attacking', 'Begin');
        }
        else
        {
            GotoState('Guarding', 'Begin');
        }
    }
    else
```

```
        if (IsInState('Attacking'))
        {
            GotoState('Attacking', 'Begin');
        }
}
defaultproperties
{
    CurrentGoal = None
    GuardDistance = 300
    AttackDistance = 500
    Threat = None
    GuardRadius = 1000;
}
```

Creating Enemy Guard Bot Pawn

Next, we need to create the pawn class for the enemy guard. Listing 11–24 shows the code.

Listing 11–24. *GuardPawn class*

```
class GuardPawn extends BotPawnCh10;

event TakeDamage(int Damage, Controller InstigatedBy, vector HitLocation, vector
Momentum, class<DamageType> DamageType, optional TraceHitInfo HitInfo, optional Actor
DamageCauser)
{
    PlaySound(HurtSound);
    Health = Health - Damage;
    if (Health <= 0)
    {
        PlaySound(DeathSound);
        destroy();
    }
    BotControllerGuard(Controller).Threat = InstigatedBy.Pawn;
}
defaultproperties
{
    Health = 500;
}
```

The most important feature in this new pawn class is that the guard's Threat variable located in the bot's controller class will be set to the pawn that causes the guard damage.

Creating the Heads Up Display

Next, we need to create the class for our custom Heads Up Display, shown in Listing 11–25. This HUD will display the power generator's health, the player-controlled ally bot's health and the player's health. Key changes to the code from previous versions of the HUD in other chapters are highlighted in bold print.

Key things to notice in the following code listing:

- The HUDInfo structure holds the data for a text label that will be displayed on the screen.

- The DrawHUDItem() function actually draws the information to the screen for an individual HUD item.

- The DrawHUD() function is the hook where we can draw extra information to the HUD in addition to the standard graphics which include things like the virtual joysticks. DrawHUDItem() is called from this function.

Listing 11–25. *Custom HUD*

```
class Ch11HUD extends UDKHud;

struct HUDInfo
{
    var string Label;
    var Vector2D TextLocation;
    var Color TextColor;
    var Vector2D Scale;
};
// HUD
var HUDInfo HUDHealth;
var HUDInfo HUDAllyHealth;
var HUDInfo HUDObjectiveHealth;
var HUDInfo HUDGameOver;

simulated function PostBeginPlay()
{
    Super.PostBeginPlay();
    HUDHealth.Label = "Health:";
    HUDHealth.TextLocation.x = 1100;
    HUDHealth.TextLocation.y = 50;
    HUDHealth.TextColor.R = 0;
    HUDHealth.TextColor.G = 0;
    HUDHealth.TextColor.B = 255;
    HUDHealth.Scale.X = 2;
    HUDHealth.Scale.Y = 4;

    HUDAllyHealth.Label = "AllyHealth:";
    HUDAllyHealth.TextLocation.x = 600;
    HUDAllyHealth.TextLocation.y = 50;
    HUDAllyHealth.TextColor.R = 0;
    HUDAllyHealth.TextColor.G = 255;
    HUDAllyHealth.TextColor.B = 0;
    HUDAllyHealth.Scale.X = 2;
    HUDAllyHealth.Scale.Y = 4;

    HUDGameOver.Label = "Objective Killed";
    HUDGameOver.TextLocation.x = 300;
    HUDGameOver.TextLocation.y = 300;
    HUDGameOver.TextColor.R = 255;
    HUDGameOver.TextColor.G = 0;
```

```
            HUDGameOver.TextColor.B = 255;
            HUDGameOver.Scale.X = 7;
            HUDGameOver.Scale.Y = 7;

            HUDObjectiveHealth.Label = "ObjectiveHealth:";
            HUDObjectiveHealth.TextLocation.x = 0;
            HUDObjectiveHealth.TextLocation.y = 50;
            HUDObjectiveHealth.TextColor.R = 255;
            HUDObjectiveHealth.TextColor.G = 0;
            HUDObjectiveHealth.TextColor.B = 0;
            HUDObjectiveHealth.Scale.X = 2;
            HUDObjectiveHealth.Scale.Y = 4;
}
function DrawHUDItem(HUDInfo Info, coerce string Value)
{
    local Vector2D TextSize;
    Canvas.SetDrawColor(Info.TextColor.R, Info.TextColor.G, Info.TextColor.B);
    Canvas.SetPos(Info.TextLocation.X, Info.TextLocation.Y);
    Canvas.DrawText(Info.Label, ,Info.Scale.X,Info.Scale.Y);
    Canvas.TextSize(Info.Label, TextSize.X, TextSize.Y);
    Canvas.SetPos(Info.TextLocation.X + (TextSize.X * Info.Scale.X),
Info.TextLocation.Y);
    Canvas.DrawText(Value, , Info.Scale.X, Info.Scale.Y);
}
function DrawHUD()
{
    local int Health;
    super.DrawHUD();
    Canvas.Font = class'Engine'.static.GetLargeFont();
    // Objective Health
DrawHUDItem(HUDObjectiveHealth,ExampleCh11PC(PlayerOwner).ObjectiveHealth);

    // Ally Bot Health
    Health = ExampleCh11PC(PlayerOwner).AllyBot.Pawn.Health;
    DrawHUDItem(HUDAllyHealth, Health);

    // Health
    DrawHUDItem(HUDHealth,PlayerOwner.Pawn.Health);

    // Game Over
    if (ExampleCh11PC(PlayerOwner).bGameOVer)
    {
        DrawHUDItem(HUDGameOver, "");
    }
}
defaultProperties
{
}
```

The new custom HUD is shown in Figure 11–1.

Figure 11–1. *New HUD*

Creating the Power Generator

Next, we need to create the class for the power generator that will be the player's objective to destroy. The key code is in the TakeDamage() class which is called by a weapon's projectile when it hits the generator. If the generator is attacked by the player or the player's ally bot then the enemy bot that is guarding the power generator will attack that pawn.

Listing 11–26. *Power Generator*

```
class Generator extends Actor
placeable;

var ParticleSystem ExplosionTemplate;
var ParticleSystemComponent Explosion;
var SoundCue HitSound;
var int Health;
var Pawn Guard;
event TakeDamage(int Damage, Controller InstigatedBy, vector HitLocation, vector
Momentum, class<DamageType> DamageType, optional TraceHitInfo HitInfo, optional Actor
DamageCauser)
{
    PlaySound(HitSound);
    Explosion = WorldInfo.MyEmitterPool.SpawnEmitter(ExplosionTemplate, HitLocation);
    BotControllerGuard(Guard.Controller).Threat = InstigatedBy.Pawn;
    if (InstigatedBy.IsA('ExampleCh11PC'))
    {
        Health = Health - Damage;
    }
}
event Touch(Actor Other, PrimitiveComponent OtherComp, vector HitLocation, vector
HitNormal)
{
    WorldInfo.Game.Broadcast(self,"Generator Has Been Touched by " @ Other );
}
defaultproperties
{
    Begin Object Class=StaticMeshComponent Name=StaticMeshComponent0
        StaticMesh=StaticMesh'Pickups.Health_Large.Mesh.S_Pickups_Health_Large_Keg'
        Scale3D=(X=5.0000,Y=5.0000,Z=5.000)
        CollideActors=true
        BlockActors=true
    End Object
    Components.Add(StaticMeshComponent0)

    Begin Object Class=CylinderComponent NAME=CollisionCylinder
        CollideActors=true
        BlockActors=true
        CollisionRadius=+0140.000000
        CollisionHeight=+0140.000000
    End Object
    Components.Add(CollisionCylinder)
    CollisionComponent = CollisionCylinder

    bCollideActors=true
    bBlockActors = true
```

```
HitSound = SoundCue'A_Gameplay.Gameplay.A_Gameplay_ArmorHitCue'
ExplosionTemplate = ParticleSystem'Castle_Assets.FX.P_FX_Fire_SubUV_01'
Guard = None;
Health = 300;
}
```

The Power Generator is shown in Figure 11–2.

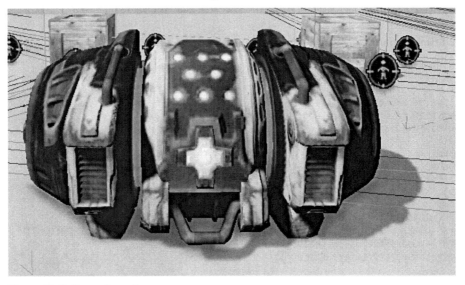

Figure 11–2. *Power Generator*

Configuring the Game Type

Next, we need to set up this new example for compilation and for playing on the mobile previewer. In the configuration directory located at

```
C:\UDK\UDK-2011-06\UDKGame\Config
```

(it will be different if you are using a different UDK version), change the UDKEngine.ini and Mobile-UDKGame.ini configuration files to the following:

```
UDKEngine.ini
[UnrealEd.EditorEngine]
ModEditPackages=ExampleCh11
Mobile-UDKGame.ini
[ExampleCh11.ExampleCh11Game]
RequiredMobileInputConfigs=(GroupName="UberGroup",RequireZoneNames=("UberStickMoveZone",
"UberStickLookZone","UberLookZone"))
```

Save the configuration files. You may need to write protect them to preserve the contents since the UDK sometimes overwrites them.

Bring up the Unreal Frontend and compile the scripts.

Creating the Level

Next, we need to create the level for this game framework.

1. Start up the Unreal Editor.

2. Load the level you created for Chapter 10, the one with many vendor crates surrounded by cover nodes. (You also can find the level—ExampleCh10Map.zip— with the source code for this book.)

3. Save the level as a new level by selecting **File ➤ Save As** from the main menu and entering a new filename for the map. You can use whatever filename you wish.

4. Select the Actor Classes tab in the Generic Browser.

5. Search for **generator** in the Actor Classes tab.

6. Select the generator class in the Actor Classes tab.

7. Right Click on an empty area and select Add Generator Here to add a power generator to the level. Position the generator so that it is just above the ground.

8. In the Actor Classes tab search for **botspawnpad** in the search area. Select the botspawnpad class and right click to place this item in an empty area in the level. Adjust the pad so that it is just touching the ground. The level with the generator and botspawnpad should look something like Figure 11–3.

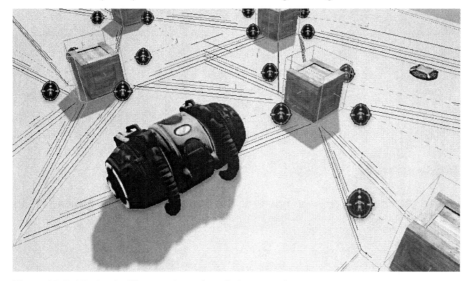

Figure 11–3. *The level with generator and one botspawnpad*

9. Save the level.

Running the Game

Now, we are ready to run our game. Follow these steps:

1. Select **View ➤ World Properties** from the Unreal Editor main menu. This would bring up the World Properties window.

2. In the World Properties window set the Default Game Type under the Game Type category to ExampleCh11Game.

3. Select the **Play ➤ On Mobile Previewer** option to run the game on the mobile previewer form the Editor.

4. Once the game is running move your character around the level and your ally bot should follow you around.

5. Click on your ally bot to select it as indicated by the orange arrow hovering over the bot and to activate the bot command mode (see Figure 11–4).

ObjectiveHealth: 300   AllyHealth: 100   Health: 100

Figure 11–4. *Selecting your ally bot*

6. Next, direct your bot to a position nearer to the enemy guard bot by clicking on an empty area closer to the generator (see Figure 11–5).

Figure 11–5. *Direct your bot to move to a location nearer the enemy guard bot*

7. Next, click on the ally bot again to select it and then click on the enemy guard bot to have your bot attack it. After the attack is finished the ally bot should return to following you.

8. Repeat this process until the guard is killed.

9. Finally, destroy the power generator by firing your weapon at it until the objective killed message is displayed, as in Figure 11–6.

Figure 11–6. *Power generator is destroyed.*

Summary

In this chapter we covered a game framework that is suitable for a third-person shooter or a third-person shooter / adventure type game where you control other team members that have special abilities and you need to direct them to accomplish specific tasks. We first covered an overview of the game framework discussing features of the framework in both general and code specific terms. Then we created the actual framework. We created new code, discussed how to set up the game to run on the mobile previewer, discussed how to build the level, and finally we gave a walkthrough of this game framework that showed you how to accomplish the goal of destroying the power generator.

Chapter 12

Top-Down Shooter/RPG Game Framework

In this chapter we will create a game framework suitable for a top-down shooter/role playing type game.

Of course, role playing games do not need to be from the top-down perspective. However, the old roleplaying games such as the original Ultima series featured a 2D top-down view of the playfield and used 2D icons for characters. This is the sort of feel we want to create here in this game framework although everything will be in 3D. Elements in the framework presented in this chapter that specifically relate to role playing games are:

- The ability to display and save individual character statistics such as hit points, experience, and so forth.

- The ability to direct members of the player's group to perform actions such as attacking an enemy and moving to a new location.

First we give a general overview of the framework and then code-specific details of the implementation. Next, we create the actual framework. We create new code for the game, modify an existing game level we created in Chapter 11, and adapt it to our new game framework. We also configure this new game type to run on the mobile previewer and then demonstrate the completed framework.

The game framework in this chapter specifically consists of:

- A top-down view of gameplay

- The ability of selecting player- or bot-specific information and displaying it on the HUD by clicking on the character.

- An ability of commanding a bot to move to another area of the level or to attack an enemy bot.

- The ability to save and load character information by having the player's pawn touch a statue.

Game Framework Overview

In this section we will discuss the game framework in general and specific terms. First we give you a general overview of the game framework by listing its main features. Next, we give you a more code-specific overview of the framework as to how exactly the general features are implemented in code.

General Framework Overview

This framework provides for a top-down view of the playfield and player's pawn. You can adjust the distance the camera is from the ground and set whether the camera rotates with the player or has a fixed rotation. Another feature of this framework is a custom Heads Up Display or HUD that allows the player to display the statistics specific to the player or a member of the player's group by clicking on that Actor. You can extend this HUD by adding or deleting entries including those specific to the type of pawn being selected.

In a shooter type game you might extend the HUD by adding the amount of ammo or other physical items that the player is carrying. In an RPG you might add intangible items like character traits such as strength, agility, dexterity, endurance, and negotiating skills.

This framework also provides for a bot under player command that the player can direct to move from one location to another in the game world and can direct to attack an enemy. You can build on this by adding other bots to the player's squad or modifying the code to change the exact behavior of the bot. For example, you can add in new code to make your bot repair damaged structures. For a role playing game you might add in the ability to use magic to attack enemies and to heal members of your party.

Additionally, the framework includes a method to load and save character statistics for the player and the player's ally bot. You can extend this method by adding in more data for the characters that will be saved and loaded or by changing the exact method that character data will be saved. Currently, character data is saved or loaded when the player's pawn touches a statue in the game world. You can change this by using some kind of menu system to load and save character data. You can also customize this method by loading and saving other data besides character data, including the game state such as the player's location. For a shooter type game you could save the character's physical possessions, and for a role playing game you could also save the character's intangible traits like magic ability, spell casting experience, combat experience, and so on.

Specific Framework Overview

The top-down view is implemented in the player's pawn class which is the PlayerPawnCh12 class. The function CalcCamera() is the function that actually changes the camera's view from the default first-person view to the new top-down third-person viewpoint. A top-down third-person viewpoint means that the player's viewpoint is above the player's pawn and is looking straight down at the player's pawn and the game playfield. This viewpoint should remind players of the older 2d role-playing style games such as the original Ultima series for the Commodore 64 and Apple II. More recent examples of top-down style role playing games are Across Age, Dungeon Hunter, Inotia 2: A Wanderer of Luone, Rough Touch, Sword of Fargoal, and Zenonia. All of these games are available for the iPhone.

The custom HUD for this class is implemented in the Ch12HUD class. This class depends on the HUDPawn variable located in the ExampleCh12PC class to determine which Pawn's information should be displayed on the HUD.

The SaveMarker class implements the 3d mesh graphic that the player's pawn needs to touch in order to save his own as well as his team member's character info. The SaveMarker class calls the SaveSquadInfo() function located in ExampleCh12PC class that implements the actual saving of the character data.

The LoadMarker class implements the 3d mesh graphic that the player's pawn needs to touch in order to load in his own as well as his team member's character info. The LoadMarker class calls the LoadSquadInfo() function located in ExampleCh12PC class that implements the actual loading of the character data.

Hands-On Example: Creating a Top-Down Shooter / Role-Playing Game Framework

In this hands-on example we will create a game framework suitable for a top-down shooter or a role-playing game. We add to the functionality of the game framework presented in Chapter 11 for a third-person shooter game. For this framework you again control a bot that you can move to different locations and command to attack an enemy bot but you do it from a top-down perspective. In addition, you can click on the bot or player and bring up character specific statistics such as hitpoints (which is health) and experience and display these on the HUD. Also, you can load and save the character data of the player and the ally bot by having the player's pawn touch two different 3d mesh graphics that represent the load and save markers.

In a role-playing game, saving your progress through the game world is essential. One reason it is essential is that one characteristic of a role-playing game is building up the character's attributes, such as experience points, strength, magical ability, and so forth, in order to defeat more powerful enemies and progress through the game. Since it is unlikely you will be able to do this in one play session, you need a method to save your character's status. We have chosen the marker method; however, you can extend this framework if you wish and develop some kind of menu system to load and save character data based on what you have learned from this book.

First we need create some new code such as a new game type, player controller, player pawn, ally bot pawn, enemy bot pawn, character information class, save marker, load marker, and HUD.

Creating the Game Type

The first thing we need to do is create a new directory for the code for this project. Create the ExampleCh12 directory under your default UDK installation directory at `C:\UDK\UDK-2011-06\Development\Src`. If you are using a different version of the UDK other than the June 2011 UDK then this default directory will be different. Create a directory called Classes under the new directory you just created and put all your source code files in this directory.

Then create the following class (see Listing 12–1) and save it under the filename "ExampleCh12Game.uc". Again as with all previous examples in this book the filenames must match the classnames and the file extension must be ".uc".

Listing 12–1. *Game type*

```
class ExampleCh12Game extends FrameworkGame;

event OnEngineHasLoaded()
{
    WorldInfo.Game.Broadcast(self,"ExampleCh12Game Type Active - Engine Has Loaded
!!!!");
}
function bool PreventDeath(Pawn KilledPawn, Controller Killer, class<DamageType>
DamageType, vector HitLocation)
{
    return true;
}
static event class<GameInfo> SetGameType(string MapName, string Options, string Portal)
{
    return super.SetGameType(MapName, Options, Portal);
}
defaultproperties
{
    PlayerControllerClass=class'ExampleCh12.ExampleCh12PC'
    DefaultPawnClass=class'PlayerPawnCh12'
    HUDType=class'Ch12HUD'
    bRestartLevel=false
    bWaitingToStartMatch=true
    bDelayedStart=false
}
```

The key code is highlighted in bold. Note that the `PlayerControllerClass`, `DefaultpawnClass`, and `HUDType` are set to new classes created for the game framework in this chapter.

Creating the Player Controller

Next, we need to create the player controller for this game framework. This player controller builds upon the one in Chapter 11. The new code is shown below. In the interest of saving space, we have abbreviated this code so that only key important changes from the controller in Chapter 11 are shown. Each function listed below is complete with the changes or additions highlighted in bold. However, there are functions that have been eliminated from this listing but are in the full source code for this book.

The important functions employed in this framework and their roles include the following:

- The key functions that involve saving character data are the SaveSquadInfo() and SaveCharacterInfo() functions.

- The key functions that involve loading character data are the LoadSquadInfo() and LoadCharacterInfo() functions.

- The key function involving changing the player controls so that moving the player forward moves the player up the screen and moving the player side to side in a strafing manner moves the player left and right across the screen is the PlayerMove() function located in the PlayerWalking state.

Listing 12–2 contains the first segment of controller code and deals with class variables and the functions that load and save character data to a file on the iOS device.

Listing 12–2. *Loading and Saving*

```
class ExampleCh12PC extends SimplePC;
var Pawn HUDPawn;
var CharacterInfo CharacterFile;
function SaveCharacterInfo()
{
    class'Engine'.static.BasicSaveObject(CharacterFile, "CharacterInfo.bin", true, 1);
}
function LoadCharacterInfo()
{
    class'Engine'.static.BasicLoadObject(CharacterFile, "CharacterInfo.bin", true, 1);
}
function SaveSquadInfo()
{
    CharacterFile.PlayerHitPoints = PlayerPawnCh12(Pawn).Health;
    CharacterFile.PlayerExperience = PlayerPawnCh12(Pawn).Experience;
    CharacterFile.AllyHitPoints = BotPawnCh12(AllyPawn).Health;
    CharacterFile.AllyExperience = BotPawnCh12(AllyPawn).Experience;
    SaveCharacterInfo();
}
function LoadSquadInfo()
{
    LoadCharacterInfo();
    // Put data back into variables
    PlayerPawnCh12(Pawn).Health = CharacterFile.PlayerHitPoints;
    PlayerPawnCh12(Pawn).Experience = CharacterFile.PlayerExperience;
    BotPawnCh12(AllyPawn).Health = CharacterFile.AllyHitPoints;
    BotPawnCh12(AllyPawn).Experience = CharacterFile.AllyExperience;
}
simulated function PostBeginPlay()
{
    Super.PostBeginPlay();
```

```
    CharacterFile = Spawn(class'CharacterInfo');
}
```

The important things to notice in the preceding listing are

- The HUDPawn variable holds a reference to the pawn that will have its statistics displayed on the HUD.

- The CharacterFile variable will hold the character data for the player and the ally bot that will be written to a file.

- The SaveCharacterInfo() function uses the BasicSaveObject to save the character data for the player and the ally bot located in the variable CharacterFile into the file "CharacterInfo.bin".

- The LoadCharacterInfo() function uses the BasicLoadObject to load in the data from the file "CharacterInfo.bin" into the variable CharacterFile.

- The SaveSquadInfo() function sets the CharacterFile variable with the player and the ally bot's statistics and saves them into a file by calling the SaveCharacterInfo() function.

- The LoadSquadInfo() function loads in the player and ally bot's data and puts them back into the correct player and bot ally variables. The LoadCharacterInfo() function actually loads in the character data from a file and is called first.

- The PostBeginPlay() function was added so that a new CharacterFile variable will be created when gameplay starts. This variable will hold the data for the characters.

The next piece of code, shown in Listing 12–3, involves the PlayerWalking State and changes made within that state to the PlayerMove() function. The additions are in bold print.

Here the PlayerMove() function is overridden in the PlayerWalking state. It is in the PlayerMove() function that the player's controls are remapped so that moving forward is moving up the screen and moving side to side or strafing is remapped to moving the player left and right on the screen in the top-down view.

Listing 12–3. *PlayerWalking State*

```
state PlayerWalking
{
ignores SeePlayer, HearNoise, Bump;

    function PlayerMove( float DeltaTime )
    {
        local vector X,Y,Z, NewAccel;
        local eDoubleClickDir DoubleClickMove;
        local rotator OldRotation;
        local bool bSaveJump;

        if( Pawn == None )
```

```
        {
            GotoState('Dead');
        }
        else
        {
            GetAxes(Pawn.Rotation,X,Y,Z);

            // New Custom Code
            NewAccel.y = PlayerInput.aStrafe;
            NewAccel.x = PlayerInput.aForward;
            NewAccel.Z = 0;
            NewAccel = Pawn.AccelRate * Normal(NewAccel);

            if (IsLocalPlayerController())
            {
                AdjustPlayerWalkingMoveAccel(NewAccel);
            }

            DoubleClickMove = PlayerInput.CheckForDoubleClickMove(
    DeltaTime/WorldInfo.TimeDilation );

            // Update rotation.
            OldRotation = Rotation;
            UpdateRotation( DeltaTime );
            bDoubleJump = false;

            if( bPressedJump && Pawn.CannotJumpNow() )
            {
                bSaveJump = true;
                bPressedJump = false;
            }
            else
            {
                bSaveJump = false;
            }

            if( Role < ROLE_Authority ) // then save this move and replicate it
            {
                ReplicateMove(DeltaTime, NewAccel, DoubleClickMove, OldRotation -
    Rotation);
            }
            else
            {
                ProcessMove(DeltaTime, NewAccel, DoubleClickMove, OldRotation -
    Rotation);
            }
            bPressedJump = bSaveJump;
        }
    }
}
```

Listing 12–4 includes the functions that spawn bots. In the SpawnGuardBot() function the
enemy bot has a new body which is in the form of the GuardPawn2 class. In the
SpawnAllyBot() function the player's ally bot has a new body in the form of the
BotPawnCh12 class.

Listing 12–4. *Spawn Functions*

```
function SpawnGuardBot(Vector SpawnLocation,optional Vector Offset)
{
    SpawnLocation = SpawnLocation + Offset;
    GuardBot = Spawn(class'BotControllerGuard',,,SpawnLocation);
    GuardPawn = Spawn(class'GuardPawn2',,,SpawnLocation);
    GuardBot.Possess(GuardPawn,false);
    GuardPawn2(GuardPawn).AddDefaultInventory();
    GuardPawn2(GuardPawn).InitialLocation = SpawnLocation;
    GuardPawn.SetPhysics(PHYS_Falling);
}
function SpawnAllyBot(Vector SpawnLocation, optional Vector Offset)
{
    SpawnLocation = SpawnLocation + Offset;
    AllyBot = Spawn(class'BotAllyController',,,SpawnLocation);
    AllyPawn = Spawn(class'BotPawnCh12',,,SpawnLocation);
    AllyBot.Possess(AllyPawn,false);
    BotAllyController(AllyBot).SetCommand(Follow, Pawn);
    BotAllyController(AllyBot).BotOwner = Pawn;
    BotPawnCh12(AllyPawn).AddDefaultInventory();
    BotPawnCh12(AllyPawn).InitialLocation = SpawnLocation;
    AllyPawn.SetPhysics(PHYS_Falling);
}
```

Listing 12–5 involves the SetHUDPawn function and its use in the SwipeZoneCallback()
function:

- The SetHUDPawn() function sets the Pawn which is set in HUDPawn that will have its statistics displayed on the HUD.
- In the function SwipeZoneCallback() the function SetHUDPawn() is called every time the user touches the screen in order to determine the pawn that will have its statistics displayed on the HUD. Either the pawn will be the player's pawn or the ally bot's pawn.

Listing 12–5. *SetHUDPawn*

```
function SetHUDPawn(Actor TouchedActor)
{
    if (IsActorAllyBot(TouchedActor))
    {
        HUDPawn = Pawn(TouchedActor);
    }
    else
    {
        // Set Default to Player Pawn
        HUDPawn = Pawn;
    }
}
function bool SwipeZoneCallback(MobileInputZone Zone,
                               float DeltaTime,
                               int Handle,
                               EZoneTouchEvent EventType,
                               Vector2D TouchLocation)
{
```

```
    local bool retval;
    local Actor TempActor;
    local Vector HitLocation;
    local TraceHitInfo HitInfo;

    retval = true;
    if (EventType == ZoneEvent_Touch)
    {
        // Code for Setting Bot WayPoint
        TempActor = PickActor(TouchLocation, HitLocation, HitInfo);
        ProcessTouch(TempActor, HitLocation);
        SetHUDPawn(TempActor);
    }
    else
    if(EventType == ZoneEvent_Update)
    {
    }
    else
    if (EventType == ZoneEvent_UnTouch)
    {
        // Stop Firing Pawn's weapon
        StopFire(0);
    }
    return retval;
}
```

> **FRAMEWORK NOTE:** You can easily expand this class to load and save additional character data
> for your own game by modifying the functions SaveSquadInfo() and LoadSquadInfo().

Creating the Player Pawn

Next, we need to create the player's body or pawn (see Listing 12–6). The key things to
notice in this listing are

- Player statistics are added here in the form of the variables
  CharacterName and Experience.

- The function CalcCamera() does the actual work of changing the
  camera view to a top-down view with CamOffsetDistance distance the
  height of the camera from the ground. The pitch which is the up/down
  movement of the camera is set to –90 degrees which points
  downward.

- If the bFollowPlayerRotation is true then the camera turns (yaw
  changes, left or right) to track the player when the player turns.

- The function GetBaseAimRotation() sets the aim rotation for weapons
  firing to straight ahead, which means the pitch is 0.

Listing 12–6. *Player's Pawn*

```
class PlayerPawnCh12 extends JazzPawnDamage;

var bool bFollowPlayerRotation;
var string CharacterName;
var int Experience;

////////// Top Down View ///////
simulated function bool CalcCamera( float fDeltaTime, out vector out_CamLoc, out rotator
out_CamRot, out float out_FOV )
{
    out_CamLoc = Location;
    out_CamLoc.Z += CamOffsetDistance;
    if(!bFollowPlayerRotation)
    {
        out_CamRot.Pitch = -16384;
        out_CamRot.Yaw = 0;
        out_CamRot.Roll = 0;
    }
    else
    {
        out_CamRot.Pitch = -16384;
        out_CamRot.Yaw = Rotation.Yaw;
        out_CamRot.Roll = 0;
    }
    return true;
}
simulated singular event Rotator GetBaseAimRotation()
{
    local rotator   POVRot, tempRot;

    tempRot = Rotation;
    tempRot.Pitch = 0;
    SetRotation(tempRot);
    POVRot = Rotation;
    POVRot.Pitch = 0;
    return POVRot;
}
defaultproperties
{
    bFollowPlayerRotation = false
    CamOffsetDistance= 1500.0
    CharacterName = "Player"
    Experience = 0
}
```

FRAMEWORK NOTE: You can expand on this class by adding additional statistics to your player in this class.

Creating the Ally Bot Pawn

Next, we need to create the pawn for the player's ally bot (see Listing 12–7). The Ally bot's statistics are added here in the form of the variables `CharacterName` and `Experience`. The `TakeDamage()` function processes damage for the ally bot and resets the experience points.

Listing 12–7. *Ally Bot's Pawn*

```
class BotPawnCh12 extends BotPawn;
var string CharacterName;
var int Experience;

event TakeDamage(int Damage, Controller InstigatedBy, vector HitLocation, vector
Momentum, class<DamageType> DamageType, optional TraceHitInfo HitInfo, optional Actor
DamageCauser)
{
    PlaySound(JazzHitSound);
    Health = Health - Damage;
    if (Health <= 0)
    {
        SetLocation(InitialLocation);
        SetPhysics(PHYS_Falling);
        Health = 100;
        Experience = 0;
    }
}
defaultproperties
{
    CharacterName = "TeamMember1"
    Experience = 0;
}
```

> **FRAMEWORK NOTE:** You can add in more statistics specific for this type of pawn here. For example, if this type of pawn is planned to have magic abilities you might add properties such as SpellCastingLevel to your list of character statistics. Although we have not discussed magic before, the general idea is that the character will have some power such as healing, or the ability to cause damage to enemies using some supernatural ability not based on a physical device or weapon. In terms of the property SpellCastingLevel, this variable would denote the ability of this character to use magic with a higher number indicating a greater ability. For example, a higher number would perhaps make special types of spells available.

Creating the Enemy Bot Pawn

Now, we create the pawn for the enemy guard bot (see Listing 12–8). The `ExperienceValue` variable is the value that is added to the experience statistic of the character that kills this pawn. The character must be either the player or the player's ally bot. The TakeDamage() function is where the experience points are actually added to the character that has successfully killed a pawn of this class.

Listing 12–8. *Guard Pawn*

```
class GuardPawn2 extends BotPawnCh10;

var int ExperienceValue;

event TakeDamage(int Damage, Controller InstigatedBy, vector HitLocation, vector
Momentum, class<DamageType> DamageType, optional TraceHitInfo HitInfo, optional Actor
DamageCauser)
{
    PlaySound(HurtSound);
    Health = Health - Damage;
    if (Health <= 0)
    {
        PlaySound(DeathSound);
        /*Add experience points to player or member of player's group
          if this pawn is killed by one of them*/
        if (InstigatedBy.IsA('ExampleCh12PC'))
        {
            PlayerPawnCh12(InstigatedBy.Pawn).Experience += ExperienceValue;
        }
        else
        if (InstigatedBy.IsA('BotAllyController'))
        {
            BotPawnCh12(InstigatedBy.Pawn).Experience += ExperienceValue;
        }
        //destroy();
        SetLocation(InitialLocation);
        SetPhysics(PHYS_Falling);
        Health = 100;
    }
    BotControllerGuard(Controller).Threat = InstigatedBy.Pawn;
}
defaultproperties
{
    ExperienceValue = 100;
}
```

Creating the Character Information Class

Next, we need to create the class that actually holds the character information for the player's squad that will be saved to the character file. See Listing 12–9.

Listing 12–9. *Squad Information Class*

```
class CharacterInfo extends Actor;

var int PlayerHitPoints;
var int PlayerExperience;
var int AllyHitPoints;
var int AllyExperience;
```

> **FRAMEWORK NOTE:** You can expand on this class by adding in characteristics for additional squad members and/or adding in additional statistics for existing squad members.

Creating the Save Marker

Next, we need to create the 3d mesh graphic that represents the save marker and is used to save the player's squad data (see Listing 12–10). The 3d mesh for this marker is set in the StaticMesh variable and is scaled up 3 times the normal size using the Scale3D variable. The Touch() function implements the save marker's key behavior. If the actor that touches this marker is the player's pawn then a sound is played and the character information for the player's squad is saved to a file on the iOS device.

Listing 12–10. *SaveMarker Class*

```
class SaveMarker extends Actor
placeable;

var SoundCue SaveSound;

event Touch(Actor Other, PrimitiveComponent OtherComp, vector HitLocation, vector
HitNormal)
{
    if (!Other.IsA('PlayerPawnCh12'))
    {
        return;
    }
    PlaySound(SaveSound);
    ExampleCh12PC(Pawn(Other).Controller).SaveSquadInfo();
}
defaultproperties
{
    Begin Object Class=StaticMeshComponent Name=StaticMeshComponent0
        StaticMesh=StaticMesh'FoliageDemo2.Mesh.S_Statue_01'
        Scale3D=(X=3.0000,Y=3.0000,Z=3.000)
    End Object
    Components.Add(StaticMeshComponent0)

    Begin Object Class=CylinderComponent NAME=CollisionCylinder
        CollideActors=true
        BlockActors=false
        CollisionRadius=+0140.000000
        CollisionHeight=+0240.000000
    End Object
    Components.Add(CollisionCylinder)
    CollisionComponent = CollisionCylinder
    bCollideActors=true
    bBlockActors = false
    SaveSound = SoundCue'A_Interface.menu.UT3MenuAcceptCue'
}
```

Creating the Load Marker

Next, we need to create the Load Marker class. See Listing 12–11. The key points to note are

- The LoadMarker class contains a 3d graphic mesh that represents the object the player's pawn needs to touch in order to load in previously saved squad character data.

- The 3d mesh for this marker is set in the StaticMesh variable and is scaled up 2 times the normal size using the Scale3D variable.

- In the Touch() function if the actor that touches this marker is the player's pawn then the player's previously saved squad character information is loaded in from the iOS device.

Listing 12–11. *LoadMarker Class*

```
class LoadMarker extends Actor
placeable;

var SoundCue SaveSound;

event Touch(Actor Other, PrimitiveComponent OtherComp, vector HitLocation, vector
HitNormal)
{
    if (!Other.IsA('PlayerPawnCh12'))
    {
        return;
    }
    PlaySound(SaveSound);
    ExampleCh12PC(Pawn(Other).Controller).LoadSquadInfo();
}
defaultproperties
{
    Begin Object Class=StaticMeshComponent Name=StaticMeshComponent0
        StaticMesh=StaticMesh'HU_Deco_Statues.SM.Mesh.S_HU_Deco_Statues_SM_Statue03_01'
        Scale3D=(X=2.0000,Y=2.0000,Z=2.000)
    End Object
    Components.Add(StaticMeshComponent0)

    Begin Object Class=CylinderComponent NAME=CollisionCylinder
        CollideActors=true
        BlockActors=false
        CollisionRadius=+0140.000000
        CollisionHeight=+0240.000000
    End Object
    Components.Add(CollisionCylinder)
    CollisionComponent = CollisionCylinder
    bCollideActors=true
    bBlockActors = false
    SaveSound = SoundCue'A_Interface.menu.UT3MenuAcceptCue'
}
```

Creating the HUD

Next, we need to create the new class for the Heads Up Display (see Listing 12–12). The key changes from previous versions of the HUD class are highlighted in bold print.

Depending on the type of pawn in the HUDPawn variable in the player controller which is an ExampleCh12PC class then either the HUD is drawn using the DrawPlayerHUD() function to draw the HUD for the player or the DrawAllyHUD() function to draw the HUD for the ally bot.

Listing 12–12. *Heads Up Display*

```
class Ch12HUD extends UDKHud;

struct HUDInfo
{
    var string Label;
    var Vector2D TextLocation;
    var Color TextColor;
    var Vector2D Scale;
};

// HUD
var HUDInfo HUDHealth;
var HUDInfo HUDName;
var HUDInfo HUDExperience;
var HUDInfo HUDGameOver;
simulated function PostBeginPlay()
{
    Super.PostBeginPlay();

    HUDHealth.Label = "HitPoints:";
    HUDHealth.TextLocation.x = 1100;
    HUDHealth.TextLocation.y = 50;
    HUDHealth.TextColor.R = 0;
    HUDHealth.TextColor.G = 0;
    HUDHealth.TextColor.B = 255;
    HUDHealth.Scale.X = 2;
    HUDHealth.Scale.Y = 4;

    HUDName.Label = "Name:";
    HUDName.TextLocation.x = 600;
    HUDName.TextLocation.y = 50;
    HUDName.TextColor.R = 0;
    HUDName.TextColor.G = 255;
    HUDName.TextColor.B = 0;
    HUDName.Scale.X = 2;
    HUDName.Scale.Y = 4;

    HUDGameOver.Label = "Objective Killed";
    HUDGameOver.TextLocation.x = 300;
    HUDGameOver.TextLocation.y = 300;
    HUDGameOver.TextColor.R = 255;
    HUDGameOver.TextColor.G = 0;
    HUDGameOver.TextColor.B = 255;
```

```
            HUDGameOver.Scale.X = 7;
            HUDGameOver.Scale.Y = 7;

            HUDExperience.Label = "Experience:";
            HUDExperience.TextLocation.x = 0;
            HUDExperience.TextLocation.y = 50;
            HUDExperience.TextColor.R = 255;
            HUDExperience.TextColor.G = 0;
            HUDExperience.TextColor.B = 0;
            HUDExperience.Scale.X = 2;
            HUDExperience.Scale.Y = 4;
}
function DrawHUDItem(HUDInfo Info, coerce string Value)
{
            local Vector2D TextSize;

            Canvas.SetDrawColor(Info.TextColor.R, Info.TextColor.G, Info.TextColor.B);
            Canvas.SetPos(Info.TextLocation.X, Info.TextLocation.Y);
            Canvas.DrawText(Info.Label, ,Info.Scale.X,Info.Scale.Y);
            Canvas.TextSize(Info.Label, TextSize.X, TextSize.Y);
            Canvas.SetPos(Info.TextLocation.X + (TextSize.X * Info.Scale.X),
Info.TextLocation.Y);
            Canvas.DrawText(Value, , Info.Scale.X, Info.Scale.Y);
}
function DrawPlayerHUD(Pawn HUDPawn)
{
            local string CharacterName;
            local int Experience;
            local int HitPoints;

            CharacterName = PlayerPawnCh12(HUDPawn).CharacterName;
            Experience = PlayerPawnCh12(HUDPawn).Experience;
            HitPoints = HUDPawn.Health;

            DrawHUDItem(HUDExperience, Experience);
            DrawHUDItem(HUDName, CharacterName);
            DrawHUDItem(HUDHealth, HitPoints);
}
function DrawAllyHUD(Pawn HUDPawn)
{
            local string CharacterName;
            local int Experience;
            local int HitPoints;

            CharacterName = BotPawnCh12(HUDPawn).CharacterName;
            Experience = BotPawnCh12(HUDPawn).Experience;
            HitPoints = HUDPawn.Health;
            DrawHUDItem(HUDExperience, Experience);
            DrawHUDItem(HUDName, CharacterName);
            DrawHUDItem(HUDHealth, HitPoints);
}
function DrawHUD()
{
            local Pawn HUDPawn;
```

```
        super.DrawHUD();
        Canvas.Font = class'Engine'.static.GetLargeFont();

        HUDPawn = ExampleCh12PC(PlayerOwner).HUDPawn;
        if (HUDPawn.IsA('PlayerPawnCh12'))
        {
            DrawPlayerHUD(HUDPawn);
        }
        else
        if (HUDPawn.IsA('BotPawnCh12'))
        {
            DrawAllyHUD(HUDPawn);
        }

        // Game Over
        if (ExampleCh12PC(PlayerOwner).bGameOVer)
        {
            DrawHUDItem(HUDGameOver, "");
        }
}
defaultProperties
{
}
```

Configuring the Game Type

Next, we need to set up this new example for compilation and for playing on the mobile previewer. In the configuration directory located at

```
C:\UDK\UDK-2011-06\UDKGame\Config
```

(it will be different if you are using a different UDK version), change the UDKEngine.ini and Mobile-UDKGame.ini configuration files to the following:

```
UDKEngine.ini
[UnrealEd.EditorEngine]
ModEditPackages=ExampleCh12
Mobile-UDKGame.ini
[ExampleCh12.ExampleCh12Game]
RequiredMobileInputConfigs=(GroupName="UberGroup",RequireZoneNames=("UberStickMoveZone",
"UberStickLookZone","UberLookZone"))
```

Save the configuration files. You may need to write protect them to preserve the contents since the UDK sometimes overwrites them (see the section "Configuring the Game Type" in Chapter 9).

Bring up the Unreal Frontend and compile the scripts.

Creating the Level

To create the level for this example, complete the following steps:

1. Bring up the Unreal Editor.

2. Load in the level you created for the game framework in Chapter 11 (see the section "Creating the Level"). (You also can find the level—ExampleCh11Map.zip— with the source code for this book.)

3. Save a copy of this level by selecting **File ➤ Save As** to bring up the windows save dialog and typing in a new name for this new level then saving it.

4. Next, select the Actor Class tab from the generic browser and search for savemarker in the search box. Select the SaveMarker class when it comes up.

5. Right click on an empty area in the level and select Add SaveMarker Here to add the marker to the level (see Figure 12–1).

Figure 12–1. *Adding the Save Marker to the Level*

6. Next search for loadmarker in the search box in the Actor Classes tab. Select the LoadMarker class when it comes up.

7. Right click on an empty area in the level and select Add LoadMarker Here to add the marker to the level (see Figure 12–2).

Figure 12–2. *Adding the Load Marker to the Level*

8. Save the level.

Running the Game

Now, we are ready to run our game.

1. Select **View ➤ World Properties** from the Unreal Editor main menu. This would bring up the World Properties window.

2. In the World Properties window set the Default Game Type under the Game Type category to ExampleCh12Game.

3. Select the **Play ➤ On Mobile Previewer** option to run the game on the mobile previewer from the Editor.

4. Select your bot ally by clicking on it. The Name in the HUD should be TeamMember1, as shown in Figure 12–3.

Figure 12–3. *Selecting your ally bot*

5. Next, build up your ally bot's experience points by clicking on the enemy guard bot to attack it. Repeat this process of clicking on your bot and then on the enemy guard several times to attack it. When the enemy guard is dead it will respawn.

6. Save your squad's character statistics by having the player's pawn touch the SaveMarker statue in the level which is the rectangular statue. The round statue is the LoadMarker statue. See Figure 12–4.

Figure 12–4. *LoadMarker on Left and SaveMarker on Right*

7. Exit the mobile previewer then restart it.

8. Load in the previously saved character data by having your player's pawn touch the LoadMarker. Click on your ally bot to bring up its statistics. Note that the Experience points are the same as when you saved it previously. You should see something like Figure 12–5.

Figure 12–5. *After loading in the character data*

Summary

In this chapter we created a new game framework suitable for a top-down shooter and or a role playing game. We discussed the framework's features and then discussed how these features were implemented in terms of code. We then created the actual game framework. New code was created, a new level was created from an existing level that was made in a previous framework, the game type was then set up to run on the mobile previewer and finally we gave the reader a demonstration of the game.

Index

CPSIA information can be obtained at www.ICGtesting.com
Printed in the USA
LVOW100545190412

278260LV00005BA/4/P